TITIAN

DARIO [text obscured]

TRANSLATED FROM THE ITALIAN BY
NORA WYDENBRUCK

Biography Index Reprint Series

BOOKS FOR LIBRARIES PRESS
FREEPORT, NEW YORK

Library of Congress Cataloging in Publication Data

Cecchi, Dario, 1918-
   Titian.

   (Biography index reprint series)
   Translation of Tiziano.
   Reprint of the 1958 ed.
   1. Tiziano, Vecelli, 1477-1576.
[ND623.T7C43 1973   759.5   72-13188
ISBN 0-8369-8143-X

TITIAN

TITIAN

CONTENTS

ILLUSTRATIONS

HE was more solidly built than the others. Owing to his solitary
habits he was most given to immersing himself in those dog-
eared books of his father's, illustrated by prints depicting
religious and mythological scenes. So it happened that he conceived
the idea of acting the part of Mars, appearing with the dog at his side,
a red cloth cut from a discarded gown thrown over his shoulders:
in this accoutrement, he intended to drive away the executioners of
Sebastian.

Today, however, the dog was feeling the cold and refused to be
drawn into the game. It had curled itself up and lay shivering behind
the pile of wood at the far end of the stables, where the children were
playing as they had done on the preceding day. They had made bows
and arrows out of cords and little sticks, and were enacting the martyrdom of Saint Sebastian, just as it was shown on the picture Titian
had chosen.

Orsa had been tied to an old anvil; she was the cry-baby in that
band of young ruffians, so they had chosen her to play the saint.
Francesco commanded the company of archers, which was represented
by Caterina, and both of them were to be put to flight by Mars when
they had released their arrows. The others wanted it to be the Archangel, like the one in a little church outside Pieve, but Titian would
have none of it. Over and over again he had looked at a print depicting
Mars, a design of formidable impetuosity, and had been so impressed
by the theatrical majesty of the armed god that he wanted to represent
him at any cost. Stubbornly, the others ran away as soon as he appeared,
shouting: 'The Archangel! The Archangel!' Titian, who insisted that
he was Mars, lost his temper. He dragged the dog from its hiding-
place and forced it to walk beside him, urging it to run after the
fugitives. Then he went to free Orsa and, taking her by the hand, he
helped her to climb the pile of stacked fire-wood, in order to simulate
the Saint's ascension into Heaven. From their raised post, the boy and

girl looked down, turning their backs on a little window opening onto the grey clouds. Their figures against the light seemed very far away, almost unrecognizable.

The children were not even aware of the cold, passionately caught up as they were in the whimsicality of the game which their inherent faculties of dramatisation, equal to all the genius and the madness of a child's imagination, were now creating in the malodorous squalor of the stables. They began to improve the performance. Orsa should have been naked like the martyred saint, so she had to submit to having a dirty tattered piece of canvas tied round her middle, over her frock—and suddenly the others had the impression that her sex had changed.

They bent to pick up their bows, ready to begin again, and the game went on.

The servant-girl had already come down from the house once, her skirt thrown over her shoulders, her cheeks flushed with bending over the fire. She had ordered them to come indoors immediately; the mistress did not like them playing in the draughty, filthy stables, in this horrible weather. . . .

'We're coming in a minute!' the children had shouted back, hiding their bows and drawing together to conceal the little girl acting the martyr. In the end, Titian had shut the door in her face. But now she was back again; throwing both doors wide open, she announced, 'It's snowing!' The effect was like that of a cannon shot. Bows and arrows were thrown aside, archangels and saints forgotten, and the children pelted out into the yard to gaze entranced at the fountain, the surrounding houses and the entire countryside in its mantle of whiteness.

Titian, still wrapped in his red cloth, ran out alone into the floating, silent brightness. He hurried to the fountain and gazed at the lightly wrinkled surface of the water.

They were all calling him, the maid, his brother and his sisters, but before he turned to acknowledge them in the familiar landscape which had so suddenly been transformed, he would have liked to look through the shifting veils at the peaks of the Marmarole and the other mountains, and at Cibiano, the neighbouring village—but he could see nothing.

'Tiziano!' they kept on shouting. He turned to look at his home; Montericco rose up behind it, peopled with black fir-trees which were now outlined in white. 'Tiziano!' the maid called as she pushed the children up the outer stairs and towards the wooden gallery. The boy smiled from the centre of his stability as though he were looking down from a height instead of looking up—after all, the perspective of the world had not changed. He took off the red cloth and wound it round his neck.

The maid had crossed the gallery and opened the door to the house; one after the other, she pushed Orsa, Francesco and Caterina inside. Their faces were turned towards him and they gaped at him in amazement, already oblivious of the wonderful game in the stables. Titian saw them disappear, one behind the other, urged on by the girl who was turning them again into little children afraid of a spanking and who was now threatening to come down, seize him by the hair and drag him home. 'Tiziano!' she roared. The force with which his name rang out was enough to make the worthy community of Cadore with all its fir-trees and its mountain-tops tremble and quake, but as the last echoes of his name died away, his mother appeared in the dark aperture of the door that had engulfed the three bright little figures—gentle, silent, adorable.

'Mistress Lucia!' the maid cried out imploringly. The mistress, barely visible in the driving sleet of white, frozen, diagonal crystals, raised her hand mildly; she might have been blessing this unexpected meteorological phenomenon which provided a carpet, a mantle and a sky for the most intelligent of her sons, the most precocious, the most bashful, the most difficult to love. . . .

Yet that gesture was enough to make him move, and he began to run. Wrinkling up his face against the freezing sleet, his brow very white against the darkness of his red drapery, he trotted up the steps. For a moment he stopped to sneeze, then he stumbled on and ran blindly along the gallery. The women had gone indoors. He crossed the threshold, banged the door behind him and leant back against it with all his weight. Faced with the silent chorus aligned to stare at him, he bent low as though to make a deep, formal bow—but actually to explode into another prodigious sneeze.

In the Vecellio family, that tough, healthy race of soldiers and magistrates, a sneeze was inevitably followed by a solemn cross-examination. Having brought against himself the accusation represented by the itch in his nose, the boy looked around helplessly, his cheeks scarlet and tingling, his hair gleaming with moisture. Dropping the brave red cloth that had adorned the bellicose splendour of Mars, he prepared himself to submit without defence to the jurisdiction of the family.

The maid was loth to forgo a scolding, but the mistress, indulgent as ever, moved forward to pick up the discarded cloak and examine the damp material. Benedictions flowed from this mute and unsuspecting motherly advocate; again she beckoned to her boy and preceded him over the polished hexagons of the parquet, until they came to a large room where in the middle a fire was burning brightly on the hearth, surrounded by high-legged chairs.

Titian climbed on to one of these, like a frightened puppy that takes refuge in its basket. His mother began to dry his head with a towel. Then she unlaced his vest, while the maid threw a bundle of wood onto the flames. The other children drew closer and formed a circle round the fire, which was throwing off sparks and blazing up merrily in brilliant, orange-coloured jets of flame.

The servant-girl was scolding again. 'And this?' she asked accusingly as she disentangled Orsa from the horrid canvas of the martyrdom which she was still wearing. 'What is this?' The proceedings might well have started all over again with this charge, but that did not seem possible in the beatific atmosphere of the fire-lit room, where the children's faces glowed like shining, red-cheeked apples. In the absence of the stern head of the family, they nestled together happily under the protection of their mother, that gracious advocate to whom they owed a thousand acquittals, and pressed their icy, numbed fingers to the tips of their noses. Then they went to the window to watch the snow piling up on the window-sill.

Titian looked down at them from his high perch. His mother was now asking him why they had stayed in the stables so long, contrary to their father's orders. The boy was willing to explain, but she seemed unable to follow these fantasies beyond a certain point: Mars —Saint Sebastian—the tatters in which they dressed up! She was a wise housewife, whose feminine outlook on the things of everyday life did not admit these vagaries; for a while she fell silent. How strange this taciturn son of hers was with his self-sufficiency, his mania for flourishes and ornaments and collecting apparently useless throw-outs —nails with which he scratched drawings on little boards. He would try to colour these drawings as best he could ever since he had watched Antonio Rosso painting frescoes and altar-pieces in the churches of

Cadore, using many brushes, large and small, crocks filled with pigments and many other fascinating, complicated tools.

Since then he had instinctively attempted to transpose what he saw in the pictures he found etched or painted by others, confronting them with reality and transforming them into living stories and compositions. The saint, for instance, bearing a banner that floated in the wind, who was depicted in one of his father's books: he had seen him again as the standard-bearer at the head of a procession that wound its way through the narrow streets and up the steep paths of Pieve with chants, prayers and litanies. Or the Blessed Virgin holding the holy Child, surrounded by lights on the main altar in church—she was no different to his mother when she was standing by the fire of an evening, holding the pink, chubby, sleeping little Orsa on her arm. Ingenuously, Titian would try to set down these images with the wretched means at his disposal, drawing with a charred stick on the porous surface of a whitewashed wall. And the whole family was filled with wonder.

At other times, between Latin tasks, when he and his brother Francesco were copying pompously constructed eternal phrases which they had to memorize and recite to their father, he would cease to look at the confused medley of characters on the pages before him; then, instead of tracing words to be measured by millimetres, his hand would involuntarily amplify its movements and launch out into inexpertly resolute shapes. Francesco would lean over his shoulder, watching him, and they would remain brooding over these fantasies that intoxicated them like portents of destiny, so that the Latin task was never finished, the oration never memorized. And at bedtime, when it was customary for every member of the Vecellio family to give an account to his Maker of every action of the day, the inexorable reckoning had to be faced. In the end the boys came to imagine God to be like their father when he condemned them solemnly, towering hugely above them as he stood with his back to the flames in the circular fireplace. Like a famished Saturn, he seemed ready to devour them, simply because, in the best of cases, a metrical foot had slipped away on its own during the Latin recitation, or a conjunctive or gerundive was not clear in the text they had copied.

Then there was no escape. Master Gregorio would repeat the history of the house of Vecellio, teeming with honourable and exemplary names. The chronicle, rhapsodically recited, might either be developed from the origins of the family or followed backwards, but it invariably contained a precise and specified catalogue of the talents of all its members, living and dead: there was Master Gregorio's elder brother, Antonio, who was engineer of the Venetian Republic; his father, Conte, jurisconsult; the forefathers: Antonio, barrister; Guecello, notary; further back Cristoforo Bartolomeo; further back still Guecello, rector and mayor of Pieve, where the name of the Vecellios had originated. And yet further back to Tommaso di Pozzale, the first notary of the clan. Finally, to disperse the darkening mists of time and crown the pyramid of names worthily, Master Gregorio would resolutely place, like a beacon radiating benedictions over all the Vecellios, the bishop of Oderzo, Tiziano; he would speak in ecstatic terms of this holy man with whose name he had burdened the shoulders of his own son.

Titian, the youngest shoot to sprout from this imposing family-tree, would sit with bent head in front of the fire, while the cat rubbed itself against his legs; and to save himself from annihilation by the overwhelming proportions of his family's greatness, he would trace arabesques in ashes. This made him invulnerable and safe, and his father, surly but shrewdly discerning, now that he had given vent to his feelings would fall silent and watch him affectionately and admiringly. Then Francesco would come close to his brother, hoping to share the aura of mysterious immunity that seemed to envelop Titian.

Master Gregorio had talked to all his cronies about his son's inclination for drawing; they had all advised him, now that the boy had completed his eighth year, to take him to Venice and apprentice him to a master. Titian was aware of these conversations and consultations, but he said nothing and lost himself in his fancies.

Though Venice was not far away, it represented for the provincials of remote Cadore a fabled world, incredible and fraught with dangerous fascination. But Master Gregorio knew that his boy was a Vecellio, and that his precocious talent was no more than a renewal of the promise which every member of the family must keep to his forbears: he would never lose himself or squander his gifts.

He had also been advised to send Titian to Venice by Conte, his father, who had actually gone to that city recently as a delegate of Cadore; there he had discussed the plan with his other son, Antonio. The latter lived in Venice with his wife Daria and had sent a message

to the effect that, though they lived in the house of his father-in-law,
Giacomo Coltrini, he would willingly give hospitality to his nephew,
or both nephews, from Pieve.

Countless studios, all of them excellent, were being established
in Venice, as artists from every part of Italy came there to vie with
each other, and it would be an easy matter to find the right opening
for the two boys. Uncle Antonio was a good friend of the mosaicist
and painter Sebastiano Zuccato, the *gastaldo* or syndic of the mosaicists'
guild, and father to Valerio and Francesco, who were both able and
industrious exponents of the art. Titian was just the right age to begin
his novitiate in all matters of art, and gifted as he was, there could be
little doubt that he would readily assimilate the best that the masters
could teach him.

These informations, counsels and guarantees had created an atmosphere of suspense for the new generation of the Vecellios. The one
who was mentioned explicitly was Titian, but owing to Francesco's
habit of joining into everything his brother did, the use of the plural
was justified. While Titian became more and more addicted to
drawing, Francesco kept up with him as well as he could, though he
found it easier to help him organize a play like that of Saint Sebastian's
martyrdom. But even then Titian would sometimes appear very
strange, inebriated by his visions and he was obsessed by pictures
or with representing them. An intent look would overspread his
face, which seemed to grow older.

It worried the boy that he was unable to communicate all these
marvels; he could not even explain them to his mother, though
she was trying to sympathize and understand. He told her how he
enjoyed representing these mythological scenes, but it seemed as
though he were talking about a wretched puppet-show, a childish
game, without rhyme or reason, while keeping the entire fruitful
essence of his imagination to himself.

Sitting there before the fire, slightly embarrassed and tongue-tied,
with his hands in hers while the other children looked out of the window
at the snow, he saw his mother's lovely face through a veil of sadness,
thinking of how it would be when he had to leave her. If the departure
to Venice were really to take place, he imagined their leave-taking
to be no different: she would be holding his hands in hers, as though
to hold back the minutes that were passing and delay the moment
when they could not tell each other anything any more. There would

surely be much confusion, countless delays and parting exhortations. The cart would have to be crammed with baggage. Then, without even knowing how it had happened, they would be eager to leave, already distant, and he would see her appearing on the gallery, the petulant maid-servant beside her, waving to him, but silently, adorable but far away, inexorably far. . . .

In his childish day-dream with its pathetic prevision, he felt as though he was already far away, completely detached.

He roused himself. After slipping into the dry vest which the servant-girl had fetched, he took up a few pages on which he had copied a Latin compendium on Saint Lucy and perched himself once more on the high seat by the fire. At that moment the other children left the window at last and announced their father's arrival. The boy did not move, convinced that he would make a good impression with his extemporized zeal. Running his finger along the lines he had transcribed in the sacrosanct language of learning, he made a great show of reading.

His father came in noisily, shaking the snow from the ample cloak that enveloped him from head to foot. He stood there, stolid, insurmountable, and an enormous oblong shadow on the wall, reaching up to his shoulders, moved every time he moved.

'*Quod legis?*' he asked the boy laughingly.

'*Sanctae Luciae vitam*', Titian answered gravely, believing that he was laying up merit for the rest of the year.

'Greek, Greek, that is what you should be reading now', his father said. 'But perhaps our Titian has not studied Greek', he added, after he had told the girl to bring him some mulled wine. Then, warming his hands over the flames and striking the palms together energetically, he told them the great news of the day: they were going to Venice as soon as the good season had begun. In a couple of months, three at the most, they would leave.

Titian felt as though that moment had already come: the children in a state of trepidation, their mother remembering a thousand things, Master Gregorio shouting orders as though a minute more or less meant losing a battle. And he would be experiencing an indefinable acceleration of his heart. . . .

Even when a certain calm had been re-established in the atmosphere after this news, and everyday matters were being discussed—the horse to be taken to the smithy tomorrow to be shoed, the baby girl that had been born to Master Alo, the barber—even then he could feel nothing, could think of nothing except what was likely to become of him. A panic sense of hurry and precipitation blotted out all his sensations, so that everything seemed hypothetical, unconsummated, impossible to consummate.

When the fine season returned, the departure was suddenly upon him. He was hardly conscious as to who was with him and how he was leaving. Had he kissed his mother? And Francesco, was he there?

They were running to and fro on the gallery, up and down the stairs, the dogs in the square were barking like lost souls, while the neighbours leant out of their windows.

They started off.

His mother had appeared in the opening of the door with Orsa on her arm. She was waving to them. His grandfather stood beside her. As their figures diminished in the distance, the amplitude of their gestures increased. Then the maid took the little girl into her arms, for the mistress had moved aside, all alone. She was crying.

II

Venice appeared minutely vertical in the intricate architecture of the rose-coloured buildings, edged at the summit and the base by the double movement of the pale clouds that floated in the sky and their reflections in the water of the canals.

The fine season had come and the architecture was compact with animation. In the mullioned windows with two or three lights, white curtains were twisted round the graceful columns and fluttered in the breeze, like fans beckoning to the passers-by. Men and women looked down from balconies and roof-terraces, but the doors of the houses were closed, while gondolas, fishing-boats laden with salt or fish, barges, lighters and skiffs glided over the water and seemed to graze each other in order to light sparks of merriment. Only when they were clear of each other and each craft had set off in the opposite direction, the occupants would turn and salute each other with banter and hilarious curses. Then, suddenly, vertical wedges of silence formed a perspective of parallel canals and not a sigh could be heard.

All the way to Casa Coltrini Titian could hardly find time to draw his breath, so intent was he not to miss the slightest detail of the marvellous and incredible new scene. From the gondola, he could see as in a theatre, solid, moss-grown boxes edged with pale stones, groups of students and young men wearing black caps and satin cloaks who moved around like strangely accoutred phantoms of an unknown world. Men who carried baskets and porters, their legs clad in hose of heavy cloth, came and went, burdened with merchandise; servant-girls and housewives, whose white kerchiefs, seen in profile, hid all but the tips of their noses, merchants, noblemen, idlers waiting in front of taverns, formed a varied and dense crowd; it seemed an intimidating population and he felt sure that it must speak an entirely different language and have entirely different customs to those of his poor, solitary Pieve. Even his own father's voice sounded unfamiliar when he named a palace, a famous church or a well-known bridge.

They were about to reach their destination, and had entered a narrow canal. Tense with expectation, Titian leant forward and saw a gondola gliding towards them. A woman's voice, accompanied by a lute, was singing softly. The other occupants of the gondola were laughing and joking, but the sound of the lute was indescribably, agonizingly sweet. The two vessels passed each other swiftly, nearly touching. Titian got up to peer into the other gondola, but the curved baldachin of black serge hindered him from satisfying his curiosity. He turned round to follow it with his eyes, trying to grasp the essence of these tenuous threads of sound that seemed to imbue the water with love and the air with a slow, powerful sense of joy.

'Good-for-nothing idlers,' growled Master Gregorio, and pointed ahead to the house where they were about to land. The boy could not tear himself away from the melodious trail of the apparition which had awakened an unknown emotion in him and was now vanishing among the intricacies of the bridges, into bars of shadow, into the silence. It was the first time he had heard such music; the mystery of its origin and its cause seemed to portend unknown revelations; it disturbed him and made him feel slightly feverish and light-headed. He believed that from now on his life must suddenly become fantastic.

They had arrived at their destination.

★　★　★

Casa Coltrini, with its air of being a solid, well-to-do dwelling, seemed to ring with echoes all the time.

When a prolonged exchange of compliments had taken place and the travellers had been assigned their rooms, Titian suddenly realized that his home-life was going to be very different from Pieve. From now on he would be alone, in a peculiar kind of solitude which would increase as time went on. The presence of Francesco, who had always tagged at his heels, was no more than a habit, as automatic as eating, drinking and sleeping and attending to the tasks of every-day life. Titian accepted it with indifference; he knew that in future his thoughts would centre seriously and exclusively on his own personal life.

Antonio and Daria, his uncle and aunt, appeared as symmetrical personages, intent on cherishing their little son and expecting everyone else to like him. This was Toma Tito, an ingenious little rascal who seemed to be responsible for all the echoes that sounded through the silent rooms. With a strip of tin-foil, with a little bell without a clapper that he had picked up somewhere, even with the knuckles of his thin hands, he was always producing some slight sound: tic, toc, tac. . . . Titian started, taking up the *la* of that mysterious musical vibration that had been enveloped by the sable hangings of the gondola at the moment of his arrival.

Daria also seemed vaguely connected with the episode of the gondola. Though she was irreproachable as a mother and housewife, she had a way of appearing late for meals or any other family gathering, cool and self-possessed, demanding, as it were, the privileges of her femininity. She was always concerned for the welfare of her husband, her son and her father and unfailingly attentive to her guests, but there was something in her simple yet studied elegance that struck Titian as exceptional. His own mother had accustomed him to picture the mother of a family as always in the house, passing from room to room, followed, preceded or accompanied by the servant-girl. But Daria, although she did not neglect the affairs of her household, had a life of her own and spent many hours in rooms which he had never entered.

One morning she appeared at breakfast with her face flushed and her tawny hair gleaming and kept passing her hand over her temples and patting the tresses coiled in the nape of her neck. Titian gazed at her. All the others round the table were also looking at her, and Master Gregorio began to jest about a certain fashion among the ladies of Venice, asking her how long she had stayed on the roof. Daria laughed, pretending to make a mystery of it, and went on passing her hand through her hair. Titian was at a loss to understand what they were talking about, but later he begged Toma Tito to take him up to the belvedere on the roof.

Yes, they would go up there, his cousin said, but there was always some delay or postponement, and in the meantime new echoes, nonexistent or deafening, superimposed themselves. Titian pondered on the feminine element in his new home, so different from the bearing of his mother; it became another pretext for solitude, something which cut him off, forcing him to repress his emotions in his behaviour to himself and to others.

They talked about his future, about Venice, and his uncle Antonio immediately launched into a panegyric:

'*Ah, Vinetia. . . . Vinegia. . . . Vinexia grande*!' A city that comprised a hundred and ninety thousand souls, possessed three thousand ships, three hundred galleys, innumerable industries and factories, and all those art-schools! Where was another city such as this to be found? As he said it, it seemed as though these figures enhanced the value of his hospitality. While he enumerated all the famous artists in Venice, Titian began to familiarize himself with the names of the brothers Bellini, Vittore Carpaccio, Vivarini, Antonello da Messina, Cima da Conegliano.

As a family they had certain pretensions, and they amused themselves by discussing those members of the art-world whom they knew personally or about whom they were well informed: one of their favourite subjects was the house of Gentile Bellini, his valuable art collection, the beautiful objects he had brought back from Constantinople in 1480, such as the Venus attributed to Praxiteles and other priceless statues. Describing Gentile's journey to the orient, they repeated—probably for the hundredth time—the story of his dispute with the Sultan Mahomet II, how Gentile had painted the severed head of St John the Baptist, and the Sultan insisted that the head did not fit the neck. To prove his point, he ordered the head of an unfortunate slave to be struck off there and then, before the eyes of the horror-struck painter.

They would also discuss the work which was occupying the artists most prominent at the moment: Gentile was painting a large canvas representing the procession on the Piazza San Marco, Giambellino decorating the hall of the Great Council, and Carpaccio had been commissioned to illustrate the life of Saint Ursula. Jestingly they asked Titian which of these artists he would have preferred, and which honours he himself would have liked to win. In the meanwhile, they promised to take him to see St Mark's Cathedral, the wonder of wonders, next day. Later they would arrange a meeting with their friends, the Zuccatos, to discuss what was to be done about him.

Titian was bemused with this wonderful city of Venice, of which the greatest wonders were yet to be revealed to him. In his youthful impatience, seeing that it was not as easy to leave the house as it had been at Pieve, he begged Toma Tito to take him up to the roof as soon as he was awake and dressed the next morning. But his cousin explained that they were not allowed to be up there alone, and said they would ask the maid-servant to take them. The maid-servant was busy. They would ask the house-boy, but the house-boy was out shopping. They would have to wait till later, when Toma Tito's mother went up, in the middle of the morning.

While he waited, Titian went to stand at the window and watch the phenomenon which struck him as a poetical and fantastic whimsy—the sight of the gondolas floating between the houses in the canal below. He felt as though time itself had become fluid and the hours were floating past without being defined in his consciousness, while he crouched there, watching from his safe coign of vantage.

Tic, toc, tac. . . . Toma Tito was back.

Together they climbed to the roof up a staircase so dark and narrow that Titian felt as though his eyes had been bandaged. Suddenly they emerged into the full blaze of the sunlight and found themselves standing on a paved square at the top of the world, among the clouds. Surrounded by a few sweet-smelling plants, Daria was sitting there, dressed in a loose wrap, her head framed by a halo of straw from the sides of which her golden hair streamed out. The whole of Venice lay around her, surrounded by a turquoise-blue sea.

Daria laughed as she saw the two boys, and Toma Tito ran forward to embrace her and touched her hair with his thin, white hands. Titian remained standing a little further away and contemplated the scene.

The woman appeared to be enthroned above the city, or to be holding it in her lap, so triumphant and majestic was her beauty in the dazzling light. From time to time she dipped a comb into an earthen vessel and passed it through her hair with a slow, an everlasting gesture—the ritual gesture by which she created her fair-haired, golden loveliness. Golden veins of light were floating round her, forming a phosphorescent shell of indefinable motes vibrating in the air, as close-knit as the spokes of a rapidly rotating wheel.

The city looked immense, and the heat seemed to plunge it into a beatific torpor. This planimetric triumph, this vertiginous splendour and Daria's fragrant beauty made Titian remain spellbound in contemplation.

From the top of the bell-towers the sound of the bells sank down into the lagoon, and a light breeze fluttered the curtains on the surrounding roof-terraces. At last Daria rose to her feet and lifted the hoodless straw brim from her head. She shook her hair forward, and, singing softly to herself, she began to unravel its golden curls with her fingers.

III

LITTLE by little, Titian began to find his bearings in the artistic world which was the pride of Venice. He soon felt at home with the Zuccato family: Sebastiano, the *gastaldo*, had examined him in the art of drawing and then, correcting his hand, kept him around so as to accustom him to regular work; Sebastiano and his sons Valerio and Francesco had frequently taken the boy with them to San Marco and the Palazzo Ducale, where there were always crowds of architects, consultants, painters and artisans, while panting work-men, rendered speechless by the effort, were lifting up the perforated marble slabs. They might have been moving gigantic insubstantial blossoms—a fantastic flowering, forming and fertilizing new and unheard-of art-forms. Titian watched; he was beginning to penetrate into this atmosphere with a vigilance that equalled that of the sculptors who were raising the stone flowers into space. Seen through these shining arabesques, the glitter of the golden tesserae in the mosaics on the arches seemed like air, hoarded and refined in the course of many centuries.

The Zuccatos, in their workshop, were in a continual ferment as they hatched out their plans for similar backgrounds; sometimes the whole place seemed to glitter and vibrate as the tesserae were aligned, or as a couple of apprentices, holding their breath, applied gold-leaf to one of the caskets which Master Sebastiano decorated so exquisitely that they were much sought after as wedding-gifts.

Sometimes Titian was assigned to verifying the numbers of the tesserae—newly gilded, or consisting of malachite, or sometimes resembling emeralds. He dropped them in a bag, passing them from one hand to the other, and he thought they were like the very heart of the dissected colours, a heart that had hardened. Absorbed as he was in the attempt to discover some new inflection in their tonality, he became absent-minded and found himself forced to empty a bag in the middle of his counting and start all over again. In the meantime, the Zuccatos had been rolling up large designs or finishing the preparation of mastic and putty, and in the end, they would all leave for San Marco.

Other boys, bigger than Titian, but following the same occupation —tyros and apprentices, whispering gangs of lads and youths carrying portfolios and bundles of paper, crowded round the various shops in the Mercerie where paintings of religious subjects, done by the pupils of Gentile and Giovanni Bellini, were exhibited. Some of them could already claim to be regular professionals—as, for instance, Giovanni Mansueti, Girolamo Bernardino or Cristoforo dei Temperelli, who had all been working since 1485 in the Sala del Gran Consiglio for a monthly fee of three ducats. Others, students who were just learning to use their brushes, or tyros beginning to grind the colours, came armed with some vile drawing imitating a Madonna of their masters' and took up their pitch near the Fondaco dei Tedeschi, hoping to catch the eye of one of the foreign traders. The fat German merchants could be seen, snorting like stallions on a landing-stage as they breathed in the damp dense air of the evening while their agents concluded their business deals.

In Venice, a great number of Germans were continually coming and going. The Venetian government had assigned the Fondaco to them as their exclusive abode, with the understanding that they refrain from doing business personally, or in any other place. Three officials, known as the *Visdomini*, directed all proceedings and ruled over a crowd of dependents: *messeti*★ or brokers, dispensers, packers, weighers, cooks, servants, porters and boatmen.

It was the custom to appoint the foremost artist of the city to the post of overseer of the salt stored in the storehouse near the Fondaco; this lucrative appointment did not call for any particular effort and brought a revenue of some three hundred scudi a year. From September 1474 the beneficiary of this office had been Gentile Bellini, but when he went to the court of the Sultan Mahomet II in Constantinople in 1479, the commission to carry on the decorations of the Sala del Gran Consiglio as well as the agency had been awarded to his half-brother Giambellino.

★The *messeti* at the disposal of the German merchants were chosen by drawing lots, with ballot-papers out of a hat. They had to hold themselves at the disposal of their temporary masters who had been assigned lodgings with adjoining warehouses by the steward of the Fondaco. A merchant might also employ two brokers, according to the importance of his business, and during his entire stay in Venice he was always accompanied by them. They not only did all his business, they also had to keep the foreigner under constant observation and report all his activities to the *Visdomini*, who served the highly organized and extremely mistrustful Venetian Government as informers.

The traffic, teeming like a wasps' nest round the Fondaco and the neighbouring Piazza di Rialto, formed a centre similar to that of the Piazza San Marco and the Mercerie. Towards evening, as the heat diminished and before the gondolas had set out for the open sea, courtesans, wearing widows' weeds to deceive their prey more easily by the disguise of modesty, promenaded around with slow, measured steps. In the mornings, members of the aristocracy and the Senate would meet near the church of San Jacopo or on the Piazza di Rialto, conversing under the porches, where Florentine, Turkish and Genovese merchants of cloth and silk displayed their wares and the schools of painting and music had their head-quarters. Here could be seen a map of the world in relief, showing the routes through which the city of Venice plied her trade.

Titian felt as though wings were sprouting on the soles of his feet, but with a great effort of will he remained close to his master, the *gastaldo*; although he found the latter's company wearisome, he realized that he could learn much from it—the best rules of perspective, the rules for grinding colours, the technique of transferring a drawing onto a prepared board with the silver-point.

On the subject of pigments and technique, the master launched out from time to time into a lamentable rigmarole of complaints. The main reason for his suspicion and displeasure was the vogue for oily varnishes and ultra-finished surfaces which Antonello da Messina had imported from Flanders. A revolution, he called it. He was the head of the painter's guild, as Giacomelli del Fiore, the teacher of Carlo Crivelli, had been before him, and the old-established, valid systems were good enough for him. However, heated discussions and arguments about technique were continually flaring up in the house: Valerio and Francesco, who were both intransigent mosaicists, reinforced their theory that even the art of stone could not be destroyed by the salt atmosphere of Venice by hotly defending the new practice of painting in oils; they argued that even if the necessity to employ oily pigments that could resist humidity did not arise in other parts of Italy as it did in Northern countries, this was exactly what was needed in Venice. Had not the frescoes by Guariento in the Sala del Gran Consiglio gone to rack and ruin, owing to the moisture in the atmosphere? And though Gentile Bellini had done his best to restore them, the fire that had finally destroyed them a year ago was probably the best thing that could have happened. Master Sebastiano objected that the Flemish painters did not deserve the credit of having re-discovered the use of oil; already in the year 1100 the monk Theophilus had taught how to dilute pigments with oil, and a century later Pietro di Sant-Aderamo still mentioned it in his treatise *De coloribus faciendis*—and finally, had it not always been a usual practice to cover paintings in tempera with a varnish consisting of one part of sandarac dissolved in three parts of linseed oil? The Flemish technique demanded the use of an extremely liquid pigment, which was obtained by successive glazes of a small amount of linseed oil and a large quantity of amber varnish, an extremely laborious procedure. Gentile and Giambellino had not just adopted this method automatically, but had studied it thoroughly and adapted it with great ingenuity, changing the proportions of the solvent, augmenting the quantity of oil and diminishing that of varnish and for the glazes substituting a method of touching-up with fine brush-strokes of thin paint.

Finally the young Zuccatos said that Giambellino, even more than Master Gentile, was now preparing the triumph of the new school by his work on the decorations of the Sala del Gran Conciglio; Gentile had already begun to replace the frescoes in the hall by tempera paintings on canvas, and now that the work had been taken up again after the fire, Giambellino had done the rest with much greater intensity.

It was only natural that Titian felt more and more attracted to the so-called 'revolution'. The months of his apprenticeship, while he had practised the art of laying on a tint with the brush or shading with curving strokes the drawings which he constructed with so much discernment, had certainly not led him to take part in the mosaicist activity that predominated at the Zuccato workshop. Now Francesco and Valerio took it upon themselves to inform Antonio Vecellio that his nephew was indubitably ready to join the ranks of the Bellinis' pupils. Gentile and his half-brother Giambellino more or less shared the studio: what with the increasing zeal of their disciples and the fame of the antiques Gentile had collected, no school more apt to perfect the artistic education of a youth could be imagined.

Old Zuccato thought that it was only right and proper that a lad at the beginning of his career and so obviously gifted, should be initiated in his art by the recognized leaders of the Venetian school. He had promised Antonio and Gregorio Vecellio to do everything in his power so that the boy should develop his potentialities, and therefore he made an appointment with the Bellinis. One morning, at the pre-arranged hour, he was preparing to go to their house with Titian—and as usual, Francesco was nowhere to be found. Yet somehow this strange little personage, who was always on the point of being left behind, managed to emerge from nowhere at the decisive moment. Now again, he suddenly re-appeared and rapidly quenched his thirst. His papers were more or less in order, and he prepared to participate in his brother's destiny. Together they started off, following the *gastaldo*.

Master Gentile Bellini was not in the studio. One of the students volunteered the information that he was upstairs, and sent someone to fetch him. The youth immediately began to gossip: Master Gentile's son-in-law Mantegna in Rome, had received a certain sum for his son Ludovico from the Pope. . . . Master Gentile's daughter, Niccolosa, had arrived in Venice yesterday to spend some time with her father. In the meantime, the other students had got up ceremoniously to salute the old *gastaldo*—and at the same time they threw critical glances at the two boys.

Titian looked round; he felt as though he had strayed into a vast, silent torture-chamber, where truncated statues represented the galvanised corpses of beauty, and the mosaics the petrified winding-sheets of colour, while every activity was subject to the most complicated, scientific rules, systematized to utmost perfection.

The apprentices were at work: one was grinding colours, another, stripped to the waist, was posing near a brazier; a third, with his right arm tied to his body at the elbow, painted with minute, incessant brushstrokes, moving his hand gently by millimetres.

Now Master Gentile arrived from the upper rooms, and with him was Giambellino who had come from the Palazzo Ducale to greet his half-sister.

'*Maestro Zintil, buon di,*' intoned one student.

'*Ser Zuane, buon di.*'

'*Maestro,*' repeated half the chorus.

'*Ser Zuane,*' responded the other.

'*Ser Zintil.*'

'*Maestro Zuane.*'

Francesco and Titian looked at each other, but they maintained a profoundly serious demeanour. The Bellini brothers saluted Master Sebastiano respectfully, though their courtesy was a tribute to his venerable age, and not an expression of the customary familiarity between colleagues of equal rank. However, this attitude was so veiled that the *gastaldo*, thick-skinned as he was and profoundly convinced of his own authority, failed to notice it.

A couple of paintings by Gentile which stood on the easel were then displayed, and Master Sebastiano inspected them with the air of a man who finds himself among his peers, indulging in interminable monologues. At last Gentile, who had made a rough guess at the reason for this visit, turned the conversation to the two boys before his visitor could pry into other paintings. Zuccato ordered the boys to unpack their drawings and showed a few of them, selected for various reasons, to the Bellinis.

While the masters were talking, first one, then two, three, and finally five of their grubby-looking disciples had risen and gathered round inquisitively to look at the drawings. They commented on them with expressions of admiration which betrayed a certain spiteful irony. In a whisper, they asked Titian where he had come from.

'From Cadore.'

'Ah, from the mountains. . . .'

Then they began to talk in whispers about the Zuccatos, their mania for gold, and how with their caskets, their mosaics and their way of intermingling gold with their paint, in the outmoded manner of Crivelli, they used more of the precious metal than the foremost goldsmith in Venice. It was a meretricious way of achieving effects, they said, and such profusion was contrary to the standards of good taste—neither gold nor precious stones that appeared in a painting should actually be gold or stones. And they raised their eyes to Heaven, as though to thank the Lord that here they were doing serious work, not plying a handicraft. After having cooled down the ardour of the neophyte with this first cold douche, they went back to their easels, smoothing their long hair.

The door of the studio opened and a smiling woman appeared on the threshold. 'Here I am, Zinevra', said Giambellino, as he went to meet his wife who was accompanied by Niccolosa. The couple, who lived at Santa Marina, took their leave; Gentile and the *gastaldo* also went outside. Titian, followed by Francesco, walked behind them with his accustomed grave demeanour, that gravity he shared with all the sons of the mountains and which seemed to increase, so that he appeared like a person who had taken a certain vow.

IV

AT the school of the Bellinis, Titian could doubtless have learnt, with less effort than anyone else, to make ordinary paint appear like real gold. It was the least he could have done, seeing that the master gave the same advice to his pupils every day: 'Do as I do, all of you, if you want to succeed as an honest man.' This singular manner of beginning in the plural and concluding in the singular seemed to promise an ideal goal to the one who attained it alone, in legendary isolation as he himself had done, and not by a collective procedure.

Titian worked with a will, but he was beginning to detach himself from the manner of Gentile. The master continued to paint crowded representations of the religious festivals of Venice, the processions on Piazza San Marco, for instance, and he was always sending out his students right and left to make exact studies of the architectural features he intended to represent.

His head bent over his drawing-board, Titian would often ponder over this circumscribed activity of his, and the character of his master's work. As long as the latter received commissions for his pictures of public ceremonies, he himself would be obliged to go around sketching details of houses, balconies, and portals, taking notes of the façades, even down to the ornamental patterns with which the Venetian chimney-tops were decorated. And the result of all this industry was only too well known: insolent critics maintained that in the picture of the procession, the arbitrary perspective had four vanishing-points!

Nevertheless, Titian got to know the city through his frequent explorations of it, he got to know the life of the streets, the moods, anxieties and rumours that were always in the air. Francesco was by his side and sometimes the two boys would sit on a step, executing a drawing divided in two sections so as to save time. When they had sat motionless for a long time, they would become slightly bemused and their thoughts would stray to the last outing they had taken together in Pieve, many, many months ago; they became aware of the passing of

27

time and remembered the feast days that would soon return to plunge
Venice into a turmoil. They remembered that over a year had gone
by since they had started working with the Bellinis, and, rather
redundantly, Titian inscribed the date 1491 onto the margin of the
drawing he had just completed. They listened to the people gossiping
at the street-corner, and looked at each other in amazement as they
heard that '*do zovani*'—two youths—had been arrested the night
before after having been found in bed with some nuns at the convent
of San Spirito. Titian returned to his work, bending down so that
the shadow of his hair fell over his face, but there was no holding
Francesco: he rushed away in hopes of picking up more of these
salacious news-items.

Titian laid his own finished drawing aside, picked up Francesco's
rough attempt and applied himself with the protective patience of a
saint to the task of improving it.

Francesco returned in great excitement: 'It's true—two boys—
really with the nuns! Marco Balbi and Francesco Tajapietra!'

Titian held the corrected drawing under his nose and said curtly:
'Shut up now and let us go home.'

Francesco was now fifteen, a year older than Titian, but already
he was beginning to seek distractions from the rigours of the routine
of work to which his brother applied himself willingly. The others
had talked about it to Titian in the workshop, saying that there was
little to be expected of Francesco's future if he went on like this.

There was little Titian could do about it. Venice offered incessant
temptations, irresistible to a feckless youth like Francesco. He was
always hanging round the principal taverns of the city—the 'Capello
Nero' on the Piazza, the 'Sturion' on the Rialto or the 'Campana'.
During the fine season, he would stray to the rough quarters of the
city, where wharf-porters and drunkards could be found playing the
game known as the bare-headed hunting of the cat, a game in which
a man threw himself head foremost against the belly of a wretched cat
tied to a wall and crushed it with one blow, to the delighted shouts
of the surrounding idlers. Or he would stand entranced watching
the perfumers burning essences on the Piazza San Marco.

It had always been like this: Francesco was like a will-o'-the-wisp
who could appear and disappear as though by magic. Perhaps he would
spend his whole life in this manner, forever hovering on the margin
of the concrete tasks of existence.

In his free time, Titian liked to go and see the Zuccato brothers, whom he usually found immersed in designing mosaics, tissues and all kinds of ornaments. Or, with Master Gentile's permission, he would look through the pages of the sketch-books that had belonged to the latter's father, Jacopo, the founder of the school. It contained studies of architecture, of warriors, of St Jerome with his lion, of St Christopher; notes of Latin inscriptions had been set down next to drawings of armour, and ever and again there were studies of lions and lionesses. All this evoked the heroic, romantic mood in which Titian delighted.

He gazed at these pictures with the kind of beatific calm which always filled his spirit when he had a long time before him in which he could do as he liked. He experienced a similar sensation to the one he had felt at Pieve—how many years had gone by since then?—when he had been inspired by the engravings of Mars or the print of that clumsy little picture of St Mark. Serenely, he began to copy one of the lions, and then put away the precious collection which Gentile treasured as reverently as a holy relic.

*   *   *

One day his master had charged him with a message and he went to Giambellino's house in Santa Marina, as he had already done several times. Inside, a voice was singing—an angelically virile voice. He listened, unable to bring himself to speak. With a gesture towards the house where the voice continued to vibrate as though seeking an outlet into the open air, Giambellino said:

'Go along—it's Zorsi.'

Zorsi? Titian had never heard of him. He entered the studio.

A painting by Giambellino had been set up on the easel. With his back to the door, a young man stood before it, grinding his colours and singing, his powerful legs apart like a watchman who sings to the moon. He interrupted his song to ask who was there.

'I, Tiziano Vecellio.'

'Ah, you work with Master Zentil', said the other, adding that he had been told that Titian was one of the best pupils there, and that he had convinced himself of it when he had seen him in the courtyard putting out some of his work to dry. But why not rather come to work with Giambellino? he asked suddenly. Then, putting aside the colours he was grinding, he began to point out the beauties of the painted allegory on the easel, extolling them as enthusiastically as though he had been displaying a painting of his own, something improvised in a moment of inspiration. 'Look,' he cried. On a sumptuous pavement composed of the most polished inlaid marble, figures of children and adults, both nude and draped, stood united in mysterious silence. The very atmosphere was religion, space had been transmuted into the pure poetry of perspective, and the colours into intelligence. On that pavement with all its perfections the void had been constructed, but the very breath of the landscape was atmosphere, a magic which neither Gentile, nor Carpaccio nor Mantegna could have evoked so movingly.

'The Blessed Virgin, Saint Jerome, Saint Sebastian . . .,' young Vecellio began.

His companion explained that the picture was an allegory of the Tree of Life; then he began to grind his colours again, moving his ochre-daubed hands as though he were unravelling threads of honey.

'I am Zorzo da Castelfranco,' he remarked, and then began once more to pound up ochre and honey, singing as he worked.

Titian gazed at him in silent admiration. This young man filled the whole room with the power of his presence and his voice, a voice that was both manly and exquisitely sweet as it rose to the sky, wandering among the green and brown tints of the painted landscape as though it were itself an element seeking communion with the other elements of nature.

Giorgione, as they called Giorgio da Castelfranco, was only slightly older than Titian, but far more developed physically. His fine neck supported a strong head with a mop of wavy hair; his eyes were large, deep and melancholy; his powerful body seemed impelled by an agitation which was soothed by the gentle radiance of his voice. A hole in his hose revealed, like a jewelled plaque, a patch of white skin above the right knee. The situation was one of almost magical suspense: Titian was at a loss for words, moved as he was by the painting and the singing voice.

Now Giorgio interrupted his song again to ask what he was now working at with Master Gentile.

'On a picture of a ceremony.'

'What, not again?' the other exclaimed. Then he went on to say that magnanimous as the Gran Consiglio might be, it was the ruination of art. The Doge cultivated the arts, but he extinguished any inspiration in the artists by obliging them to carry out works of this kind. And private individuals could not make up their minds to take the initiative and decorate their houses as they thought fit, with paintings of different subjects. 'The Government . . . the Church . . . the Church . . . the Government. . . .' Giorgione hummed angrily. Artists needed commissions, but they needed freedom too. In Venice, the glorification of the state was assuming excessive proportions. It was up to the patricians to make an end to this mania for collecting old rubbish and ancient miniatures. One or the other of them, like Grimani, had started to buy paintings by Memling and Bosch, but the main reason was their rarity and their foreign origin—while it was the duty of the rich to support the Venetian artists.

Again he contemplated Giambellino's 'Allegory'. Giorgione recapitulated his praises of the conception, the poetic movement, the depth of the content; he enumerated the painters who had worked in Florence, collaborating with poets and writers—Botticelli, Piero di Cosimo, Pollaiolo. . . . It was a Parnassus, unique in its way.

'I cannot continue to sing liturgies for the rest of my life!' he cried, and went on to explain that the artist must be free to celebrate the beauty of his own inspirations and the delight of the senses. Had not Master Gentile been obliged to go and live with the Turks in order to paint amorous scenes and unclothed figures? he terminated, alluding to the fact that Mahomet II had commissioned Gentile, among other things, to paint some libertine pictures for him.

Titian listened entranced, like one hearing messianic tidings. In a flash, this mysterious singer daubed with honey, this painter stained with ochre, had stirred and stimulated all his profoundest intuitions.

Twilight was gathering, and they made haste to put everything back in order before darkness fell. Without lighting the lamp, they left the house together. The building outside appeared deeper and richer in colour, enhanced by the scattered gold of the sunset reflected in the canals.

'I would like to paint every one of these facades, to decorate them with angels and heroes. I would like to paint every house in Venice!' Giorgione said, looking up at the women leaning out of the windows and pointing out one and then another to his companion. He stepped along lightly, a fine, broad-shouldered figure.

The women were beginning to come out of the houses now, closely veiled, walking slowly on their high *calcagnetti* or *zibre*, the wooden shoes covered with satin or embroidered velvet which raised them as much as two hands from the ground. Like midgets transformed into giantesses, supporting themselves with one hand on the shoulder of a maid-servant and with the other on that of a twin companion, they plodded along painfully, dominating the entire width of the alleys and obstructing them like slow-moving, limping heifers. Not infrequently one might see one of them lying on the ground, her gown pitifully spoilt, sometimes even having marred her face or broken a bone. But when they walked, they were grandiose, abundant apparitions; panting as they moved on their high stilts, they proceeded, turning their faces up to the young moon from time to time. Now every window was outlined in light. In the end the women stopped at a landing-stage and their cavaliers assisted them to install themselves in the gondola.

The air was full of love, and Giorgione's nostrils quivered like those of a lonely stallion nostalgically scenting all the secret beauty of the prairie. . . .

V

Nᴏᴛ for the first time Titian experienced a strange emotion, an uprush of blood that set his cheeks on fire. A mere nothing sufficed—the attitude of a woman, an insinuation of Francesco's, for instance that story about the two youths and the nuns—and he felt as though the flush that throbbed through his veins was spreading over the whole of Venice, tinging his cheeks with the consciousness of a repressed emotion and colouring the city with countless tints of sweetly dangerous, wanton tenderness.

He understood all this better now that he frequently kept company with Giorgione, who revealed many secrets to him. He was far more developed physically, exuberant and extremely handsome, and he had already thrown off all restraint in amorous matters.

Titian looked up to him as to a superhuman hero, though Giorgione was not ostentatious about his prowess. But he often sang in the studio, sang more divinely than any lover could have loved, for his song was the quintessence of love, and when he fell silent as he worked, his silence disturbed Titian even more profoundly. Giorgione seemed to have his being in well founded, floating musical harmonies, and his companion involuntarily endowed the entire city with these harmonies, interpreting nature. Love, the love of the senses, seemed invincible, wearing down the spirit so that it crumbled, like the plaster on the houses that shed their scales like serpents in the sunshine.

The distant snows of Pieve symbolized a morality, made up of bigotry and senatorial pride, to which Titian still adhered faithfully. That Alpine background of family trees against which his father, Master Gregorio, stood out in his exemplary and stubborn attitude, repeating for the hundredth time his dissertation on the dynasty of the Vecellios and their supreme principles of good conduct, constantly re-appeared to give his lungs great gusts of health-giving fresh air and re-evoke the memory of bygone purity.

Far removed from snows and family trees, Venice basked in the seductive sunlight, panting in a barely concealed frenzy of living. Under the Venetian sunlight lay many ships built of sturdy, robust trees—neither the snows nor the oppressive family-trees of the provinces. The ships landed and sailed away, having disgorged into the city their riches and conspiracies, carpets and slaves, parrots and perfumes. In the steadily increasing heat of the summer, the boys in the populous quarters plunged naked into the canals, tucking their long hair behind their ears, the women on the terraced roofs sat in the sun until they were exhausted, and in the evening, other women alone in their houses leant out of the windows with a rushlight beside them that illuminated their neck and shoulders; Titian often came upon a couple locked in a passionate embrace in narrow alleys like dark dank passages; all this enraptured him.

Love and lust was everywhere, scaling the façades of palaces and convents, intoxicating the foreigners. The Senate yelped ineffectually and the religious authorities did what they could to check the immigration of nuns and women pilgrims, for once they had come to Venice, they inevitably ended as harlots. Galleys weighed anchor, armies sailed to fight in distant lands, but the city continued to unfurl her majestic rituals of pride and sensuality.

Segregated patrician ladies paraded like arrogant peahens, erect on their stilts and loaded with jewels, when the Doge celebrated his nuptials with the sea, or when mummers and clowns were performing. Courtesans, expert in the arts of love, could be seen smiling from under their veils, revealing sparkling teeth that had been rubbed with a mixture of gum Arabic, aloes and alum, while their eyes cast languid or flashing glances around. Splendid young men appeared, noble as thoroughbreds, and, when it came to amorous adventures, as touchy as rival turkey-cocks; or curious apparitions of which even the sex was indistinguishable—girls concealing their feminity under masculine garments and ample, mushroom-like head-dresses, or pretty boys parading in women's clothes.

In the vast, dark silence of the night, while this motley world of lost souls was frenziedly immersed in its own pleasures and interests, it often happened that an unexpected fire broke out and an entire quarter of the town echoed with desperate screams. It was not unlike a Venetian festival with fire-works when, during one of these tragedies, sparks rose up and flaming rafters were submerged by the waters of the canals; the universal confusion recalled the most perverse and terrifying moments of the ancient Saturnalia. But then the implacable humidity, the silence and solitude of the lagoon absorbed every echo, every flash of light, every movement. Another day of sunshine—and once again the rapacious features of the citizens would reflect their silent jealousies and their silent intrigues, their calculated generosity and their ruthless speculations.

There could be no doubt that a sense of crazed, burning complicity, generated by the mania of conspiracy, by a mere whisper, a mute understanding or simply by a caprice, yet powerful enough to sweep away love itself, was obvious even to the innocent eyes of the most harmless spectator. They all spied on each other and informed on each other. A mute sensuality pervaded the strange city where men, bereft of horses, bestrode other human beings and the sons of the people assumed heroic poses, rowing with tensed muscles. Propelled by the vertical force of their own body poised in equilibrium, like an heraldic symbol of procreation they flew over the waters. Insatiably, passionately, unceasingly, they made love.

The custom of free love was universally accepted, as the nuptial solemnity, though frequently celebrated, was a prerogative of the great families and their descendants. Concubinage and the adoption of sons by mistresses or *mamole** was sanctified by usage.

They made love insatiably. No restraint was imposed on the natural instincts, yet an unnatural element was continually meandering through the silence. The waters communicated the silence, but they exasperated the senses. A sibilant whispering, like that of the waters, filled the city: in whispers the people plotted, discussed business, made love or announced that an epidemic had broken out.

Young boys played a game which they called, in their Venetian dialect, *zogar a portarsene*, which Titian watched in amazement. One boy sitting astride another who pretended to sell salt or fish would have his buttocks ceremoniously pinched by others playing the buyers, who then ran away with the wares they had acquired by pinching hard. Another boy mimed a goat-herd leading his goats to pasture; the boys playing the goats bent their heads and hopped along on all fours, bleating merrily until they were caught by the goat-herd and the

---

**Mamola*—a housekeeper and concubine. Though she occupied a subordinate position domestically, she fulfilled all the duties of a wife without being bound by marriage vows. Content to live in obscurity, she was a good mother, but also a lover, often the unassuming companion of an artist devoted to his profession who felt unable to endure the ties of matrimony.

purchasers of milk, who pretended to milk them by twisting their genitals. Some ran away to avoid the pain caused by the spite or roughness of their playmates, only to return on the following day, covered with bruises but ready to begin all over again, unable to resist the call of a curious attraction towards each other.

Before the crowded, fabulous background of little bridges and narrow canals, Titian had been leaning against a wall stippled by the last rays of the sun on an afternoon early in April. He left his post of observation and walked towards the Palazzo Ducale, where he was to meet Giorgione. A dense crowd had collected round the two famous columns, the columns of justice. All the people converged towards one spot, but most of them were as silent as spectators waiting for a performance to begin. Titian found himself next to the house-boy of an inn who was showing a stranger round the city, so he had to listen to the boy telling his client the history of the columns while the crowd surrounding them pressed ever closer.

Originally there had been three columns, the boy began. They had been shipped from Constantinople, and while they were being brought ashore, one of them fell into the water and remained there. The other two were left lying in a corner and had stayed there so long that it was a wonder they had not been worn away by the backsides of the idlers who used them as benches. It had not been possible to find an engineer capable of setting them up, until at long last a native of Lombardy, Nicolo Barattiere, succeeded in erecting them. He was rewarded not only by a premium, but by obtaining permission for gamblers to play games of chance at the foot of the columns without incurring the legal penalty. . . .

'Are they gambling now?' asked the stranger, pointing to the crowd seething round the columns.

'No, they're going to execute a criminal,' the boy replied and was about to continue his story when he was interrupted by a confused clamour arising in the crowd. The condemned man was being led to the centre of the open space. 'Sodomite!' shouted some, while others yelled: 'To the devil with him!'

The house-boy began again, pointing to the bronze lion on the left column, but the stranger interrupted him. 'Who is the criminal?' he asked.

'One Bernardino Correr. They are hanging him because he wanted to force Master Hieronimo Foscari to commit sodomy, and cut the laces of his breeches at night, in Ca'Trevisan at San Bartolomeo,' said the boy, and continued calmly to explain the statue of St Theodore on the other column: the saint was holding his shield on his right arm instead of on the left to show that the Republic was armed for defence only. . . .

'But are they really going to hang him now?' insisted the horror-struck stranger.

'Certainly, and afterwards they'll burn him,' the boy reassured him, hoping that his client would be satisfied at last and let him earn his dues. Keeping his eyes fixed on the poor wretch about to suffer the supreme penalty, he chattered on imperviously, explaining how the privilege Barattiere had obtained for the gamblers was withdrawn by the Doge because of some incident or other; and that was how the nickname *barattieri* had stuck to the petty thieves and idlers who had been the habitués of that open-air gambling den. . . .

Now the halter was being laid round the condemned man's neck.

'I refuse to stay here!' shouted the stranger who, instead of being allowed to enjoy the beauties of Venice, was being forced to witness a hanging.

'It won't take a moment,' the boy assured him. But the stranger turned to go, and Titian followed him and his companions.

They were now hanging the condemned man.

By sheer force, they succeeded in pushing their way through the crowd and reaching the confines of the Square, where the spectators were thinning out.

'Zorzo!' Titian cried, for now he saw Giorgione with several other friends. He was a head taller than all the people around him, and now came forward with a smile.

They all went to have a supper of fried fish, sitting at a table illuminated by a tallow-candle and looking out at the night which was falling on the smooth waters of the lagoon.

Giorgione announced that Lorenzo Magnifico had died in Florence. Giambellino had repeated many stories about him, which he had heard from Poliziano when the latter had come to Venice in June, a year ago.

Poliziano was enchanted with the city and admired the talents it had produced, but he had spoken in great detail about Florence, her famous and still unknown men of genius, including a marvellous young sculptor called Michelangelo who had been carried home more dead than alive one day, when a rival sculptor had smashed in his nose. The aggressor was Pietro Torrigiani, and he had to flee Florence, so as to escape being punished by the Magnifico. Poliziano, during his travels, had hastened to send exact reports to the great Lorenzo on his meetings with notable Venetians, the most interesting of which he considered the meeting with the famous Cassandra Fedele, a lady as gifted for languages as she was for science, who had written a treatise on the different schools of philosophy entitled *De scientiarum ordine*.

'That is what we need—to know men and women of genius, to frequent personalities of great family and great talent, and not to come down to eating fried fish by the light of a tallow-candle!' they all repeated together. Venice must be great, it was up to them to make her great and admirable. They were ready to decorate the whole of the city from top to bottom, covering the walls of every house with glorious visions of nudes glowing in the sun. . . .

With a slow movement, Giorgione opened his arms wide to the night, as though to sing his passion for life, to embrace all life's voluptuous, ineffable delight, to surrender to the raptures of living.

VI

POLIZIANO had spent his time vaunting the charms of Florence while he was staying in Padua and Venice and visiting the libraries in order to acquire Greek books, which were still hard to come by in Toscana, for his patron Lorenzo Magnifico. In Venice he had commissioned Giovanni Rhosos to copy a treatise on the Resurrection of the Dead by Atenagora and a lexicon by Stephen of Byzantium, both of which formed part of Cardinal Bessarione's collection. Unfortunately, Lorenzo was not to enjoy these possessions, for the copies were not finished till the end of March, 1492, just a week before his death.

The ships arriving now from the East were not only disgorging parrots, slaves and perfumes into the city, but also flooding it with Greek scholars and books. Ever since 1453, the year of the fall of Constantinople, when many learned Greeks had fled to Venice, the patricians who dwelt along the lagoon had begun to receive them in their palaces as teachers. Little sons of the nobility, instead of playing at *zogar a portarsene* like their contemporaries in the populous quarters, were being led by the hand by tutors and taught to recite the Greek alphabet from alpha to omega and vice versa. This alphabet, which Master Gregorio would so dearly have loved to teach his sons, had now become the dominant note of culture most in vogue throughout the city. To this fashion of an elevated Olympian intellectuality the mythological allegories devised by Giorgione, together with Giambellino, may be attributed.

Titian knew little or nothing about Aristotle, from whom, however, the scholars of Padua had culled only very confused ideas until the advent of Almorò Barbaro, who unleashed something amounting to a revolution in the world of letters by going back to the best Aristotelian commentaries and translating them faithfully and competently. Barbaro, the leader of this cultural movement, was supported by Gerolamo Donato and by the majority of the Venetian nobility until the Senate decided to promote the opening of various schools in Venice.

These were schools of Aristotelian philosophy, of Latin, painting and music. A circle of friends of compelling prominence began to form around Giorgione, inspired by his intentions and aspirations. Almorò Barbaro, the son of Clara Vendramin, who was the deceased Doge Vendramin's daughter, and wedded to Zaccaria Barbaro, introduced Giorgione into his mother's family. Through the Barbaros, he was received by the Barbarigos, the kinsfolk of Agostino, the then reigning Doge, and they recommended him to Cardinal Grimani, a great amateur of the arts. Thus it went on, until success and ambition developed Giorgione's personality to such authority that he became capable of influencing even Master Giambellino, who still availed himself of his collaboration or passed on to that of Titian and Basaiti.

Other links of friendship went to form a precious chain: Tuzio Costanzo, a friend of Almorò Barbaro, took Giorgione under his protection: Aldo Manizio, the printer, became a friend of all three and knew Pietro Bembo well. Pietro Bembo often came to Venice and, now friends with the four of them, was joined by the etcher Giulio Compagnola, so that the group numbered six. These were joined by Sebastiano Veneziano and Torbido: together with Titian, these were Giorgio's comrades, among whom Palma and Catena can also be numbered.

They gathered together to make music in the evenings, to perfect the pursuit of love and to seek in the sublimation of this perfection the dominant mood of their life and their taste; thus an ideal society began to be formed.

Contemporary landscapes, where Aristotle could have activated the impassibility of his mind by contact with nature, lay around them between the gardens of Murano: in Venice, leafy boughs overhung the waters where the houses of chosen families were illuminated by torches: fire and air, water and earth—Aristotle, Hippocrates, Seneca.

Women were seated there, profile against profile, and seen among the torches in these nocturnes, in all their gentle softness, they seemed to swell like ripe fruit, while the conversation turned round hyperboles of winged figures and myths of demi-gods.

From time to time, the ladies would slowly turn their full faces to each other and exchange a word of two about their youngest babies, who had been given names of the latest fashion:

'How is your Sofonisba?'

'Thanks be to the Lord God, she is sweeter even than sugar. And your Elena, your Giovano?'

'They are my fortune and my happiness!'

It was natural to begin with these illustrious patricians and make them change their habit of ordering devotional pictures in favour of commissions for painted facades, painted wardrobes and chests, decorated with the fanciful subjects which Giorgione preferred rather too overtly, as he sang:

'Luna, Paris, Cupidine'. . . .

The illustrious patricians became increasingly interested in books, as though to confirm the ideals of grandeur they had about themselves, in sculptures and even more in paintings, where the ideal images of spiritual beauty were visibly demonstrated, and most of all in music, to refine the quality of their emotional pathos.

'Luna, Paris, Cupidine. . . .' 'Son of Venus.'

These names were beginning to make the pomp of Carpaccio's oriental processions appear faded, and Giorgione, with his sonorous and serenely disturbing song, seemed to be releasing new uncharted worlds of the imagination:

'Luna, Paris, Cupidine. . . .' 'Son of Venus.'

As the sounds vibrated through the air, stirring the senses, and the spirit expanded happily under the stimulation of ideas, the blue-black stagnation of the night was traversed by summer lightning that lit up the drowsy green distance of Torcello.

'Luna. . . .'

★　　★　　★

But suddenly, unexpectedly, every voice was repeating another word—the word 'war'.

The violent breath of time which can, in the course of an interminable day or of a brief year, destroy or pile up events, appeared for one eternal moment to embitter the temper of the new generation. War. . . . Yet the immutable exterior life of Venice, constructed out of the silence of eternal and yet fleetingly brief years, drawing its energy from the disproportion between European events and its own magical physiognomy, now began, captiously and triflingly, to fasten with increasing voracity on what was happening in Italy, and story after story was told in every alley and on each successive day about the invasion of Charles VIII and his armies.

Notwithstanding all this, the Supreme Council superintended, as jealously as a lady abbess supervising a convent, the most negligible developments of the smallest details: for instance, was the work of the Bellinis at the Ducal Palace being carried out with all due zeal? On the 24th December, 1493, the order was given that: *Master Bartolomeo Bon, foreman and overseer, must hasten with all diligence each day to the Great Hall of the Palace, to see that the painters make haste to work.'*

In the meantime, great piles of money were being accumulated with which to pay the militia and the most excellent commanders were there to command the troops.

Those were strange years; news came to the Coltrini family from Cadore: Master Gregorio had been elected captain of the Pieve company now under arms. And one evening at the Oltrino home, Francesco, inspired by his father's example, announced his intention of giving up painting and joining the soldiers.

That happened in 1495, a brief year like the one that preceded and the one that followed it. Fourteen ninety-six was a year that passed in a flash, although it consisted of many interminable days. In the warmth of the sun, Titian painted a figure of Hercules on the facade of the Morosini palace.

Giorgione was also painting the exterior of palaces, beginning with his own house at Campo San Silvestro, in order to attract clients: musicians, poets, groups of boys, emperors and other phantasies, painted so well that they appeared to be alive, shivering in the damp air of winter and basking in the summer sunshine, ideally placed above the passage of time like superior onlookers, impervious to the noise of the city, to the sorrow, the lives and deaths of men. Soldiers were dying, princes were dying. In Milan, Beatrice d'Este died, the same Beatrice who had been so sumptuously entertained years ago in Venice. In France, Charles VIII died. In Florence, the vanities were being burned on the main square: a great pyramid had been erected with piled-up rose-coloured masks, lutes inlaid with ebony and ivory, pieces of damask, portraits of great courtesans, books by Petrarca, Boccaccio, Pulci: before the fire was kindled, while the sound of trumpets and bells and the voices of boys dressed as angels were re-echoed across the square, a cynical Venetian merchant offered twenty thousand gold florins for all these gifts of God. But he just escaped being burnt himself. A year later, they burnt Savonarola.

Louis XII of France, the cousin of Charles VIII, proclaimed his titles to Milan. Venice, fearing that the French might land at Pisa, committed errors which filled her allies with suspicion. Proud, suspicious Venice had sent a message to the effect that the lords of Venice had broken the King of France, but the credit for having made Charles VII strike his tents was due to the Spaniards. There was nothing left to the lords of Venice than to accept the fact that, from now on, the two invincible powers in Europe were Spain and France. Venice, poisoned and forced back domestically into the intimate life of the circumscribed city boundaries and the calendar of its long days besieged by the waters, attempted to heal the last scars of the ferocious *morbus gallicus*, the infection which had spread everywhere—the only legacy the French had left.

Caterina, the wife of Gentile Bellini, died: the widower took Maria Trevisani as his second wife. Giambellino's wife Zenevra died. Francesco Vecellio was ailing after being wounded in the war and went to stay in Pieve. But Titian and Giorgione, gazing at the allegories they had painted, felt the energy of eternal youth welling up in them. The first germs of rivalry between them were beginning to develop but, early in the morning of the first day of the year, Titian was standing in front of the beautiful facade of Campo San Silvestro and called out: 'Zorzo! Get up, Zorzo! Our century has begun!'

It was the first day of the year 1500.

VII

THE Turks had declared war against Venice, and war it was, no matter how hard the Venetians tried to conceal the significance of that word from themselves and ignore the daily reminders of it. The gondolas, like dolphins with their serrated teeth, glided over the water slowly, unceasingly, as though all the world were at peace.

A rumour went round that in one of these gondolas, Leonardo da Vinci had passed along the Grand Canal on a certain morning in March. His admirers hastened breathlessly to get more information. Had it really been Leonardo? Who had first spread the news? An austere-looking gentleman accompanied by a strikingly hand-some youth and another gentleman, had been seen in a gondola. Possibly it had only been a merchant with his minion, or a foreigner, two foreigners, accompanied by a lad. But before nightfall the news had been confirmed from several quarters: it was Leonardo with one of his models, and a high-ranking personage who had already made contact with engineers and authorities of the Great Council. Toma Tito had received the news through his father and he informed Titian that the personage accompanying Leonardo was Loca Pacioli, and the handsome curly-headed youth who had attracted so much atten-tion was called Andrea Sala, *il Salaino*, the great master's favourite pupil. The next day Leonardo was to have a confidential interview with the directors of the Arsenal and the members of Senate, concerning certain plans of his for measures of offence and defence for the navy, in which the government were extremely interested. Toma Tito added in a whisper that it was possible their friends the Barbarigos might arrange a meeting with the inaccessible, mysterious Leonardo, once the discussions with the Senate were over.

However, the negotiations were slow and difficult; the plans were examined and the estimates studied with exasperating hesitancy and suspicion. In the end, the Great Council, which in 1485 had refused to support the venturesome voyage of Christopher Columbus, turned

44

down Leonardo's plans as well. The news spread through the city that he was leaving Venice immediately.

Il Salaino, the handsome Andrea, who had spent not only his time but also the money he had pilfered from his master buying materials, perfumes and antiques, laid great stress on the fact of Leonardo's imminent departure, hoping to ingratiate himself with the Venetians. He supplemented his indiscretion about the plans by telling everybody that the master had made a wonderful drawing in Mantua, shortly before he came to Venice: it was an unfinished portrait in black chalk and sanguine of Isabella d'Este, the sister of Beatrice, and was later to be executed in oils.

Lorenzo da Pavia discussed it with everybody, and Andrea readily anticipated the questions people asked him by revealing details about Leonardo's painstaking and complicated technique. Everybody asked him to obtain permission for them to view this wonderful drawing. He arranged appointments, but it was obvious that this only irritated Leonardo, who refused to see anybody. The possibility of visiting the studio depended on Andrea's resources. By a miracle, he finally received the Master's permission to display the renowned work and invited Giorgione, Titian, Palma, Sebastiano and others to admire the profile of Isabella with its effects of light and shade, as well as other studies which Andrea had secretly taken from the master's portfolio.

Critical comments were arrested in mid-air. The silence, created both by Leonardo's absence and the presence of his personality, and the dim light of the late afternoon, plunged inanimate things and living faces into a tenuous shadow; the charming youth, slightly embarrassed, slowly turned over the drawings while a faint smile curved his lips as he peered from under his eyelids at the masterly chiaroscuro of the drawings for which he had posed and where infinite variations of his own features had been immortalized. A comparison of these portrait sketches with the model showed Leonardo's mastery; even in the slightest study he succeeded in conveying a sculptural quality. A cheek appeared modelled by a delicate veil of shading, like a cloud that is imbued by its own suspended volume even as it vanishes into space. There were other drawings where one could not discover any definite outlines, but nebulous shadows of varying intensity gave a modelling both fluid and deep to the features of that multiple countenance which, from drawing to drawing, summed up the unique face of Salaino.

This profound three-dimensional power seemed to come from within, from far away, from a distant inward world.

As they discussed the drawings, they remembered the shading on some of the faces painted by Giambellino, which was not to be compared with what they were seeing now. The breath of life was in the chiaroscuro of these images, even to the contours created with light; they initiated a new sense of form and expanded the limits of modelling.

'The Master is late', the handsome Andrea kept on repeating, but they all felt sure that he was in the next room, waiting for them to go away.

They took their leave. In the silent alleys with their diminishing perspective, the men's faces appeared, in the light of the afternoon, to be modelled by shadows such as Leonardo had created. Titian turned his eyes from one to the other without a word, like one who sees some strange sight for the first time.

*   *   *

He was often to remember these drawings.

When he looked at his studies and sketches at night, when the light of his oil-lamp flickered behind the magnifying lens of a bulging glass jar filled with water, he would become absorbed in the interplay of mass and volume. It was augmented as the little flame grew bigger and its light shone steadily in the lens of the glass. The darkness of the spaces around him, unbroken and monotonous, seemed equally magnified. Beating like a pulse, he could feel his will and the ardency of his life increasing.

In this expansion of every dimension, he felt inspired to transform the arid landscapes of Giambellino's allegorical tradition into stronger compositional constructions, giving far greater authority to the figures he represented. He took the decision to look at everything as intently as though he were to portray it.

He had just completed a votive picture commissioned by the Pesaro family, depicting Alexander VII at the steps of St Peter's throne, presenting Cardinal Baffo to him. The *cognoscenti* considered that this work owed everything to Bellini. But now he was in complete agreement with the ideas of Giorgione and Palma, intent on conquering space and rendering depth in a monumental reality which must be continually verified by contact with reality. For instance, the image of Daria bleaching her hair on the roof was still one of those memories which seemed to him a vision to be realized. He hesitated whether he should call her Goddess or Madonna, but he foresaw that what he would paint was going to be an elementary and mysterious figure to which he would give the tangible attributes of beauty, the intrinsic quality which every human body possesses as a creature of solid flesh and blood, with a whole history written in its eyes. A portrait, therefore—not one, but many portraits. A figure, perhaps even two or three together—such were the ideas that floated through his mind.

Giorgione had painted compositions. The study of the formal classicism of antiquity had caused rather too manifestly a revival of the spirit of formal sylvan allegories. Memories of Pieve, of journeys to Asolo and Padua, towns on dry land in the green countryside, imparted new strength to certain simplifications with which Titian was now beginning to free himself from the influence of Giorgione. The latter continued to paint figures possessed of a certain mysterious fascination. Indifferently, he let them be called Ptolomy, Pythagoras and Archimedes, the three Magi, the three Ages of Man, Virgil, Aristotle and Averroes, or Evander, Aeneas and Palladius. Young Lotto had painted a Danae and other mythological subjects. Now Isabella Gonzaga, who had so great a preference for the works of Mantegna, was insisting that Giambellino should paint a symbolical picture of an antique subject for her. She had also ordered paintings from Perugino, demanding that they be executed with perfection and diligence, so that they might bear comparison with the subtle style of Mantegna, which she appreciated so highly.

Mantegna had created a mythology all his own from the antique visions, in a nervous, compact style: the sound of the curving shells into which his nude demi-gods, their bulging muscles garlanded with acanthus leaves, were blowing, had now found an echo on the Nordic hunting-horn of Albrecht Dürer.

Titian's mythology was clearer, based on the credibility of historic events and, above all, on the traditions of Rome; thus it was more provincial, but more dramatic. Choosing a theme, such as Lucrece, Pompey and Tarquinius, he would search for his models in real life, studying the attitudes of people in the crowd who stood watching a wedding cortège of gondolas or the fireworks at one of the fiestas of the Compagnie della Calza. Many people were prepared to lay bets on his success as a painter, even though the Senate had no use for him as yet and employed artists of the older generation to carry out the decorations in the Sala del Gran Consiglio—Giambellino and Alvise Vivarini.

The seasons came and went as he sat by the little flame that shed its light through the belly of the water-jug, either with the window open to the night during the heat of early summer, or barred and bolted to keep out the cold of winter. As time went by, the slightest claim to superiority might easily have led from a harmonious conjunction to an absolute supremacy. Any occasion could bring it about.

A spark only, this light, a spark that fired up or subsided in the tepid belly of the jug. . . . Giorgione and Titian were both working hard and delighting in each other's generous vitality, but Titian was aware of the spark of their rivalry. He saw it every night in the crystal globe. Zorzo's songs would come into his mind and a pang of jealousy would grip his heart like a vice.

'Zorzi, Zorzon!' was what all the women called Giorgione. Now he was again hearing those melodious phrases, far away in the night.

Outside someone was singing, possibly Giorgio himself. There were other voices on a deeper note—one could have been that of Sebastiano, who also loved to sing, and several others, a chorus. Slowly, Titian felt soothed and his inner restlessness subsided. He leant back in his chair and sank into a pleasant torpor.

In the empty space of the night, the voices extended their range without separating from each other, then again they faded and the sound of one high voice alone re-emerged, like a sweet cry. A deep, buzzing murmur, a choral lament and a thousand echoes. . . .

Shaking his head, he attempted to persuade himself that he was hearing these sonorous accents in his mind only. Then he caught one word—one cry that chilled his blood, and a furious jangle of bells rent the silence. Titian started up and leapt to his feet.

'Zorzo!' he called out unconsciously and instinctively. He ran to the window and threw it open. In the gust of cold air that rushed in, all the sharp cries seemed to turn to ice on his skin, the cries which, between sleep and waking, he had been transforming into the sweetness of songs. People were screaming and shouting, and from every side the bells were clanging desperately.

'What's on fire?'

'The Fondaco! The Fondaco dei Tedeschi!'

In a sudden panic, he found himself running down the stairs—he could not have run faster if he had learnt that his own home was on fire. Then he remembered the burning wick, the spark of inspiration and discord: breathlessly he ran back to his room and blew it out before he rushed into the street.

People were running in the dark alleys, asking for information as they bumped into each other. When they came into the neighbourhood of the Rialto they had to stop, for here an enormous crowd had already gathered.

The building of the Fondaco had been burning for more than half-an-hour and even the surrounding alleys were piled high with a confusion of salvaged goods, sacks, chairs, luggage, silverware, all bundled together, weapons, clothes, capes, furnishings that had been spoilt by the flames and were impregnated with the stench of burning.

The woodwork of the Rialto bridge had been saved from the fire, but the crowd was howling as though it had been overtaken by the deluge.

The German merchants were cursing in their own language and trying to pile up the goods they had salvaged from the burning warehouses. One moment they were driving back over-zealous helpers who got in their way, the next blindly accusing others of stealing their property. Truculent brawls developed: a procuress, who fed all the cats of the district and was in the habit of accosting the merchants, fared badly in one of these. Boats had been overturned when several tenants started throwing their property out of the windows into the canal below. Several things had gone to the bottom, others struck people near the landing stage and wounded them, others had been fished up by anonymous profiteers who had quietly disappeared.

The *Visdomini* and the other authorities directed the operations like officers taking a fortress by storm. Porters were carrying salvaged goods to the nearby Loggie of the Rialto or to the Lipomano Palace; at the windows of the houses near the Fondamento, in the intermittent light of the fire, one could distinguish excited people putting on their clothes and loading themselves with goods and chattels. From windows further off, images of Saint Mark, reliquaries, rosaries and holy pictures were being held out towards the endangered area, and a chorus of voices implored: '*Sancto, Sancto Marco in hora mortis nostrae*', invoking rain, snow, frost, all the cataracts from heaven that can come down in January. But those who shouted most and were having the time of their lives were a few over-dressed, cynical young men, from whom in

D

the past some of the foreign merchants, before parting with a ducat, had demanded every form of perversion: now that their parsimonious admirers were besides themselves with frenzy, they avenged them by mocking them, splitting their sides with laughter.

The merchants, as grim-faced as mastiffs, were shouting while they lugged away useless things. For a moment, an infernal confusion reigned; an unfortunate courtesan found herself hemmed in by the crowd and separated from the servant who supported her: she fell from her stilts, hurt herself, was first insulted, and then assisted and taken away. A small group were cleaving through the crowd: supported and carried by helping hands, one saw three men who had been horribly disfigured by burns: they were howling as though possessed by demons.

'Marco! . . . Oh, Marco!' shouted one of them, a broker.

'Marco!' others called out.

'Marco! Sancto Marco!' they all cried out together.

'Marco! Marco mio! Marco mio! . . .' the wounded man cried out again. He was not invoking the saint, but imploring the bystanders to rescue his own brother who bore that name. Two of the lads who were with him ran back. They were calling to him from the bridge—Marco, one of the youngest brokers of the Fondaco, who had done his best to save the goods by throwing them down to the errand-boys and porters. But now he had disappeared. They were still calling out to him when, in the fierce heat of the destructive flames and the oscillating reflections of that inferno, slowly, silently, obliquely, a gentle rain began to fall. From every side shouts arose: The Almighty has wrought a miracle, Saint Mark has wrought a miracle! People embraced each other, they knelt down and held out their hands, turning their palms upwards to collect the raindrops which they kissed devoutly.

Guards and brokers implored the crowd to make way and clear the danger zone: the chain of tireless helpers who passed each other pails and buckets of water was beginning to disintegrate, and they were shouting for others to relieve them. But now the rain was falling harder, a heaven-sent aid for the cursing, sweating men.

Titian noticed the calm bearing of Bernardo Barbarigo, who had brought his man-servant to lend a hand in the salvage operations. He was able to make his way to his side and found him talking to Francesco de'Garzoni, who had succeeded him as commissary of the salt-department: while they were gazing at the scene of disaster, they were joined by Giorgione.

Titian looked at him intently, as though he were now seeing in reality someone he had known for a long time in his dreams. As in a reverie they stood in silence in front of the flames that were now dying down.

'No one will profit by this calamity except you, the architects and painters,' Barbarigo said at last.

For there was nothing left of the Fondaco except a black, smoking skeleton.

VIII

Such a disaster in a city like Venice, swarming with artists and architects, of whom every one was eager to snatch the others' commissions, plans and contracts from under their very noses, represented the most splendid opportunity that had been offered for many years.

A few days passed, while a quarter of the city's inhabitants kept to their beds, nursing the bruises, wounds, burns and colds they had incurred during the night of the 28th January, 1505. Then, when the German merchants and the *Visdomini* had been settled in the Loggie di Rialto and the palace of the Lipomani family rented for the occasion and the scene of the disaster cleared of the débris, which threatened to collapse, the authorities announced a competition for the erection of a new edifice. Those who entered the lists were Giorgio Spavento, a civic architect whose talent was universally recognized, and Girolamo Todesco—in other words, 'German Jerome'—equally gifted and highly favoured by his compatriots, the merchants.

The architects went to work and handed in their plans, their elevations, their estimates and sketches for the marble decorations. These schemes became the talk of the town, even though Venice's chief title to fame remained the continual work for the embellishment of the Sala del Gran Consiglio, and the interior of Saint Mark's.

Summer had come while the two names, Spavento and Todesco, and their plans, were being considered. Finally, Todesco's plan was chosen. The Senate, with a solemn but diplomatically-worded decree, declared that, owing to the solicitations of the merchants from Germany, the plans of their compatriot had been accepted, but it was specifically stated that 'no single thing in marble should be made in that Fondaco, nor was any carving to be done in secret'.

'So they'll make it of paper, with painted doors and windows!' commented Giorgione, leaning his head on the shoulder of his mistress,

52

the beautiful Cecilia. 'Of paper—so that it can burn down more easily!' he added, laughingly.

Cecilia drew her fingers through his thick brown curls; the friends sitting round the table, where the ruby-red wine glowed in the goblets and the dishes shone like full moons, burst out laughing. Those nearest to him were Giorgio's followers, the latest of whom had come from Florence. This was Pietro da Feltre, known as Zarato, but nicknamed 'the corpse' by Giorgione, owing to the deathly pallor of his face and the blueish tinge of the skin over his sunken orbs.

Titian was spending a short holiday at Pieve; it had to be short because he hoped that some good might come to him from the affair of the Fondaco, and also because Giorgione, laughing and self-confident, was waiting for what his self-confidence promised him.

Owing to the restrictions and in order to gain time, elaborate marble work was out of the question—therefore it was to be expected that the walls of the Fondaco would be painted. That was what everybody in Venice was saying, and what Titian was repeating in Pieve; he promised himself every day that he would leave on the morrow, return to the city and solicit the support of Bernardo Barbarigo, who had been commissary of the salt works before joining the Council of Ten.

When he mentioned his friends and patrons, the faces of the worthy provincials lengthened in amazement. When they all sat together in the contentment of the long, light summer days, old Conte, Andrea and Tiziano, his parents would ask about his departure, which he kept announcing and postponing, and he hinted how happy he was to be with them here, where his intense nostalgia was at last appeased, where he could recapture his happiest memories—here, in Cadore. Yet it was not impossible that new fuel had been added to both nostalgia and memories. Cecilia, the daughter of Master Alò, who had come into the world during a snowstorm long ago, was now a young girl of such radiant loveliness that Titian could not bear to think of the day which would force him to say goodbye to her. She did many little jobs in the Vecellio home, and Titian had persuaded her to pose for him several times. During the long silences while he was working she remained immobile, a frightened little girl, but the fact that he was looking at her filled her with courage and ambition.

Then the day came when Titian had to announce his departure on the morrow, and this time he was in earnest. Cecilia arrived and brought him some shirts which she had sewn for him, and while Titian was carefully varnishing the portraits he had painted of Master Gregorio and his mother, the girl was twisting and crumpling the shirts between her hands and twisting and muddling her words in her confusion. She looked like a pure lily, a little saint, and yet the blushes, caused by the uncontrollable emotion that terrified her, stained the milk-white skin of her cheeks.

'You must sew many more shirts for me', Titian said, and she blushed even more deeply. He added that she would have to sit for him for all the saints of Paradise, when he was comissioned to paint them, and she was on the point of fainting with emotion. Once already, he had caressed her and said that he would take her with him as soon as he had a home of his own in Venice. 'Will you come?' he asked. Now she was weeping as she clasped the last of the shirts to her breast, as though to restrain the wild, painful beating of her heart.

'With you, *Titian*? . . .' she murmured in her dialect, and then fell silent, suspended on the brink of an existence for which she hardly dared to hope.

'With me. D'you understand?'

'With you. . . .'

'With me.'

*　　*　　*

When he got back to Venice, he found that Alvise Elmo had succeeded Garzoni in the direction of the salt-works. Girolamo Todesco had received an order at Cattaro, and so he had lost that of reconstructing the Fondaco. Giorgio Spavento had now begun to work on it.

Titian saw all his companions again. The Coltrinis, the Barbarigos, the Zuccatos, Sebastiano Luciani, Palma, Giambellino, who was paint-ing the portrait of Bembo; he saw them all, because they all knew that he had returned, and he also lost no time in seeing Giorgione; although they talked frankly to each other about their work, they both knew that the passionate sincerity of their friendship was now a thing of the past.

One day, with other friends, they met before Giorgione's house at San Silvestro; Giorgio knocked at the door and told Titian to keep his eyes open, for he would now see the most beautiful picture that had ever been painted appearing on the façade.

'Cecilia,' he called.

Between the wonderfully coloured figures of the frescoes, there now appeared in the frame of a small window a more dazzling vision than all those painted ones that absorbed the light.

'Cecilia. . . .' The strange coincidence struck Titian with a kind of incredulous amazement. Now she came to open the door, with a tiny black kitten on her arm, curled up like a sleeping baby. She was laughing, and the white bosom revealed by her low-cut dress seemed to be laughing too—only the kitten remained dark and silent. They wanted to caress it, for in her arms it seemed like a strangely bewitched child, and to touch it lightly, calling 'Pst, pst, Diavolin!'

The girl bent backwards, for fear that the kitten might scratch her; against the tapestry-like background of the sunlit, painted wall, she seemed to be the only creature modelled in the round, worthy of the heroic physique of her lover, who was standing beside her. The physical beauty of these two was such that one could sense the fierce and silent urge that drove them towards each other, by the yearning of their flesh, a mute, voracious passion.

*　　*　　*

In the meantime, beams of the best timber were rising to the sky: people were saying that the laying of the new foundation for the Fondaco and the construction up to the first floor was to take twelve months, at a monthly cost of three hundred ducats.

The merchants gazed admiringly at the work and puffed themselves up proudly when they stood talking in front of their future dwelling with Albrecht Dürer, who had been to Venice already in 1491 and had now returned in order to complete certain of his sketches of perspective and to paint an altar-piece for the church of San Bartolomeo. In the meantime he was going into the matter of the exterior of the Fondaco.

'He can have San Bartolomeo, but hands off the Fondaco!' said the artists, who were longing for the honour of competing to do these decorations. And before the German merchants ventured to manoeuvre openly in favour of their compatriot as they had done for Todesco, the decoration had already been commissioned and the work had begun. Tenacity usually achieves its purpose and so it soon came about that on the scaffolding of the façade of the Fondaco, as well as on the west and north side, Giorgione was hard at work, while Titian painted the façade looking towards the Merceria. Morto da Feltre was also with them, as their assistant.

Giorgio's scheme of decoration consisted of figures appearing against a background of painted niches which alternated with the windows. These figures were chosen to symbolize for all eternity the meteorological conditions and the events of the city. As he finished his sketches, tried out the colours and traced the outlines, he visualized the serene, impassive figures, watching the world move by.

The world was the same as ever, with its dead, its wars, its disappearances and substitutions.

Mantegna was dead: now Gentile Bellini was drawing up his last will and testament: a short time later he also died.

But it was life that Giorgio and Titian were painting. Giorgio a reclining Venus, Titian a mighty Judith. Again they were filled by the force of eternal youth while they were preparing their final throw to win the stakes of artistic fame.

Possibly Giorgione was already regretting that he had given way to the pressure Barbarigo had brought to bear on him, concerning Titian's collaboration in this work: he did not relish having him as a competitor, even though he had reserved the lion's share for himself.

Titian had thrown himself into the enterprise like a madman. He was even letting his beard grow. His Judith, the portrait of the Levantine, and that of the associate of the Confraternity della Calza which he was now painting, could be enjoyed most of all by the tenants of the first floor opposite, so narrow was the alley. All the better for them, he said to himself, and he painted with so much zest, perfection and naturalness, in a style of such sturdy simplicity, that when the scaffolding was taken down and people first began to satisfy their curiosity and looked at the fantastic things painted by Giorgione on the wall facing the Grand Canal and the mighty Judith on the side, which was so magnificently contributed, they complimented Giorgione, and not Titian.

Obviously this intrigue, due to erroneous information, was followed by a mischievously provoked quarrel, owing to the seeds of discord which had been sown, half in jest, by those who were perfectly capable of discerning between the work of Giorgione and Titian. They were all the more vexed and pretended to be amazed when Giorgione was forced to rectify the matter. As to Titian, nothing could have delighted him more than this unexpected personal success of his.

One day while he was there supervising the selection of a colour for the plaster over the entrance, Toma Tito arrived, greeting him with his usual 'buon di', as he had done countless times when he had faithfully visited him during the progress of the work. Pointing to the sword which the seated female figure was brandishing, he suggested that this was indeed the sword of Justice. 'Justice that has been rendered to your art.'

But the reason for his coming was to tell Titian that his great-uncle, Tiziano di Andrea, had just arrived in Venice on a mission concerning the fortifications of Pieve and was actually at their house now.

They met in Casa Coltrini. Titian became increasingly distressed as his great-uncle prophesied a terrible fate for Cadore, their beloved home, which was continually threatened by the Germans. Ranting like the lawyer he was, he launched into a flood of rhetorical oratory that caused his neck to swell, discoursing on the misfortunes of the country and the defence of the principles of justice: here in Venice they were embellishing the Fondaco dei Tedeschi, the Warehouse of the Germans, while the Germans, led by Maximilian, might descend on Cadore at any moment.

And thus it came to pass. The whole of Cadore was invaded: Pieve surrendered.

Snow was on the ground, a limitless expanse of snow. The horses pawed the whiteness; men's faces and eyes tingled. Captain Sistraus, the commander of the invading troops, stopped a long time in front of the Castle of Pieve to give his orders. His eyes were steel, each of his hands consisted of ten tapering daggers: he raised the incised sleeves of his hauberk, bawling in his terrifying language, and slipped his cruel hands back into his gloves. Cowering behind the shutters of every window in every house, men and women, the aged and the children, thus learnt their fate: they had to leave their homes, and when they had hurriedly collected a few belongings they went up into the hills at night to join the fugitives who were already hiding there in ramshackle huts and shelters.

Holding their breath, Lucia, grandfather Conte, Orsa and Caterina came out at dusk. Andrea led the way as far as the beginning of a path where a boy, one of the sons of their friends, the Constantinis, was waiting for them. Lucia was weeping bitterly at parting from her home. She sobbed out recommendations concerning the house, invok-

ing blessings for her absent loved ones—Master Gregorio on the rock
of Botestagno, Titian in Venice.

'Hurry, hurry . . .', urged Andrea.

From up there they could see the whole of Pieve lying at their feet,
like a poor, abandoned hen-house, and all around it the tents and camp-
fires of the troops, glittering on the whiteness of the snow. Two shadows
appeared on the whiteness, and they fell silent in terror. But the newcomers were only a young girl and an old man, muffled up to the
eyes: they recognized Cecilia and her father.

'Cecilia,' they whispered.

'Master Andrea! Mistress Lucia . . . Orsa! 'They drew close together
like a black flock of lost despairing creatures.

*　*　*

When the incorporation of Cadore into the Tyrol had been refused,
the leaders of Pieve constituted themselves into a party known as the
'Fifteen'. It comprised Matteo and Agostino Palatino, Oliviero Genova,
Bernardino Constantini, Lorenzo di Giacomo, Andrea and Tiziano
Vecelli. They were to report to the Venetian authorities immediately
on the situation and the intentions of the enemy.

As soon as Constantini's report had been received in Venice,
Bartolomeo d'Alviano was forthwith commanded to get men together
from the plains and march towards Cadore, while Girolamo Sarvognano had orders to march with his troops up the Tagliamento valley.

The 'Fifteen', having been advised of the arrival of the liberators,
sent Andrea and his son to meet Sarvognano and inform him about
the enemy positions. The meeting took place at Lorenzano and the
commander of the Venetian troops ordered the intrepid pair to act
as liaison with d'Alviano, who was now at Longarone. It seemed an
impossible undertaking, but one of Sarvognano's son generously offered
to accompany the Vecelli on their mission.

Up and down the rocks, climbing and sliding, hurrying like scalded
cats through the icy cold, they traversed an inferno of difficulty and
discomfort.

'Holy Cadore!' panted Andrea to keep himself from cursing, but
he felt as though he was hurrying to rescue his own family. He really
hoped to rescue it, and also its treasures: like the other inhabitants of
Pieve, they had concealed them in the rocks before the unfortunate
capitulation.

Near Longarone, they found d'Alviano, who charged them with a message for Sarvognano: as soon as the reinforcements had come from Venice, he was to take the route that had been indicated to him and confront the Germans. The three went back the way they had come, invoking all the saints to keep up their spirits despite the risks, the cold and their exhaustion.

On the pre-arranged day, with four mountain cannons and the reinforcements led by Giorgio Cornaro, the army marched towards the enemy. They stopped at Cibiana towards evening, intending to wait for the arrival of Sarvognano's troops, which they expected on the morrow.

They cleaned their arms, fed and watered their horses and prepared themselves to bivouac in the dark. The Stradiots, the fierce Greek and Albanian riders who followed the Venetian army, thumped their padded coats and terrified the peasants with their curving swords. The soldiers went into the houses to look at the cheerful flames on the hearth, and unlaced their breastplates—but they were to see more than they had reckoned with, for the flame of a fire which had been stoked to excess flared up a narrow chimney and caught the roof, nearly setting fire to all the village.

The whole valley appeared to be alight to the eyes of the astonished Germans, who could see the opaque mirror of the snow illuminated by a tremendous blaze. They sounded the alarm and assembled their troops. D'Alviano, fearing that the fire might be disastrous, had roused the Venetian troops and rushed to the spot where the remains of the hut were still burning: with kicks and blows, he ordered his men to assemble and attack.

The soldiers hurled themselves at each other like wild beasts. The horses, maddened by the spurs, stumbling over the stones hidden under the snow, rushed into the melée, neighing and foaming. The men hewed each other to pieces as though to draw blood in this cold could replace fire, life and warmth. Sarvognano and his men were not there —every one must fight for two, the soldiers of the Serene Republic yelled to each other. They confronted the Tyrolean brutes with the vehemence of David fighting Goliath. Ranieri de' Signori della Sassetta, the Tuscan captain, cursed louder than all the others, laughing furiously in the midst of the ghastly massacre: he hurled himself on Sistraus, lunging at his mount and at him, and literally cut them to pieces.

The Germans had already been drawing back and now, when they saw their leader was slain, they gave up. They fled as far as Rocca di Pieve, and the others were massacred on the field.

One thousand and eight hundred corpses were counted, and among them were found the bodies of three women, armed like the others, fair-haired, soaked in blood. Mistresses or wives, they had been obsessed by their passion to the point of following their men on to the battlefield rather than part from them, and now their lifeless bodies lay there, livid with bruises and cold. The soldiery who were collecting weapons and going around to put the dying out of their misery with a *coup de grâce*, gathered incredulously round those three pathetic bodies. They uncovered the flesh and bared the breasts, but against the blood on the trampled snow these breasts appeared so tender and dazzling that the men were seized by uneasy horror and, to put an end to it, they pushed the bodies into a hollow, covering them with snow, bushes and stones.

It was then that Sarvognano and his men came on to the frozen, torpid field of death. The soldiers mocked the newcomers, telling them they had arrived to find the work already done, and demanded wine to wash down the banquet of human flesh they had prepared for them. Then marching side by side, they covered the short distance to Pieve, blowing their trumpets with all the might of their lungs.

The refugees from Pieve came down from the mountains with leaps and bounds, embraced the soldiers, cheering and shouting victory; they went back to their houses, to find whether they had been robbed or mercifully spared, lighting great fires to restore themselves from the cold and hunger they had suffered, while the soldiers helped to chop wood, dropped their weapons and threw themselves down to sleep, wrapped in their cloaks, covering their feet with warm ashes.

Lucia and her children, accompanied by Cecilia, returned to their home. The Vecellio house, like those of the other families of the 'Fifteen', was thrown open to welcome the liberators.

'What would Master Gregorio not give to be here?' Mistress Lucia kept repeating, while the Venetian leaders sang the praises of her uncle Andrea and cousin Tiziano, whose intrepid enterprise had saved the day. That evening Cornaro came to join them. A strong guard was placed round the fortress, where the survivors of the German army had entrenched themselves and, finally, late that night, Pieve sank into the sleep of exhaustion.

*   *   *

The next morning Matteo Palatini was sent to the fortress on the Rock to enjoin the enemy to surrender. The Tyrolese, under the leadership of Leonard Chorel, resisted stubbornly. D'Alviano, foaming with rage, ordered the assault. And how they resisted, those accursed fellows, defending themselves from the top of the walls, with arquebuses, stones and scraps of iron! But they could not resist concerted fire. They surrendered.

Out of more than eighty defenders, only some forty remained. Cornaro gave orders for the commander to be brought out: he would devour him, he roared, his horse would stamp him into the ground!

Chorel came out, not on foot, but on horseback: wonderfully handsome as he sat erect in his saddle, his slender body tense with the fury that contorted the fine features of his fair-skinned face. Surrounded by other riders, he halted facing Cornaro, who launched into a flood of invective, insulting him because of his idiotic useless resistance. Chorel did not utter a word, he only gripped the reins as tightly as if he were throttling his rival, and stared at him as though he could stab him with his baneful eyes.

At last he replied with a eulogy of his own valour and that of his men. He said that if Maximilian, their liege lord, were to learn how brave they had been in their resistance which was now being vilified, he would forgive them the humiliation of their capitulation. Anyway, it was a very different kind of capitulation from that of the Italian garrison! He spurred his horse, his riders sped after him like a shower of arrows and he galloped off through the village, riding down a wretched peasant who happened to be in the way.

This sudden flight, like a gust of wind arising by magic, infuriated the liberators. Cornaro uttered a brief order, and the Stradiots hurled themselves into the pursuit.

Eleven miles outside the village they caught up with the Germans, screaming like birds of prey as they dragged them off their horses into the snow. The fugitives struggled, reeling and clutching the air. Chorel, convinced that they wanted to capture him alive, leant against the trunk of a fir tree and watched them advance. But the silence of those who were encircling him, still undecided how to deal the fatal blow, how to wreak their vengeance on him, revealed the imminence of his death to him. He closed his eyes. That movement was enough to seal his fate.

They tore out his eyes, split his mouth, severed his head from his body, cut off his hands, his feet, his genitals, dismembered him and hurled the bloody remnants of flesh and armour as far as they could throw . . . far away, on to the snow, as though to mark with red on the white surface, the imaginary targets of their ferocity.

IX

WHEN Titian heard all the terrible things that had happened to his unfortunate country, he felt as though the sacred image of it that he treasured in his heart had been defiled. Thus, while the other members of the Vecellio family had been raised to eminence by the glorious pages which the enterprise of the 'Fifteen' had added to the chronicles of his home, he felt that it would not be easy for him to revisit it, as though something had mysteriously broken, disturbing him bitterly.

Possibly the real reasons were quite different. Though he was intent on winning clients and obtaining commissions, he was not yet sufficiently well-known. The best business to come his way—the altarpiece for Jacopo Pesaro, presented at St Peter's by the Borgia Pope—had not brought him into the limelight. He toyed with the idea of moving to Rome. Lorenzo Lotto had gone there, and had found work at the Vatican. He had not yet made up his mind, for he thought that the Judith of the Fondaco (his Justice) must surely bring him other commissions. So he waited.

In December, a jury selected by Giambellino assembled to assess the value of Giorgione's frescoes at the Fondaco in the presence of the proveditors of the salt-works. It consisted of Vittor Carpaccio, Vittore Belliniano and Lazaro Bastia.

Titian shut himself up at Casa Coltini with his cousin, so that he might give free vent to his agitation. Yes, he stormed, he had seen all he wanted to see when the commission arrived at the Fondaco with their noses in the air, but it made him laugh. It was a crying shame that his frescoes should be considered as no more than marginalia to Giorgione's work. He spoke feverishly about his future, about all his plans: he praised Giorgio generously, but then, in ironical juxtaposition, he enumerated the great artists in Italy—Michelangelo, for instance, who in May had undertaken a grandiose decoration at the Vatican. He, Titian, would like to do the same: he would like to paint frescoes all over Italy and he could certainly not content himself with representing mere allusions to conquests, as Giorgione had done when, among the figures of the Fondaco, he had painted two geometers measuring the globe. . . .

Toma smiled, soothing him affectionately, and at last Titian fell silent. That evening he learnt that the commission had estimated that one hundred and fifty ducats would be a fit recompense for Giorgione's work, but the proveditors had reduced it to one hundred and thirty.

*　　*　　*

The new year, 1509, brought the misfortune of a defeat to the Venetian republic. It was beaten soundly by Louis XII, the ally of Julius II; he taunted the vanquished with the message: 'The Pope gives his best blessing to his sons'.

However, the Venetians refused to be downhearted. The Carnival of 1509 was one of the most brilliant and dissolute that Venice had ever experienced. In the Celestia Convent, a band of drunken young patricians danced frenziedly all night long with the nuns, in the flaring light of the torches. Pipes shrilled and drums were banged, while the dishevelled nuns danced and watched their own shadows, high up on the walls, melting into one with those of their partners.

The Fondaco dei Tedeschi had already been inaugurated by a Mass which was said in the courtyard, but it was not yet occupied by the merchants, who now, during this wild Carnival, took the opportunity of organizing a festivity there: the chief attraction was to be the pursuit of a greased pig by blindfolded hunters.

On this occasion, the magnates inspected the fine edifice, which was approached from the Canal Grande by a landing stage surrounded by five arches resting on columns. The architect gave a minute description of every detail of the construction; there were twenty-six warehouses with adjacent lodgings for the packers, the upholsterers and the agents; eighty rooms that could be let to merchants; a hall known as the Hall of the *Stua*, dominated by a great decorated stove or '*stufa*', such as the Germans used in their own country, a hall to be used in summer, looking out on the Rialto Bridge and a courtyard surrounded by arcades with twenty-four arches. That night it was brilliantly illuminated and crowded with people in high spirits, partaking of fruit and wine and looking forward to the grotesque diversion with the pig, about which everybody was talking.

The music resounded under the arches, where the ladies were sitting, laughing gaily.

Giorgione was greeted with applause and shouts of '*el pintor del Fonteco*'. He was accompanied by Cecilia, who was dressed as gorgeously as a patrician lady. Her shameless beauty enhanced the mute sensuous appeal of her lover; all the women admired him as though he were a demi-god. But Titian, who was with Palma and Toma Tito, stared at him in silence.

The merry-making was in full swing, when in great hilarity, the unusual game began. One after another, several merchants, covered by great clumsy coats so as not to soil their clothes with the grease which was being spread all over a monstrous, enormous pig, engaged in a kind of bizarre blind-man's-buff with the animal.

The spectators roared with delight, while the pig grunted quietly in a corner and its blindfolded pursuer groped around, swaying from right to left like a drunkard. They threw apples, peels and remains of food to the hunter and the hunted. It happened that the animal was caught, squealing to the stars, and the man, in his effort not to let it go, caught hold of its pendulous ears and found himself being dragged along like a rag-doll. The crowd was helpless with laughter and shouted encouragement.

Wine was in the air and the fact of being among foreigners seemed to permit the spectators to indulge in uncontrolled hilarity. For some time already there had been shouts for one of the candidates, a stout, heavy man known as Master Albrecht, with shoulders like mountains and legs like St Christopher, but he would have none of it. Others entered the lists, yet the pig was always the winner.

'Zorzi!' a woman's voice suddenly shrilled.

'Yes! Ser Zorzon! Zorzon! Zorzoneee! . . .'

Giorgione glared furiously round the courtyard without looking at anyone in particular, as though he were asking Heaven who dared to insult him thus. The sudden, tense silence that followed was broken by a single sound—the noise of a seat being pushed back, as Master Albrecht, the gigantic gentleman, rose to his feet, for as a good German he wished to avoid anything that might cast a shadow over the festivities. He advanced into the arena like a champion, greeted by enthusiastic cheers.

The lads greased the pig again, and this time with a double ration: the merchant, majestic as an Old Testament king from the north,

E

remained standing in the middle of the courtyard. The pig was fed a handful of chilis which filled it with diabolical energy, and the merchant was given a violent shove.

The spectators were almost delirious. The Germans, all of them drunk, were standing on the tables, roaring toasts to the victory of the pig: others laughed till they cried and fell under the tables: others again groped for the young Ganymedes, catching hold of their chins, grunting '*Herzallerliebster*' and pouting out their lips.

But in the end a unanimous shout thundered through the courtyard. The competitor had subdued the pig and was holding it motionless under the weight of his own body. The crowd applauded and threw flowers into the arena, but the attendants hurled themselves on to the animal, as they prepared to slaughter it, armed with knives, cords and kitchen pots.

'No! No!' screamed the women, covering their eyes. The animal was emitting piercing squeals, then a great jet of blood gushed forth and the men around it were spattered from head to foot. They dispersed, throwing themselves on to the ground and laughing as they held up their pans like shields.

'Always the same, these Germans . . .' the spectators protested, shocked at the bad taste of ending the jolly game with this exhibition of ruthlessness.

It was already late. Giorgione was still sitting beside Cecilia, surrounded by friends and pupils—Francesco Torbido, Giovanni da Udine and others. Morto da Feltre brought the girl foliage and flowers, which she twined into a garland to crown her lover. They applauded him again, and all together drank a toast in his honour.

Titian rose from his seat: he was fondling his growing beard, a nervous trick whih he was not yet able to control. Toma followed him as he walked across to join the Coltrinis, and they all went home together.

Daria had seemed rather withdrawn all through the evening, for she did not enjoy this kind of fun, but she seemed pleased to see her nephew. She had intuitively understood his state of mind. Sending for a cup of wine, she said, in her Venetian dialect:

'I have known you when you were a child, Tuciano, and at this festival today, which is yours as well, I find you again as a man with a beard: but nevertheless you are young, Tuciano. Now, drink to your health and your fortune, and to the good health of all the Vecelli, as though they were here with you to rejoice in your work. And, if I am right', she added, with a smile, 'you will drink, I hope, secretly to the one you want to drink to!' Then, the better to underline the significance of her gesture, she rose and offered him the cup.

He kissed her hand as ceremoniously as if she had been the Dogaressa, the queen of the Serene Republic.

X

Dᴜʀɪɴɢ the festivities at the Fondaco, a recently-finished painting of Giorgione's had been much discussed. Titian had heard that it was a wonderful allegory of Nature, which Giorgio had painted for Gabriele Vendramin, the rich soap manufacturer.

According to the descriptions, two naked women were represented in a wooded landscape, with a citadel in the background: one of them was holding a baby to which she was giving suck, the other had her legs immersed in a torrent. But later the artist had changed the composition and substituted for the figure of the bathing woman that of a man leaning on his lance. '*The soldier and the gypsy in a stormy scene*' they called the picture, because Giorgione had painted a streak of lightning across the heavy clouds in the sky. The so-called gypsy, with the weight of her luminous plenitude, spread more radiance than the lightning in this new and audacious masterpiece.* Sebastiano Zuccato could not stop talking about it.

Titian had not yet seen the painting. He was turning over in his mind how he should react to it, but his lack of sociability and the provocation of rivalry made him long to be more isolated and find work outside Venice. He succeeded in getting the order to paint two or three frescoes in Padua, in St Anthony's church. After telling all Venice about this work of his, he left.

He experienced a sense of liberation from galling ties. Padua was fine. When he had found a place to sleep in and organized the routine of his work, he began to find himself again in the stimulating rush of new intense life, made up of frugal sparing meals and fervent new

*As regards this alteration undertaken by Giorgione, we refer to the study by Antonio Morassi ('*Esame radiografico della "Tempesta" di Giorgione*', in '*Le Arti*' anno. *I fasc. VI*) in which it is proved that, instead of the shepherd or soldier that we see now, the original figure was that of a nude woman bathing; either the customer or the artist himself had decided to substitute the masculine figure, whose head, for instance, is painted over the foliage of the thicket in the background. Some variations in the landscape were also brought to light by the radiographical examination.

friendships. He felt that he was becoming young once more, courage-ously able to defend himself alone, relying on his own unaided strength like a boy confronting an obstacle.

Domenico Campagnola and others were working beside him at the decoration of the church. They would borrow a few copper coins from each other and find an outlet for their temper in frequent laughter. Then they would stand for hours on end and gaze at the monumental figures of Giotto, that expressed the spirit of the earth with all the power of their vitality. Those were marvellous days.

Titian painted three frescoes, then four—large, simple compositions, doing his best to give his figures the solid stability he admired in Giotto's work. In the Scuola del Santo he represented three miracles of Saint Anthony, and in the Scuola dei Carmini, the meeting of Anne and Joachim.

His new friends, the Cornaros and the poèt Sperone Speroni, came to see him at his work. With the subtle understanding of experts, they admired the freedom with which he had tackled these religious subjects. There was nothing academic about his compositions, which were painted as though they represented a realistic, every-day tragedy —a jealous husband stabbing his wife. With one voice, they assured him that this was indeed a forceful and amazing innovation.

When a painter hears words such as these, time seems to stand still for him.

Titian looked upon this fresco as something not quite his own and yet born at the same time of the desire to fix in an enclosed form, as simply as possible, the poetic tension of a drama. He asked Sperone, who admired him sincerely, to comment on it in detail, and the latter, who had seen his Judith at the Fondaco, assured him that he was making wonderful progress.

He was offered the work of decorating the façade of a palace. He had actually intended returning to Venice for some time, but when he received the news that some cases of bubonic plague had occurred there, he accepted the commission and began to work immediately. These first tidings were soon succeeded by others, and whole families of refugees arrived.

*　　*　　*

Venice was putrefying. When some miserable rags were burnt in a courtyard, the black smoke would rise and spread its foul stench over the walls of the palaces, the mullioned windows and the terraces on the roofs.

Through the narrow, squalid alleys, physicians, wrapped in long blue cloaks, went from house to house, followed by attendants, whose garments were distinguished by a cross on the chests and backs. They appeared to be taking part in a grotesque masquerade. Their clothes had been disinfected with juniper berries, their hats were pulled down over their faces and they wore masks with long noses, through which they inhaled medicinal odours. In the midst of death, the appearance of these lemures with their hooked beaks, seen through the broken glass of a tiny window or the folds of a curtain, spread panic and terror. Those who were delirious imagined that the devil had already come to fetch them. They howled, but they were taken away and the door of the house was nailed up.

Some families concealed their sick stricken members, so that they should not be taken to the lazar-house: they bolted their doors for fear of medical investigations and gave no sign of life. In that way, whole families died, hiding their gold in secret boxes, infecting each other, forsaken by their servants, unknown to the parish priests. The sanitary authorities were obliged to force their way into houses and palaces, and every quarter of the city was reconnoitred in the most rigorous manner.

The patrols had already knocked once at the doors of Giorgione's house in San Silvestro. One evening they came back. There was no one there, an old woman who lived next door assured them—an old woman who seemed to be the only survivor in the world. There was nobody there, she repeated: the painter had probably left and followed his mistress, who had forsaken him and fled with Morto da Feltre, his assistant.

They knocked again. 'There's no one there, not a soul,' repeated the old woman. They forced the door and went into the house. Several rooms were locked, but they forced their way into all of them. Finally they climbed the stairs to the bedchamber above and broke down the door, hesitating for a moment as the light of the torch flickered in the enclosed air, which was heavy with the stench of putrefaction.

Fragments of a broken jug were scattered on the floor. The wine that had flowed from it formed a pool and had not yet dried up—in the dim light it looked like a pool of blood.

The lovers had been thirsty, but they had not been able to drink the wine: they lay dead on the wide bed from which the curtains were drawn back. One of Giorgio's hands dangled inertly over the mattress marking a moment of suspension into all eternity, seemingly arrested in the motion of seizing the jug.

They had not been able to drink. Perhaps hour after hour, in their agony, they had gazed at the wine of life spilt on the paved floor, until it vanished in the darkness of night.

Perhaps Cecilia had died after her lover, perhaps she had died first. Her body lay across his, her head half-hidden. An open box containing small trinkets stood beside her on the rumpled sheets. They had made love until the ultimate moments of their life, masking the death towards which they were going with love.

The men drew near to remove the bodies, and all around, one above the other, elongated shadows like desiccated corpses rose up. In the dramatic light of the torches that filled the low-ceilinged room, with the stifling smell of burning tallow, now that the first spell of the horribly fascinating apparition was broken, the dead lovers were suddenly transformed into a couple of pitiful, dishevelled corpses, destroyed by a death common to all. . . .

The sheets were drawn away, the pillows tied up, ready to be burned. The two bodies fell apart. Giorgione's beautiful head hung over backwards, the face darkened by a sprouting beard, the open eyes fixed into the void, the powerful bare chest—the chest of a tunefully singing warrior—hollow, emptied out. The girl's eyes were closed but for a mere slit: the detached strand of an ornament studded with precious stones lay on her bare skin like the shining coils of a serpent. As the men went about their business and the flames of the torches flared, they might have been already preparing the funeral pyre that was to consume the corpses on the Island of Poveglia.

PART II

I

TITIAN heard the news of Giorgione's death while he was in Padua, but it was only when he returned to Venice that he learnt that he would never see Daria Coltrini again. And when Toma Tito told him that it had not saved her to leave Venice, as she had not been able to return, he rebelled against the injustice of fate. On the night of the feast at the Fondaco, Daria had toasted his future success; Giorgione's death was tantamount to the removal of the chief obstacle to his career. But now her own death seemed, just because of that propitiatory toast, to be so closely connected with the disappearance of his rival that it struck him like an ironic combination of destiny.

Now it was Titian's turn to occupy the position of the first artist of Venice. The commission to complete a Venus which Giorgione had left unfinished was the first sign, but he discovered other portents as well and hoped for their confirmation. He worked, worked, worked.

When the beautiful Violante, Palma's favourite model, was not posing for the latter with violets in her hair, he would paint her. She was the very image of love, and as he contemplated her he was reminded of another image. But he decided first to establish himself with a little more decorum in the dwelling he was now sharing with Francesco. Then he went to Pieve to increase his personal comfort by fetching the new underclothes which his mother had prepared for him some time ago. And there, in the midst of the linen, he found Cecilia, as he had seen her doing once already, lovingly folding the shirts, quietly engrossed in these domestic tasks, as sweet as the lavender which scents the clean linen rooms of well-kept homes. It did not take him long to make up his mind; he took the girl, the linen and the lavender and returned to Venice. Soon his hovel was as sweet-smelling and tidy as the most ideal dwelling can be.

Cecilia had not taken long either to become accustomed to the unfamiliar face of her man, her master. She went her way quietly, putting things in order and re-arranging them, preparing food, cleaning and polishing, while he, so as to unite all the saints of Paradise in one and to keep a promise he had made her, painted her portrait, representing her as she was, serene, with her hair braided and encircling her head as was the fashion in Cadore, and wearing the garments of a Madonna.

At the same time, while he was still working at the completion of the Giorgione Venus, he received an order for an altar-piece for the church of Santo Spirito in Osola; there he painted St Mark enthroned between St Cosmos and St Damian, St Sebastian and St Rochus, the latter two to symbolize the sufferings of humanity, the blood shed in the recent wars and the loss of life in the recent plague. Furthermore, he began a composition which was truly to justify his claim to be the foremost painter in Venice; two female figures sitting by a fountain, while a little Cupid dipped his hands into the water.

Palma, the Barbarigos, the Contarinis and others frequently came to see him. They looked at the paintings by Giorgione, which he was completing.

Titian kept the picture of the two women turned towards the wall, awakening the curiosity of all those who saw the Venus of the deceased master and wondered about the other picture. Not all his visitors were allowed to see it, but when Bembo came to his workshop by appointment, together with the Great Chancellor of the Republic, who had commissioned this work, Titian displayed it in silence, suddenly turning it round to the light.

The two women, one nude, the other clothed, appeared like twins, both in the expression and the character of their faces. One was sitting on the edge of the fountain, the other leaning against it, serenely displaying their *alter ego* in the perfection of beauty.

'Do they represent celestial and mundane love?' Bembo asked, looking from the clothed woman resting her arm on a brazier to the nude one who raised a cup above the rippling folds of a drapery.

'Who knows?'

'Truth and Fable?'

'Who knows?'

The client's main concern was that his family crest should be prominently shown on the base of the fountain, where the artist had already sketched in a bas-relief showing Love being scourged, watched by a nude man and a nude woman. The crest was shown above them: a rampant lion, ending in an adder's tail.

'Innocence and Experience?' Bembo continued.

Titian placed the picture back towards the wall. As he was turning it round, the arm of the nude woman lifting the cup, with Giorgione's painting behind it, reminded him of Daria offering him the cup and uttering her unforgettable toast.

Daria . . . silence had fallen.

Bembo was still discussing the mysterious theme of the painting; was it the dream of Polyphilus? he began again, or perhaps the sarcophagus containing the blood of Adonis which the cupid had caught up? He chattered away, suggesting greyhounds, lovers, flocks of sheep for the background. The Chancellor, delighted that the poet should take such interest in the work, asked the artist to visit his house, so as to have another look at the family crest.

'Yes, yes', Titian said vaguely.

'And what about Violante?' Bembo enquired, alluding to the twofold feminine likeness in the painting.

At last the Chancellor went away. Crests or no crests, Titian exploded, never again would he show paintings to buyers before they were finished.

Bembo suggested that as he was not a buyer Titian had better show him the painting again. The picture returned to the light; it seemed that something had been added to it, it was now completed by an idea that had been formulated.

'This is poetry! Painted poetry!' Bembo exclaimed. Poetry, he went on in a masterly synthesis, in the manner of Ariosto, in the best style of the future. If Titian continued to paint in this manner, it would cause a sensation. Bembo gazed at the picture again and again as intensely as though he were re-reading verses of his own 'Asolani'.

The landscape was more than a mere background, it was a special kind of Olympus, cunningly constructed and profound, corresponding harmoniously with the harmony of the main personages: gardens apt for meditation, outlines of forests to overshadow the passions of human beings: he remembered the inflections his voice would assume when he had read passages of his poem tenderly and passionately, to the admirable Duchess of Ferrara, Lucrezia Borgia. . . .

No poet finds difficulty in talking about poetry, and so, in the learned circle that met at the house of Aldo Manuzio, where every member was obliged to converse in Greek with the other members of the Aldine Academy, Bembo found occasion to say that he had been privileged to see wonderful things in Titian's studio, works which were the last word in modern painting. It was a word that belonged to poetry, a poetry rich in rhymes of genius—pure poetry, he insisted, genuine poetry. Titian, *painter of poems*, was how he defined his friend.

Marc' Antonio Sabellico, Marin Sanudo, Andrea Navagero, Brother Giocondo da Verona and many others who came to scrutinize Aldo's recent editions ended by being convinced by Bembo's authoritative utterances, and they set out with him to visit the artist's studio. Thus a visit to Titian became a much-sought-after privilege for members of the Venetian intelligentsia.

Immersed in his work as he was, the artist did not relish these interruptions, but he was obliged to submit to them. He did not go out for days on end, he hardly knew what was happening beyond the threshold of his workshop. One day, when his apprentice and Francesco both happened to be away and people had been knocking at the door, he had at last decided to open it, thinking that Cecilia had not heard. He caught a glimpse of some visitors who had been let in by a little woman he did not know, who hurried away as soon as the door was closed again, and disappeared into the living-room. Pricked by curiosity, he followed her and found her supporting Cecilia, who was deathly pale.

'Tician . . .', she gasped, and implored him not to look at her. She was vomiting.

The little woman introduced herself as a neighbour and friend of Cecilia's: hastily she gave him to understand that these were the first symptoms of pregnancy.

Still clenching her hands, Cecilia raised her face and gazed at her man with the pathetic expression of an animal that has done wrong and cannot express itself. He went up to her gently and helped her to lie down on the bed. A strange silence had fallen, the silence of a gynaeceum which seemed to belong to another season and another age. Cecilia lay on the straw mattress, while the petulant little woman cleaned up the floor, opened the window, and brought her something to drink.

'You never told me', Titian murmured awkwardly, as he caressed her. He felt intimidated by the bustling activities of the other woman. It was nothing, she was quite well again, it was all over, Cecilia said, and begged him to go back to the studio and not keep the visitors waiting. She watched him hurry away. Lying there inertly, from within her humble, silent loneliness, she felt that the integrity of her heart refused to assent to the intense emotion, the incommunicable passion with which she loved Titian. The passion that agitated him was a proof that he did not belong to her, he was caught in a circle of inaccessible conditions which she was unable to understand, which paralyzed her. He embraced her hastily, he had loved her hastily, though tenderly, he had painted her with genial affection, but during all the hours he spent designing figures, landscapes, saints and serene skies, or when she heard him talking to other men in the studio, she felt absolutely excluded. The only part of the city with which she was familiar was the view from her window, and she did not know a soul except the pitiful little woman who lived next door. But Titian himself was at variance with others and playing for great stakes. Although he had been profoundly moved by the news that he was to become a father and had not hesitated to give Cecilia money so that she could have help while she was expecting her baby, he immediately became re-absorbed in his own affairs.

He had refused the proposition put to him by Bembo, who in the meantime had gone to Rome, having been appointed secretary to the new Medici Pope, Leo X, and now he was in the throes of maturing plans and decisions. At last one evening he sat down with a scribe in front of the little lamp flickering behind the water jug; he had tucked up his sleeves and had disposed around him various notes for the fateful and most important missive which was about to be penned on a large sheet of paper, as though it were the image of his destiny. Cecilia was close to the light, stitching away at little garments for the child which was now heavy within her. He dictated a letter which has been preserved: it is written in a strange mixture of Venetian dialect, dog-Latin and Italian, and begins:

'*Illustrissimo Consilio,*

1513 Die ultimo Maij in Consilio, Havendo da puto in suso, Principe Serenissimo et Signori Eccellentissimi, io Tician de serviete de Cadore postome ad imparar larte de la pictura. . . .'

He informed their Excellencies that he had begun to learn the art of painting from his childhood days, not so much for gain but in order to acquire some little fame, and to be numbered among those who have chosen that art as their profession at the present time. It was a fact that he was now getting on well and his services were being insistently sought after by His Holiness the Pontifex and other great Lords; however, being a faithful subject of the Sublime Council, he desired to leave a memorial in the illustrious city, and after having deliberated, he was prepared, if their Excellencies agreed, to use all his ingenuity as long as he lived. He suggested beginning with a picture of the Battle of the Bands on the Square, a most difficult task, which no man until that day had been willing to undertake. Then he petitioned Their Sublimities to award to him the brokerage at the Fondaco dei Tedeschi under the same conditions as it had been given to Messer Giambellino, and also to pay for two apprentices he would need, as well as for the colours and other necessary materials, as the Illustrious Council had done during the last months for the said '*missier Zuanne*'. He promised to carry out the work so rapidly and well that they would be satisfied, and ended: '*humilmente mi ricomando*'. And may the devil take them all, and all their hellish property as well, if they did not agree! he said to himself when he had finished his dictation. However, a decision in his favour was not unlikely, considering how well disposed to him some people were, notably Girolamo Contarini, who, together with Michel de Lezze and Giovanni Venier, presided over the Council.

And so it happened: his application was put to the vote and accepted. It caused a sensation such as Venice had never known in the artistic camp. Old Giambellino fell into a rage and threatened to lay a complaint, but, in the meantime, Titian had taken possession of the studio that had been placed at his disposal by the State and was already at work with his two assistants—Antonio Buxci and Ludovico di Giovanni.

The days, the weeks, the months flew by.

In the house, Cecilia went around sighing, with a wan smile- she was afraid of death, terrified of death—for was she not living in mortal sin? But she said nothing. She only begged her man to choose a fine name for the little creature that was to be born any minute now.

Pomponio—if it was a boy—otherwise Lavinia.

Pomponio was born one evening, and Cecilia lived.

II

FOLLOWING the plaint Giambellino wished to lodge against Titian, his petition was refused on the grounds that he would obtain the brokerage when his turn came. But when the payment of his two assistants was suspended, Titian himself lodged a plaint. He was awarded the sum he asked for, as well as a supply of colours and some repairs in his studio, all at the expense of the State.

He was made to realize that the authority of a personage like Giambellino was still very great. Nevertheless, he had attained as much as could be expected. Besides, Titian could congratulate himself on having refused the commissions in Rome: they represented labours which would have demanded a disproportionate amount of trouble, rivalry with artists who were already too firmly established in the good graces of the Pope, and assimilation to completely changed conditions.

The indiscretions of all the gossiping assistants and pupils employed by the painters' workshops of Venice spread news like wildfire from one end of the city to the other, as they listed the contracts in dispute between their masters. The news that old Giambellino had signed a contract with the Scuola di San Marco for a canvas representing the history of the saints was an event that caused vast excitement among his disciples and those of his rivals. Every time they met when they were purchasing canvases or colours, they started to discuss it anew— as Giambellino had not yet completed his picture for the Duke of Ferrara, how was he now to finish this new work, old as he was?

They suggested that Titian would certainly be called upon to complete it. Most certainly not, others retorted, because to judge by precedents, it would be finished by Vittore Belliniano. Then they went their separate ways, carrying fine rolls of canvas and parcels of colours under their arms.

In that competition between the two rivals, between the respect due to the old hermit and the increasing popularity of Titian, the latter felt that he was already the recipient of universal sympathy. He let people talk and continued to paint in the Hall of the Great Council. Simultaneously he had begun to work at some amazing portraits.

The models talked while they were sitting, one in resounding tones, another hoarsely, a third shrilly. They filled the studio with the echoes of life from the four cardinal points of the city. He seldom said anything: they did the talking—about money, deals, dowries, speculations. Money was what they talked about most—always, eternally about money.

The sonorous-voiced sitter told him, with shouts of derisive laughter, about Pietro Bernardo's eccentric testament in which he had laid down that his dead body was to be washed in vinegar and perfumed with musk to the value of forty ducats. . . .

'Forty ducats!' he thundered: 'Forty ducats! I ask you——'.

The hoarse one, wheezing like an owl, reported how much the last feast in his house had cost him, holding the accounts in his hand while he was posing, his eyes fixed on a point in space, turning over every calculation in his niggardly brain.

The shrill-voiced man found it impossible to sit still: he was making up a dowry of antique and subtly chosen objects of virtue for his daughter, who was soon to be married.

'A square chandelier—listen—two ducats. . . . A parrot's cage, two ducats. . . . A gilded curtain, six ducats. . . .'

Men were apt to catch that fever in Venice. Titian saw them panting, their hands like claws, ready to clutch even the gold of the sunlight on the marble of the palaces, on the impalpable waters beside the immense flanks of the houses. In portraits he painted, he expressed the dominant theme of veiled greed, of matured powerful pomp. He painted spiritual faces, but pivoting on bodies spread out in the attitude of one who wishes to dominate, hands that were stealing from under the magisterial amplitude of the cloaks which concealed those elbows with which they were pushing their way to eminence.

Fashion had already changed, simultaneously with the evolution of the pictorial arts. Gowns, capes and sleeves became wide and abundant: the human figure appeared monumental in the heavy gowns of damask in all the colours of the peacock, in the sumptuous fur capes *alla romana* which the ladies were beginning to wear in the house. Like the mundane beauty Titian had painted by the fountain, whom Bembo called 'the Fable', the clothed and gloved lady, so the 'honourable courtesans' presided over their salons, and sang or recited verse for the benefit of their admirers.

Titian's figures, acquiring and propagating the air of majesty, appeared as though they were meant to be carried over the waters to the almost inaudible swishing of the gondolas, surrounded by silence: figures that seemed to watch life around them as though it were a spectacle, on whose actors the dignity of the individual imposes a touch of assumed indifference; figures of men and women who never walked—heavy, solid, vital and static.

The swiftness of their progress in the gondolas flattered the complexion of their skin, soothed by the breeze, and mirrored in the indolent possessiveness of their gaze.

It was only Cecilia, majestic too, but quivering with modesty as she sat with down-cast eyes, whom he still painted as the Madonna. She was gravid again; as she sat there, holding sturdy little Pomponio, who was to represent the Divine Child, the pregnancy which anchored her to herself was slowly perfecting a ripe type of womanly beauty, still shining with traces of youth. Beside the portrait of Cecilia as the young Mother of all mothers, Titian painted another: not a twin sister of equal beauty, like the two women at the fountain, but in luminous counterpoise—a Saint Bridget, mellow, with bleached golden hair. He had painted himself as Saint Ulfo, in armour, with brown, wavy hair, a short thick beard and the straight nose that was later to become aquiline.

Blending the archetypes which he saw in the ever-renewed reality of the images he painted, he succeeded in presenting them with such authority that no one could doubt the opulence of his inspiration and his success.

One solemn feast-day, when he happened to be almost near enough to touch the members of the Doge's cortège as they defiled across the Piazza San Marco, with all their standards and drums, he experienced a feeling of happy elation as he noticed how many people were anxious to display their friendly feelings towards him.

Men in the crowd took off their hats, calling out to each other as the various officials came past.

'The Secretaries', they announced, and these worthies appeared in their caps and capes, walking behind the austere Patriarch of Venice, resplendent in his sumptuous chasuble. Some of them greeted Titian.

'The Chaplain . . .'. He was followed by the keepers of the ducal chair and cushion, and they also acknowledged him.

Then came the Grand Chancellor, walking alone in front of the Doge; as he turned towards the spectators who were bowing to him, he made a sign of greeting to the painter of the lovely fountain. He was followed by pages: then, accompanied by genuflexions, came His Serene Highness the Doge under the precious umbrella.

'The Speakers, the Ambassadors'—and many of them who often came to his studio, recognized Titian and waved to him.

Finally, the *Illustrissima Signoria* was announced: two by two the members of the Great Council walked past, making futile remarks to each other, so as to strike an attitude or give the impression that they had vastly important matters to discuss; among the homage of the crowd they noticed Titian's restrained salute and returned it, with benevolence.

The rear was brought up by the eight banners, the six silver trumpets, the attendants of the Ambassadors and of the Doge.

Titian walked away in the opposite direction, going about his business with an air of tranquillity and the authoritative demeanour of one who leads a procession on his own behalf; now it was his turn to exchange signs of greeting with those among the crowd who recognized him. The first to salute him was his friend Palma. They walked on together, while the other procession tailed off in front of the gilded arcades of the cathedral.

It is not surprising that a man as industrious and ambitious as he was, when he happened to be perusing some bleak text in Roman history at night, would see far more interesting personages defiling before his inner eye, and dream about them like a miser who cannot stop counting his gold: the occasions to advance on the path of his artistic destiny were punctually awarded—the first contacts with the Court of Ferrara, the death of Giambellino, and finally the commission to paint a great altar-piece—the Assumption of the Blessed Virgin.

III

However carefully Titian tried to regulate all his movements and enterprises, exercising his self-control to the utmost, so as not to take any hasty decision, events were now beginning to take his life by storm.

Orazio, his second son, was sucking Cecilia's breasts as greedily as a gondolier gulps down his wine between two voyages, and Pomponio, supported by a girl from Cadore, staggered about pursuing the cat. It happened that Jacopo Tebaldi, Alfonso d'Este's secretary and ambassador to Venice, proposed to Titian that he should stay awhile at the palace of his master at Ferrara. After Titian had seen to it that the price for the great picture which he had to finish was fixed by the Great Council (instead of four hundred ducats he was to be given only three hundred) he decided, last but not least in order to have a respite from Orazio's whimperings and Pomponio's pursuit of the cat, to go to Ferrara, taking his assistants with him.

The art students who had wagered that Titian would complete a work of Bellini's won their bets when it was understood through Tebaldi's advances that the Duke of Ferrara was commissioning Titian to do a series of pictures for his alabaster cabinets, under the condition that he should also complete Giambellino's painting of the Feast of the Gods. In this picture the aged master, who had now almost attained the term of his days, displayed his ability for bringing his work up to date and adopting the lyrical mode which Giorgione and Titian had brought to such perfection. Titian started off on his journey.

'To think that we shall now see the Duchess, the famous Lucrezia Borgia', the two apprentices whispered, as they muffled themselves up against the biting wind of February. Yet in Ferrara they found fireplaces where one could have burnt an entire grove—one of those groves so beloved by Bembo. But Bembo was now in Rome, and his adored Duchess, immobilized by her pregnancy, was sitting beside her husband in front of one of those tremendous fires. And naturally they talked about Venice.

The Duke remembered a certain little balcony, an extraordinary little balcony he had once seen in Venice. Now he could no longer locate it exactly: he had asked a member of his court who must certainly know it, and then he had remembered Titian—who might trace a rough sketch of it for him. A balcony, in Venice, an extraordinary balcony. . . .

That was the first contact in front of that fire, evoking a memory which he seemed to have cherished for centuries: the Duke indicated that his predilection for it lay far back in the past, as he expressed this first wish of his with gentle discretion. Yet this discretion was somehow contradicted by a pair of rapacious restless eyes. While his hand —the hand of a maniac for artillery—tugged nervously at his little beard, and he fell silent, one could hear the wind howl, sucking up through the cowl of the chimney the bright soul of the whole burning grove. Finally, a brief preliminary hint at the work for the precious alabaster cabinets sounded a very different note of controlled impulsiveness, entirely turned towards the future. On that note, rising to his feet, he said goodnight: the ladies in waiting surrounded the Duchess solicitously, and the Duke's attendants preceded them, lighting their way through the icy, high-ceilinged decorated galleries.

The next day Titian's two assistants, opening their eyes as wide as they could, commented to the master on all the marvellous things they had seen and were seeing: this was not merely a castle, it was a fairy-tale palace, they exclaimed. What cannon! (The Duke's guns were his favourite hobby.) And what stables! (Stables invariably impressed anybody accustomed to live in Venice.)

'Behave with restraint', was all the master said.

'*A Mò Tuciano, depintore alozato in Castelo, boche 3*' . . . the entry made on the 13th February, 1516, by the collector on the register of the Ducal expenses, began. 'To Master Titian, painter lodged at the Castle, three mouths . . . salad, salted meat, chestnuts, oranges, candles, cheese. . . .'

'Behave with restraint', had been Titian's advice to the two dependent 'mouths', although he had expected a more spontaneously hospitable treatment with regard to himself. In the meantime, he had already discussed various projects with the Duke.

They had set to work and the days passed. The two apprentices were disappointed that the famous alabaster cabinets were not really alabaster: besides, despite the fact that they had kept their eyes glued to every movement of the Court, they had not yet succeeded in catching even a glimpse. So they behaved with restraint, working hard and willingly. There was nothing one could do except behave at that Court, where everything was subject to a rigid time-table. The Duchess lived in seclusion, dividing her time between her devotions and the care of her children—Ercole, who was now eight, Ippolito, six, and Eleonora, who was not quite one year old. Owing to her renewed pregnancy, she never appeared except in the chapel.

Titian himself took little part in the court life, and spent the greater part of his days working with his two assistants, except for frequent interviews with the Duke.

Alfonso missed the company of an artist; he hinted at the welcome possibility of Ariosto's permanent return to Ferrara, and sometimes his haughty reserve disappeared when the painter revealed his taste for mythology while they discussed the decorations of the cabinets. Yet his reserve was not unlike the tone of authority which was natural to Titian and made the latter seem such a great gentleman.

Titian had gone round Ferrara, contemplating the works of Cossa. He made studies for portraits of the Duke and Duchess and came to an agreement about the scheme for the allegories that were to be companion pieces to Bellini's *Festino*: the Duke, even though he still hoped that Raphael would paint the Triumph of Bacchus for him, ordered a *Bagno* from Titian, which he was to execute immediately he got back to Venice.

Then the day of departure arrived. With assurances of profoundest gratitude and promises of diligent care, recommendations by the Duke concerning certain trifles to be sent to him from Venice and assurances by the artist that he would fulfil these missions punctually, Titian started on his return journey on the 22nd March.

Taking them by and large, these enterprises were hard work and he felt it was a priceless privilege to stay in his own studio wearing his carpet-slippers. But this kind of labour represented the best kind of publicity an artist could hope for, and the benefits derived therefrom were far from negligible. A year earlier, at Bologna, Leonardo had actually accepted a pension from King Francis I of France and the right to reside at the Château de Cloux, where he had betaken himself at once, possibly taking leave of Italy for ever.

In the meanwhile, in Venice, the interest of the artistic circles was increasingly centred on the subject of Michelangelo. Legates coming from Rome, had brought engravings of the ceiling of the Sistine Chapel: ambassadors and merchants who had seen it all described its passionate impetuosity as something unheard of, never before conceived by any artist or any famous school: apocalyptical figures, monumental Old Testament prophets that struck the spectator with terror. Here a daemon had engaged on the creation of man: he would sweep away all the artists of Italy, as he had already succeeded in driving Leonardo out of Rome. It was a miracle that Raphael could still stand up against him.

Knowing that it was up to him to furnish Duke Alfonso with paintings which would harmonize with Bellini's *Festino*, Titian now threw all his energy into the completion of the great altar-piece of the Assumption for the Frari church, all the more as he did not want to be regarded as the heir and pupil of the shortly deceased Giambellino. However, he was extremely anxious to become the legitimate heir of his position in the Agency: in view of the agreement drawn up two years earlier with the Great Council, which had been signed and sealed and registered after Giambellino's death in the autumn of 1516, he was nominated on the 5th December of the same year as his successor at the Senseria del Fondaco.

A few days later, he travelled to Pieve with Toma Tito in order to spend Christmas there, and found his mother's arms open to receive him. Francesco had preceded him, accompanying Cecilia, the two little boys and the maid: he did not wish to share the success of a collective arrival with Titian and preferred to be welcomed separately by his parents and his sisters.

Neighbours and relations arrived every quarter-of-an-hour to knock at the door and welcome the arrivals. It was indeed a Christmas to warm the very cockles of the heart, with ceaseless visits and no end of story-telling. Orsa and Caterina came and went up and down the stairs all the time, to fetch in the lengths of damask Titian had brought them and to put them away again, carefully folded. These presents excited the curiosity of all their girl friends who fluttered in and out of the house, among whom was the daughter of Master Giacomo Alessandri, at whom Toma Tito was casting sheep's eyes. They all wanted information, stories, gossip from Titian, who had become the hero of the village. Had he not actually been to Ferrara, all the way to Ferrara, to the Court of the Este? . . . they could barely contain themselves.

Titian, wishing the Vecellio home to be more comfortable, set aside some money, and asked Francesco to remain behind in Pieve after he had left, to see that repairs were carried out—the roof, the furniture and other things stood in need of them. In the meantime there was an uninterrupted flux of visitors, who came to congratulate him on his appointment at the Agency, to find out in what it actually consisted and to ask whether it was true that he was going to paint a portrait of the Doge. The desire to escape all his questioners, as well as the slight feeling of idle tedium which always follows festive days, made Titian suddenly announce his departure for Venice. He would leave next day, Cecilia and the boys could join him with Francesco after a couple of weeks—but he must return without delay. Throwing a fine log on to the fire, he explained the reason for his hurry: the altar-piece of Santa Maria dei Frari was waiting for him.

With the idea of submerging the burning grief he had experienced at his first departure from home by an affectionate gesture, he begged his mother to come on to the gallery to wave to him next day: she must promise not to cry, but to stand there waving to him with a smile until he was out of sight. She could go on smiling because, as she could see, he always came back to embrace her from time to time.

IV

Hᴇ painted the magnificent upward movement of his hope. He was at work, his models draped to represent the apostles, when Brother Germano, the Guardian of Santa Maria dei Frari, came to disturb him, holding forth impatiently and staring up at the Mother of God, who was floating between heaven and an earth which was defined by nothing except a crowd of figures.

The Guardian talked incessantly. Titian also stared up, not to look at the Madonna, but in utter exasperation. The Guardian wanted to know the reason for this and for that; announced that the big marble cornice which was being made for the painting was already finished; then, as Titian, employing an unusual technique, brushed a yellow glaze over the foreshortened faces of Orazio and Pomponio, who figured among the putti and angels, he took exception to this summary proceeding and began to expostulate in his ignorance, while the artist ceased talking altogether, and kept his face turned towards the picture.

So it happened that the Guardian ended by asking everybody he could find the questions he did not venture to ask Titian: why did the figures of the Apostles have to be so enormous, of such exuberant proportions as though they were giants? And why this and why that? Thus the rumour spread that Vecellio was painting a *tour de force*, something strangely artificial and entirely outside the Venetian tradition, aspiring to copy the Michelangelesque style.

The Duke of Ferrara wrote, returning to the subject of their first conversation, to remind the artist of the sketch he wanted, the drawing of the extraordinary little balcony, which he remembered with such affection. A childhood memory, Titian, who had far different things on his mind at the time, thought to himself. Nevertheless he replied:

'Immediately I went to that little balcony and made a drawing of it. And so it should not come alone, I have also done another in the manner of the balconies of this place, which I am sending with this one of mine, and if they are not done according to the greatness of your Illustrious Serene Highness and the humble desire I have to serve you, you must pardon me and lay the blame on the wish I had to serve you as rapidly as possible, and if these do not satisfy you, I await your orders and I will do some other ones, as I have once and for all dedicated myself, body and soul, to Your Excellency's service. I know no other pleasure than to receive your commands and to prove myself worthy of executing them. I have not forgotten the 'Bath' Your Illustrious Serene Highness has ordered and I work at it all day long, and when Your Highness desires to see it, as soon as you have let me know the same, it will immediately be sent off, and until then I recommend myself humbly to the good graces of Your Highness.

In Venice, on the XIX day of February, 1517.

Of Your Illustrious Highness
the humble servant
TITIANO

From then on Tebaldi was continually carrying messages to and fro between the Duke and the painter: then the canon Malchiostro wrote to him, desiring a painting—and all the time Brother Germano, becoming more and more impatient, came back to disturb him with all his doubts and his apprehensions. At last, one fine day, when the work was approaching its end, Titian took a decision: very calmly, looking the Guardian squarely in the face, he gave him a thorough-going explanation of the movement, the proportions, the great and simple power he had striven to impart to the painting, and all the minute technical subtleties which he had succeeded in attaining. With simple words he opened the other's eyes to all the dazzling qualities of the masterpiece, into which he had poured the whole of himself: he had kept the Great Council waiting, the Duke of Ferrara, the canon Malchiostro—they had all had to wait for the completion of the Assumption for the church of Treviso. Let him look at the painting well—now it was completed. It was a masterpiece, although he himself said, so he did not need to wait for others to confirm it. Besides, it was the best answer which he could give to those who were besotted by the Michelangelesque fashion and imagined that he, Titian, was panting so as not to be left behind!

All Brother Germano's doubts were dispelled. Now he had understood, understood thoroughly. Titian's cutting assertions transformed themselves in his mind to a rhapsody of praise which he formulated into an endless monologue, as though it were a lesson he had to learn by heart. Yes, this altar-piece was a fine counterblast against those amateurs who reproached Titian for imitating Michelangelo.

When the counterblast was delivered, on the day of the public exhibition of the 'Assumption', the 20th March, 1518, Venice was amazed and carried away by enthusiasm.

Under the mighty confusion of agitated apostles and swarming nude angels, surrounding the human figure of the Virgin, an admiring, bleating crowd collected: prelates, senators, patricians, members of embassies, artists, pupils, relations and chosen friends from Cadore, merchants, even famous courtesans and pious beggars. Brother Germano aired his matured reflections in an oration, which he delivered with the full diapason of his lungs.

Then followed interminable speeches, benedictions, words and more words. Oblique rays of light filtered into the church, throwing a delicate veil over the centre round which all this chatter revolved, while its echoes floated up and remained suspended in the air. The naves were like triumphal arches, through which Titian passed serenely, welcoming the most illustrious personages or accompanying them to the portals.

The 'Assumption' initiated the grandiose manner in art which was to characterize the period in which Titian lived: he was the first to perfect its style by the harmony and brilliance of his colour.

He now lived in a frenzied rush of activity, conditioned by his ever-increasing success. The painting of the 'Bath' did not keep him from making haste to get on with his other works. The altar at Treviso brought other commissions in other places and further proposals for further plans. Yet on every enterprise, he imposed a calm rhythm in his plans of executing it, for he desired all his pictures to be masterpieces: therefore he began to make arrangements so that they could mature into masterpieces.

Now that he had succeeded in taking the full measure of his own capacity, he realized that he had not yet expressed everything which it would be necessary for him to express. He had sometimes only to snap his fingers in the motionless air of his studio, with a dry, slight movement, imperceptible, like a command—and he could almost see the magic proportions of the vision he must immortalize to attain his ambition. A slight movement, no more than laying down a brush or scratching his beard, sufficed to awaken a pictorial idea—an idea that crystallized unhurriedly, perhaps even idly—and was followed by others, countless ones. . . .

In his large workroom, standing there four-square like a mountaineer of Cadore, strong enough to cut down a whole forest, trunk after trunk, relying firmly on his computations, he let his eyes wander slowly round the room. The cat came up to him silently, encouraged by his immobility. Vision upon vision arose, unleashed by the quiet atmosphere of apparent tedium. Compositions linked up, forming ideal connections. The cat yawned and curled up to sleep in a corner: the painter set to work. He was in the mood to recapitulate visions of things that he had never seen, which he would show to other men like miracles.

Naturally the deliberation he needed to do good work could not always be made to accord with the frantic pressure of his commissions. They were the devil—a tiresome devil, which would in turn assume the semblance and the cape of the Great Chancellor of Venice, the cassock of the ever shilly-shallying Brother Germano, or the austerity of that bore, Alfonso d'Este . . . it was always the same story.

Tebaldi arrived again with messages from the Duke, and bundles of canvases and frames. Automatically, Titian began to dictate: 'Illustrious and most Excellent My Lord the Lord Duke', and continued with all the courtesy of one who wishes to maintain the best of relations with his patron, but at the same time to elude the binding agreement which the latter coveted most: that he should move to Ferrara and work exclusively for him.

The months went by while he continued to play this game of advancing and withdrawing. Tebaldi returned to the charge: Duchess Lucrezia was no more, she had died unexpectedly in labour—for that reason he had come to ask the painter to finish his work quickly, as it might afford some distraction to the Duke. But at the end of the summer, the Duke, after having waited a long time for intellectual consolations, was still vainly waiting for the artist and the paintings, and he wrote most urgently to his agent. Tebaldi flew to Titian's studio, but Titian was in Padua. Ah, this would end badly, very badly indeed, moaned Messer Jacopo. But at that moment Titian's firm steps were heard: he had come back and calmly traversed the studio. Approaching the work in question, he displayed it to his visitor, saying that if the Duke should wish to watch its definite completion, he would go to Ferrara.

It was the painting of the 'Feast of Venus'. When Duke Alfonso, trembling with impatience, saw Titian arrive with his picture of that wonderful joyous swarm of naked children who were romping on the grass, his roars of welcome were as noisy as a salvo from all his cannon.

V

IN the wake of these explosions, Messer Ludovico appeared with a serene, friendly smile, ready to admire the painting. Titian had already been informed by Tebaldi that Ariosto would be in Ferrara, and as they greeted each other, he was aware of something more than the usual curiosity between two famous men at their first meeting: the poet succeeded in conveying with what desperate impatience the Duke, their mutual patron, had been expecting the painter's arrival. It was as though he were saying in so many words: Ah: here at last is Titian himself in the flesh!

According to the law that a word can, in a delicate and majestic way, complete an image or *vice versa* a sound, architectural lines or sculptured forms, a painter has the same pleasure in meeting a musician, an architect or a sculptor. And between the painter and the poet there was the Duke, interposing his voracious control in every argument and every evocation of emotion.

During this brief sojourn their talk turned mostly round the theme of lyrical, rhymed pleasantries. The presence of Titian who, though he was not a man of letters, was known as a consummate painter of poetical visions, called forth an enduring and ever-renewed pretext for the evocation of suggestions that hit the mark.

The subjects seemed to be undetermined. It was as though one of them were to propose a conundrum, the second to complete it and the third to attempt the solution—the third being the Duke who desired clarity and tangible concreteness in everything. These riddles assumed the proportions of certain courtly artificial landscapes where pheasants perched on the topmost branches of holmoaks, whose foliage stirred in the breeze and was entwined with grapevines. There was no intoxication of beauty in the exercises, only the delight of pure technicality: while they drugged their own imagination, one would polish the form of the verbal conception and the other compose visual associations of ever-increasing felicity. Both of them seemed to be learning by heart

92

the rules whose absolute severity conditioned all their researches:

> *Zaffir, rubini, oro, topazi e perle*
> *E diamanti e crisoliti e iacinti*
> *Potriano i fiori assimigliar che per le*
> *Liete piagge v'avea l'aura dipinti. . . .*

(Sapphires, rubies, gold, topaz and pearls
And diamonds and chrysoliths and hyacinths
The flowers come to resemble what the air
Has painted on the gay, delightful shores. . . .)

The Duke, his eyes flashing vivaciously, always alert, joined image after image in his mind like a mosaic of ideas, subtle anatomies composed in a tender and tense atmosphere. And they would remember Philostratus and evoke Catullus.

But as they were taking breath during a pause in the ritual of their poetic exercises there came, among others, like echoes from a distant world, the tidings that Leonardo had passed away. His life had silently come to an end at Cloux and his great black shadow seemed to loom bitterly in the emptiness of time.

Titian took leave of the Duke with all the usual promises of promptitude and industry and said goodbye to Ariosto. These departures made the Duke even more nervous: in his letters, where he employed the royal plural ('We greet you. . . . We expect') his own heraldic plural included that of his henchman, the petulant Tebaldi, whom Titian had found waiting for him in Venice. 'We expect. We desire!'—and it was the old story all over again, the inexorable round of engagements, of promises that had to be kept, of more and more work to be done. . . . Now, however, whether it was night or day, his inspired energy knew no bounds. Boards and canvases of different sizes stood on the easels turned to the light or back to the shadow: they seemed like far-away sails palpitating on the sea, for soiled coverlets had been thrown over the figures of saints and donors when he left these paintings to dry, forgot them for a day or a week, and uncovered them again to complete and perfect them. There was Alvise Gozzi of Ragusa, the patron who had ordered a large picture for the churchs of St Francis in Ancona kneeling and looking up to the Blessed Virgin, and Altobello Averoldo, kneeling and looking up to the Risen Christ on the squared-up altar-piece which Titian had begun in Brescia.

He had few friendships and could not indulge in too many distractions. He was much criticized, but the critics could not harm him, as all he wanted was to be left in peace so that he could paint, paint, paint. Among his few friends, next to his cousin Toma Tito, the one he preferred was Palma, the well-to-do artist who would never dream of setting up as his rival and lived in calm industrious ease in his clean, light house, which his niece Margherita kept in order for him.

To be alone is not to be unique. Uniqueness consists in being the only exemplar of a particular kind. There can be no doubt that it was what Titian had always desired to attain, but before he reached this condition, he kept apart because he felt himself to be so different from the others: the only point of contact he could find between himself and anything outside was exclusively in his own work. He worked day and night, his industry was like a great machine running on inexorably in top gear, like a mill of great dreams which, ignoring all the futile accidents of the day, continued to grind out the very essence of passion. His amazed contemporaries wondered at this man's splendid isolation, his secluded, mysterious manner of working which could produce such prodigies.

One day Tebaldi's gondola stopped under the mill of his great dreams. Titian came down slowly, wrapping himself in his cloak, and together they proceeded to Murano to order jars, glasses and vases for the Duke. It was an icy February day, the sky grey with coagulated cold, and the artist panted with impatience as he looked at the lagoon and threw stealthy glances at his companion. Tebaldi was to return not once but many times. He came in Spring and again in the more summery weather, to seek a craftsman the Duke wanted to have in Ferrara to gild and finish the frame for his portrait and to submit designs for certain chisels to be used for jewellery. He came again and again, always with new commissions.

Ah! the blessed Duke! Titian put down his palette and went slowly to the window, where he and Tebaldi looked out at the June sky which, in the heat of the early afternoon, seemed to paralyse the half-deserted city. At this time of day it would have been lovely on the quiet shores of Burano or in the gardens of Murano near the tepid waters which expressed all ease of life. But his work would not wait: life was too short and it was a pity to lose even one hour, one minute. . . . Only a few weeks earlier, on the 6th April of that year 1520, Raphael had died, so young in years. The two men were silent. Titian stood motionless, still holding two paintbrushes and a painting rag in his hands, stupefied by the strong light, which seemed as sonorous as a distant buzzing of many voices. In that buzzing he heard the quiet voice of Tebaldi who was now reading aloud a letter from the Duke which he had unfolded:

'Messer Jacomo, procure an interview with Titian at once and tell him from me that he must as soon as possible portray from nature and as though it were alive an animal called gazelle, which is in the house of Magnifico Joanni Cornaro, and that he portray it on canvas lifesize, employing all diligence and that he send it to me at once, letting me know the cost. . . .'
The date was the 29th May, 1520.

Messer Giacomo's voice buzzed on in a kind of perpetual motion, from which emerged these wishes which turned into urgent commands and left the artist no peace. . . . Titian's mind was far away: when the other had finished reading the missive, down to the date, he shook himself and asked for the name of the person, the name of the house, as though he had heard nothing.

'It is the house of Cornaro.'

He could have listened to the letter being read out ten times over, like a litany, for the sunshine made him feel as languid as a lizard basking in the glare. The name of Cornaro, that had once shone with such splendid valour over the tragic destinies of Cadore, now reminded him of Pieve, but it was not a pathetic memory of the past. It was Pieve as he always thought of it, with the future before it, sound and solid, and the Vecelli established on the throne of well-being and surrounded by respect, in the atmosphere of austere power patronized by Saint Tiziano—a saint whom he was beginning to imagine with his own features, with those first white hairs of his, his own morose intransigent seriousness—the saint of his own family.

He began to talk about Pieve. To Tebaldi what he was saying now seemed indeed like an incomprehensible buzzing: he was crumpling the Duke's letter between his fingers and holding it away from the sunlight, as though it were a dazzling mirror. But Titian was now calmly reminiscing about the mountain peaks of his home, the Marmarole: Did Messer Giacomo know them? He had painted them and he would never cease to paint them, dipping them into the Venetian gold which was glimmering around them—they were his own kingdom, his eternal landscape.

There will be no Casa Cornaro and no gazelle today, Tebaldi thought to himself, holding his letter in the air like a comemmorative flag, and he understood that Titian was thinking the same, entrenched behind the theory of his impracticable landscapes. It was a duel of broken sentences, in which neither of the desperate adversaries yielded more than an inch at a time: several half-hours passed by until Titian had finally to surrender, for he could see no other way of obtaining peace than to slip into his coat and go with Tebaldi to look at the precious animal.

Although it was now time for the noonday repast, Casa Cornaro still appeared to be asleep, empty, deserted. Servants introduced them into a hall with dark hangings and informed them that the master was away from home—at Murano—and they could not see the gazelle either—it was dead. However, they went to fetch someone else. During the few minutes they were made to wait, minutes which seemed to him so many years, Titian began to curse as he always did when the Duke's wishes and commands caused him to waste half of a precious day.

At last a member of the family arrived and told them that the gazelle had died a long time ago—it was a terrible pity that it was not possible to oblige the Duke and the artist. Tebaldi, inexorable, asked whether they might not at least see his hide. Alas, even that was no longer there: the animal had been quite disfigured by the horrid malady that had killed it, and had ended at the bottom of the lagoon. But there existed a little picture by the late lamented Giambellino, representing the gazelle when it was still a thin little beast, less than a year old, at the time when it had come to Venice from the Orient: if Titian thought he could use this painting for his work, they would let him see it as often as he desired.

The artist took up his position in front of the picture with the expression of a man about to go berserk with impatience. It was no longer a question of Giambellino, or the Duke, or the gazelle, and as always the person immediately at hand had to suffer the full weight of his resentment, the person at whom he glared furiously—Tebaldi. Yet the latter dared to ask the painter quite calmly whether he cared to take notes from this rare artistic document.

That phrase might well have caused the vessel of Titian's wrath to flow over, but Tebaldi, able courtier that he was, knew full well that Titian was an artist and that a genuine artist, even in his blackest mood, will never belie himself, never lose his temper in certain situations, and never express disrespect of his own teacher. Titian

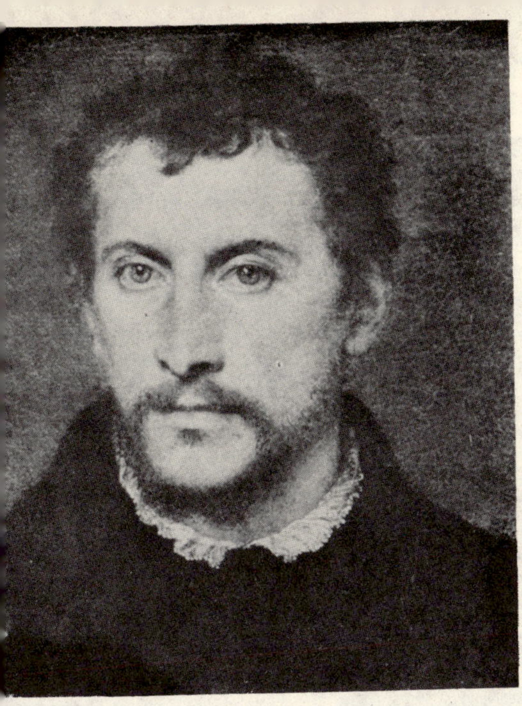

*"The man with the
grey-green eyes"*

(Pitti Gallery, Florence)

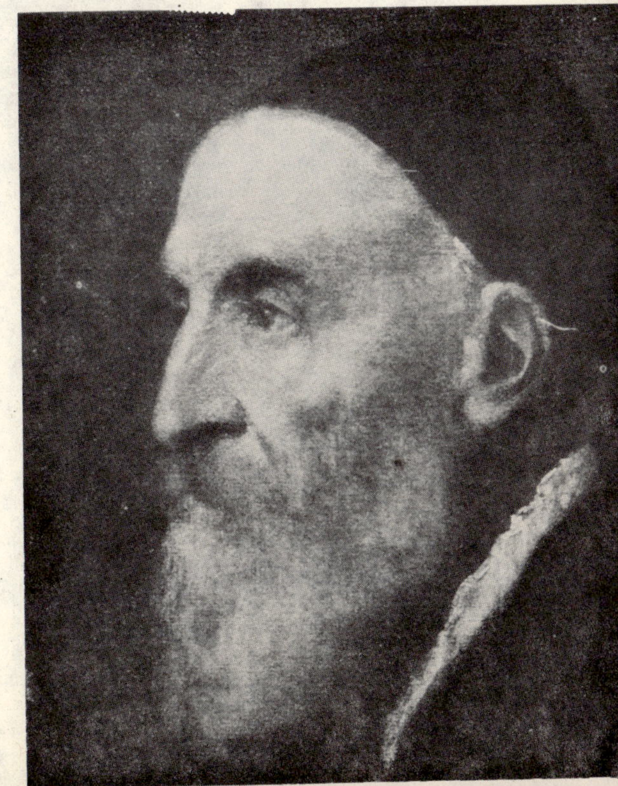

*Self portrait
in old age*—Detail

(Prado, Madrid)

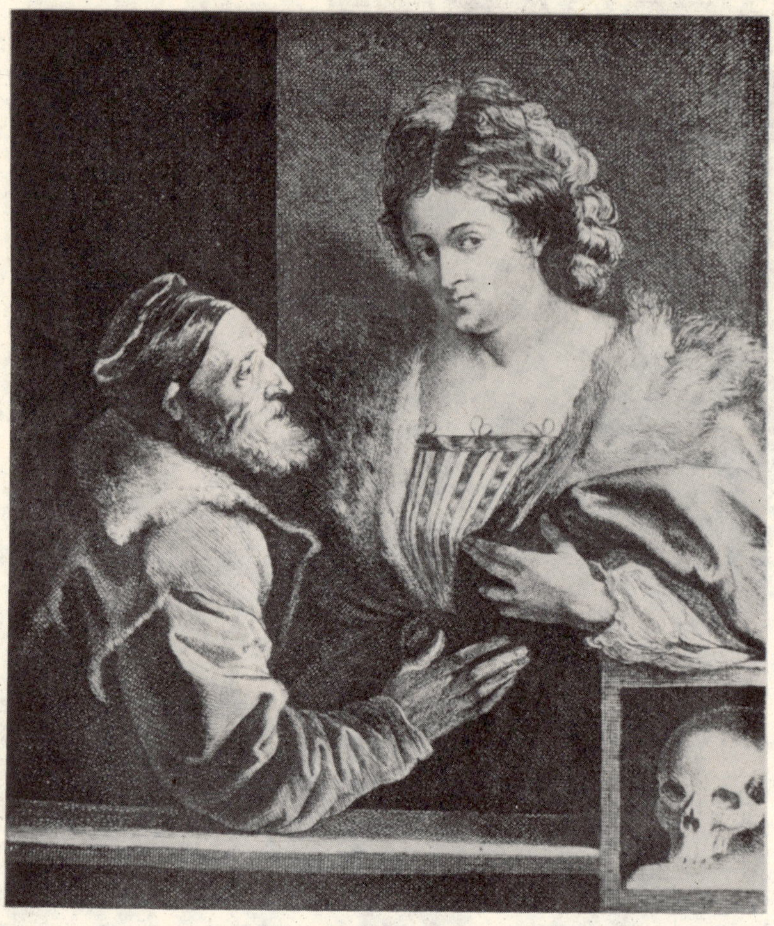

Engraving of a lost painting by Titian, of which only two prints
are known. On the margin of one appears this Italian verse:

*Ecco il bel veder! O che felice sorte
Che la Fruttifera frutto in ventre porte.
Ma ch'ella porte, o mé! Vita et morte piano
Demostra l'arte del magno Tiziano.

On the margin of the other print is the Latin inscription:

Ecce Viro quae grata suo est, nec pulchrior ulla
Pignora coniugii ventre pudica gerit;
Sed tamen an vivens, an mortua picta tabella
Haec magni Titiani arte notanda refert.

*Oh beauteous sight! Oh happy fate
The fruit-bearer bears a fruit within her womb.
Yet that she bears concealed, alas, both life and death
Is here revealed by the great Titian's art.

alluded briefly to his excellent visual memory—it was as though he had said that there had never been and never would be a more lifelike gazelle than the one he was going to paint. He thanked his host and took his leave.

The Duke's zealous ambassador, who by now knew his painter as well as he knew his own pocket, was a good diplomat. Now that he had accomplished the task of the day and had received from Titian the usual promises that he would execute the work and deliver it punctually—which he never did—Tebaldi did his best to win back the painter's friendship and goodwill. In perfect good faith, while he accompanied him home, he began to compose a verbal portrait of him, a description that hit the mark, though it was respectful: a man who found it extremely difficult to accept the idea of any enterprise that was proposed to him, and whose frequent sulks could be ascribed rather to the prejudices of a man accustomed to pursue his own aims and moral principles than to an ungenerous nature. A being one would hardly like to resemble, but one whose inspired creations must make everybody exclaim: this is truly the world for me! For example, that swarm of cupids that he had painted for Duke Alfsonso—that had given him, Tebaldi, the same delight as the juice of pomegranates or golden grapes, an intoxicating delight. . . .

He talked on and on, but Titian was no longer listening: he was counting the working hours he had lost. Titian was not listening, or appeared not to be listening. Yet actually he was listening intently. From the fortress of that inner region where he withdrew with those thoughts of his that could not be contaminated, he listened as if not to endanger his own mysterious genius.

A creature with two eyes, two ears, one mouth, two hands and a waist similar to all the other creatures on earth and yet, as Tebaldi remarked with amazement, with a natural capacity for continually fathering exceptional masterpieces: but since an artist never forgets to take all things into just consideration one might almost say that he had to restrain the signs and portents of his miracles. Therefore it was possible for him to be a man like other men. For miracles, as has been shown, can never be explained.

He produced masterpieces with alacrity, as a cobbler produces shoes. But his life tended towards infinite horizons, while the reaction of those who saw the paintings into which he put the the whole of himself required the absolute. A cobbler would stitch

G

his shoes with threads of pure gold if he were asked to do so—but he, when they asked him for a picture of Bacchus and Ariadne or an altar-piece, would simply paint a world that had never existed and never would exist except in himself: he painted ideas that materialized in the senses, and poems without names or words.

Thus the zealous ambassador of the Duke of Ferrara attempted to impersonate a kind of humorous gadfly for his princely patron and to convey his jealous opposition when Titian seemed to devote too much time to other commissions. The painter had only just returned from Conegliano, where he had been asked by the Scuola di Santa Maria Nuova to restore the frescoes, and had started to work again at the altar-piece for Brescia, on which he had already completed a muscular Saint Sebastian, when Tebaldi began worrying him again; saying that the priests were causing the artist to forget the Duke—the magnificent rewards of the priests! No, indeed, Titian protested; the work he had done at Conegliano had only yielded the lease of a house opposite the Arfosso (and he would have to redecorate it inside and out), and as to the Saint Sebastian and the other figures on the panels of the altar, they were not being paid too well. In the end he divulged how much they had brought him.

This was exactly what Tebaldi had wanted to find out; as everybody was saying that the nude figure of the saint was one of the most original works Titian had produced, he immediately wrote to the Duke to tell him about the subject of the picture and ask for the authorization to treat for it, saying that it would be a shameful waste if it were to end in the hands of the priests, in the semi-darkness of a church. He then proposed to Titian that he should paint another figure for the altar, and let the Duke have the original one. At first Titian refused to lend his hand to such a swindle, as he called it, but in the end he gave way and promised to do another painting of Saint Sebastian. The Duke had already given his consent, but one morning as Titian was going home after having worked at the Ducal Palace, he met Tebaldi, who was on his way to see him in order to read him a letter he had just received from his master:

'. . . we have thought over this affair of Saint Sebastian and we have decided that we do not wish to do this injury to the Most Reverend Legate; and let Titian be assiduous in serving us well in the work which he shall do for us, and for the time being we demand only that from him . . .'.

Included was a draft for twenty-five scudi.

This was on the 23rd December, 1521: Pope Leo X had died twenty-three days earlier, and while waiting for the election of the next Pope, the Duke did not wish to give offence in any way, especially as he was going to Rome for the occasion.

Tebaldi suggested that Titian should spend Christmas at Ferrara, seeing that he had such a great desire to visit Rome: he could work there in all tranquillity, and as soon as the news of the Pope's election came, their patron would be sure to take him to Rome in his suite. But Titian was feeling tired. He said that he would prefer to remain in Venice to finish the work in hand and he might even decide not to go to Pieve for a couple of days for Christmas.

On the 26th December, the Duke wrote to Tebaldi:

'Messer Jacomo, if you had the spirit of prophecy you could not have said a truer thing to Titian than what you told him about our plan to go to Rome. Inasmuch as, the moment we have the news that the new Pope has been elected, we in person wish to go to Rome to prostrate ourselves at the feet of His Holiness if nothing comes to hinder us from so doing, and therefore ask Titian to come soon. . . .'

But the artist had decided to go to Pieve: he did not feel well there, but he succeeded in not falling ill and returned to Venice as quickly as he could: there he took to his bed. It was nothing serious—a state of feverish exhaustion which came upon him every evening, enervating him and making him lose weight. He would never give in to trifling ailments, and after having spent a few days in bed he began to work again.

As a favour to Cecilia, he consented to rest for a short time in the afternoon and the children kept him company, especially six-year old Orazio, who was very attached to him. The little boy amused himself by learning the names of the months and then went all round the house, repeating them in every room: 'April . . . May . . . June'—then, as his childish memory failed, his father would call across from his room, guiding the uncertain progress of the little ambulant voice:

'Come on now—July!'

The child took up the refrain until at the next standstill he came back to the threshold:

'September . . . September. . . .', he stammered and began to gesticulate wildly in his confusion. Then he would start again

from the beginning: 'January . . . February . . . ' Thus the pleasant
game of the months continued for days and days, until the
father, working again and in good fettle, adopted the habit of keeping
the little boy near him in the studio, letting him play around among
the paints and brushes and watching him when he slept, curled up like
a puppy on a carpet.

Orazio had now learned the calendar of the rapidly passing months
by heart, and his father came and went: from Brescia to Venice to
carry out some commissions; from Venice to Pieve for the wedding
of his sister Caterina with Matteo Soldano; from Pieve to Venice;
from Venice to Ferrara. And here he found the Duke, who, like
Orazio psalmodizing the months, went from room to room humming
a little French song and stopping short at regular intervals, just like the
child when he could not remember the next month.

In order to please him, Titian touched up the wonderful 'Bacchanal'
that he had painted for him. On a sheet of music, lying on the grass,
forming a pivot to the harmonious intricacy of the reeling, drunken
revellers, he wrote the first verse of the little song his patron liked so
much:

Chi boit et ne reboit, ne cais qua boir soit.

A year had now gone by, and the Duke had at last received his pictures.
Accompanied by Laura Dianti, the beautiful Laura Eustochia, his
former favourite, he would often come to gaze at them, refreshing
himself, as it were, in a special enclosure of poetry that had been
created for the two of them.

Profiting by his patron's enraptured gratification, Titian took the
opportunity to travel to Mantua, to the Court of Federigo Gonzega,
whom he had known in Venice during the Carnival of 1520, and who
had since invited him to stay at his court through Giovanni Malatesta
and Braghino Croce da Coreggio, his agents in Venice. Before going
to Ferrara, Titian had equipped himself with a letter from Malatesta
to the Marquis of Gonzaga:

'The bearer is Messer Ticiano, most excellent in his art and also
modest, a pleasing person in every way; the same has laid aside many
of the works in which he is now occupied in order to come and kiss
the hand of Your Excellency according to the desire you have
expressed through me; therefore I believe I need add no further
recommendation.

Venice, XXV January MDXIII.'

Thus Titian betook himself to the court of Mantua. But how to take upon himself new tasks while that blessed painting for the Great Council was not yet completed and there were plans for a new votive picture for the Pesaro family? This was the problem that worried Titian all the more as the Duke of Ferrara had given him new orders when he left.

In order to escape from troublesome engagements and yet ingratiate himself with the new powerful Maecenas of Mantua, he did not stay there as long as he could have done, giving as his reason his anxiety to return to Ferrara so as to finish various jobs for Gonzaga's uncle, the Duke. The Marquess gave him a letter and allowed him to depart:

'To His Illustrious and Excellent Avuncular Highness. Having requested Master Tyciano, the bearer of this present letter, to carry out some works for me, he has informed me that he cannot serve me at present, saying that he has promised to paint several things for Your Excellency, which will require a long time. And for this reason I enjoin him to his obedience.

Mantuae, III februarii 1523

servus et nepos

Fredericus'

What scruples, what discipline, grumbled Duke Alfonso as he folded the letter again. He knew all about Titian and his 'obedience'. . . . The Duke seemed strangely preoccupied. However, it was actually only the question of a new intrigue with a local girl, for he was now in the habit of ravishing chosen young girls—naturally with the consent of their parents—and then, dishonoured as they were, marrying them off with a generous dowry.

In the meantime, Antonio Grimani had died and the extremely popular Andrea Gritti had been elected as the new Doge. Titian worked for only a few days and then, judging it opportune to leave the Duke to his amorous pursuits and show himself in Venice again, he returned to that city.

Francesco informed him of new commissions, of visits and projects, while the little boys threw themselves into his arms and the servants carried the luggage into the house. In the studio he found Cecilia and his fifteen-year old apprentice, Gerolamo, a zealous little painter. They were cleaning and tidying-up everything. He lost his temper —would they never leave him alone, with that mania of theirs! His first impulse was to slap the boy and lay the blame on Cecilia, for he hated to have the slightest object connected with his work touched by other people.

But the great altar-piece for the Pesaro family, waiting to be completed, seemed to dominate a completely renewed space now that the studio was shining, tidy, clean and orderly.

VI

TRULY, he was a strange person, the members of his family would sometimes say: he always came back from his journeys bad-tempered and intolerant. After a time he seemed to calm down again, but then he buried himself in his work and took no interest in anything outside it.

His entire life was concentrated in his brain, in his head: if one of his arms had become gangrenous and had to be amputated he would have cursed blasphemously, but it would not have hindered him from working on. And if he had happened to lose his right arm, he would certainly have adopted the habit of painting with his left hand.

Instead of being tested by such misfortunes, he had to submit to losing his patience when an incessant low fever returned to torment him every evening. The physician advised a change of air—whereupon Tebaldi immediately began to praise Ferrara as the healthiest place in the world. But the healthiest place in the world for him was Pieve, his beloved Pieve, high up close to God's blue sky, and not a city of rheumatism like Venice. As to Ferrara—let them send him some ultramarine blue from there, he told Tebaldi, then he would feel better at once, and possibly he would come there later.

Scornfully negligent as he was towards his own health, he could not do enough for any member of his family who had even the most trifling complaint. With equal assiduity he watched over his own financial interests—only in concentrating on these material considerations did he participate in anything outside his artistic existence. 'He's from the mountains,' people said, referring to his attitude towards the chimerical element of gold and gain.

He was indeed a son of the mountains and he himself proclaimed it every time he spoke about Cadore. What could he say about Cadore compared with the intoxicating spectacle of Venice, the sumptuous harmony of Mantua, the austerity of Ferrara? But Cadore was Cadore —the beloved body of his exiled soul, or the only soul which his hard-working body would have liked to contain. And when he counted his money or bought some precious object from Nicolo di San Matteo, the goldsmith on the Rialto, he felt that he was collecting treasure to fortify his home, as though he were taking from Venice, Ferrara and Mantua the wherewithal to enrich Pieve, his own fief. Even the Doge himself was made to serve that purpose: during two short sittings he gave Titian for the preliminary sketches for a portrait, the artist spoke of his home and his family to such effect that Messer Gregorio, who had been a member of the Provincial Council for the last year, was nominated General Overseer of the Mines, and Matteo Soldano, Caterina's husband, received the office of Chancellor of Feltre.

So there they were, these newly-elected provincial dignitaries, wearing the same old capes, their beards trimmed with just a little more care, walking heavily, their pleasure camouflaged by an air of authority and gruff friendliness, inspecting mines and fortresses, superintending administrative procedures and charges, coming and going like busy ants. And they invoked the blessings of Heaven upon Titian.

*   *   *

As soon as Titian was well again, Cecilia fell ill. A lassitude that weighed on her like a tombstone forced her to take to her bed: she lay there panting, feverish, her face dripping with sweat. A physician was sent for, visited her, prescribed medicines. He came again and found no improvement. Outside the sick-room, with great caution, he expressed the opinion that she might be going to die.

Her shrunken little face looked as though it were miles away. She already understood without being told that she might die. She was afraid of God, and her man had always been immersed in other things —that was why she feared death. She remembered how, when she had been expecting Pomponio, she had already dreaded leaving the world, burdened down with the most mortal of sins. Not even then had she been able to obtain what she desired so fervently, for she felt her own inferiority so acutely that she was unable to speak of certain things except in her silent prayers.

One afternoon, as she lay there exhausted by her long sickness, even though the fatal crisis seemed less imminent, she burst into tears, like an inconsolable child. Alone in the twilight that the curtains of the bed made darker still, she surrendered utterly to her weakness and sobbed her heart out. And perhaps the most humiliating thing of all was that not a soul heard her sobs.

That hard streak in Titian which she had hoped again and again to dissolve in the warm breath of her silent love, now seemed to rise up like a wall, a wall decorated with all the fantastic visions that he was wont to paint.

The maid-servant was out, the man with Pomponio and Orazio: Titian and Francesco were in the studio. She might have cried herself to death—but, turning her head, she suddenly saw him standing on the threshold, motionless, in mute suspense.

'*Tucian mio*,' she gasped.

'Cecilia,' he answered, and they embraced like two lost souls seeking to help each other, finding themselves in an entirely new, entirely unknown situation. They had the strength to look at each other, steadily and searchingly as they had never yet dared to look. They saw a strange flame flickering in each other's eyes, and also a pitiful, moving, terrible immobility—the things that had never been said, never uttered, never even thought.

'Cecilia!', he repeated, caressing her over and over again. She was pacified: the fires of hell that had been raging in her heart went out, she wiped away her tears and settled quietly back on her pillows to prepare herself for her fate in the turn of the tide which would last for ever. But he, as though to hold her back, to keep her alive by the force of his passion, as he had done a minute earlier, feeling a flush of shame rising to his cheeks, took a sudden decision:

'Cecilia, Cecilia . . . wait. . . .'

He went to find Francesco in the studio:

'Listen, Francesco,' he said breathlessly. 'I want to marry Cecilia, my housekeeper, out of respect, because she who is infirm has given me two sons.'

In his amazement his brother dropped the paint brushes and rose to his feet.

'I am glad, and I wonder that you took so long to make up your mind', he said.

Titian looked down at his hands, at his clothes. He might have been having an audience with the Doge himself.

'We must hurry,' he said.

'I'll go at once.'

At that moment the maid came back. Francesco went out to fetch Don Paolo, the priest at San Giovanni Nuovo, the young painter Girolamo, the goldsmith Nicolò and the stone-mason Master Silvestro.

'Ask Master Nicolò for a little gold chain, a trinket for Cecilia. . . . Hurry!' Titian called after him. He called the maid and the man, sent the girl to buy food for the whole company and ordered the man to tidy up the house and set the table.

He went back to Cecilia's room and began to take up things and put them down again, strewing them all over the room.

'What is it?' she asked, while the cat took refuge under the bed, terrified by the unwonted agitation. Titian opened the linen-cupboard and took out one of Cecilia's shifts, the best one she had, explaining that this must be her wedding-dress—she must forgive him for not having provided a better one.

Suddenly he could see her become a woman again, no longer a doomed victim, but a true woman for whom time took on a different rhythm, gentle and feminine. There was a pause during which one felt that it had become stabilized. Slowly Cecilia undid the collar of the shift she was wearing and asked him to help her. She raised herself up on the mattress, threw back the blankets and put her feet on the ground. He stood by silently, as though assisting at a ritual.

Then he lifted the shawl from her shoulders and removed the nightdress; her bare, white body in its immobility appeared like a marble statue. The cat reappeared from under the bed and clawed at the trailing draperies.

'Sssst. . . . Go away!'

Cecilia smiled. For a moment she was naked, and raised her arms to don her wedding garment, shivering slightly as the cool fresh linen touched her skin. She asked no questions—neither who was going to bless their union, nor who the witnesses would be, nor whether anyone had thought of making the necessary preparations. She merely asked for a comb and lay back on the pillows. Titian handed it to her and stooped to kiss her. She felt as though she must swoon away: she fondled the back of his neck while his mouth was fastened to her lips and the cat rolled round on the blankets, playing with the discarded shift.

They fell apart and turned towards the door. Orazio was standing on the threshold, looking at them. His father went towards him, waving the discarded gown. 'Come along with me,' he said laughingly and led the boy into the other room, where, with the manner of someone revealing a great secret, he told his son that he and Pomponio must be very good and quiet that evening: a great event was taking place in the house, he could not explain exactly what it was, but it was a very important event. Then he pushed him out into the kitchen, where the maid, who had come home laden with food, the man and Pomponio set to work with a will.

Titian changed his waistcoat, smoothed his hair and went back to Cecilia. Now everybody arrived—the priest and the witnesses. They all assembled round the sick woman's bed and she greeted them with an inclination of her head. In order to overcome the sense of strain occasioned by so unusual a ceremony, they all occupied themselves merrily with lighting the lamps, as night was already falling.

The rite was brief. Against the flickering of the little flames, at the foot of the bed, strongly modelled by light and shade, Pomponio and Orazio had placed themselves, like a pair of sculptured pages standing on guard. His sons, one twelve and the other ten, healthy and wide-awake, appeared to Titian to have been suddenly placed in the world of events in order to make him dismiss all sentimentality—they were now two little men, no longer babies to be kept in the kitchen. He kept his eyes on them as he stood there, holding Cecilia's hand in his own.

In the silence the last words of the Benediction slowly fell. From the canal below one could hear the voices of people returning to their houses, like inhabitants of a different planet.

Cecilia was worn out: the intensity of her emotion had exhausted her. They brought her some food, remaining round her so that she should have company. She smiled between one slow mouthful and the next. Then the grown-ups and the children repaired to the table to do honour to the roast meats.

'Pintorello', the little painter—that was what they were beginning to call Orazio in the house. Titian was training him to the customary discipline in his studio, for the boy was showing an ever-increasing predilection for drawing and painting. Pomponio, who was an idler and of a strangely turbulent disposition, was to devote himself to ecclesiastical studies.

Cecilia, having recovered from her sickness, often lingered to admire her own image in the painted exaltation of her milk-white, luxuriant beauty which now flowered again. It was in the semblance of the

Madonna herself that Titian had finally extolled her in the altar-piece for the Pesaros, at the foot of two tall columns, surrounded by a gentle breeze that gave movement to the clouds, to the folds of a gonfalon and new life to the colours of the marble.

VII

LIKE a rainbow spanning the earth from one pole to the other, following the trajectory of a catapult, there descended on Venice the habits, the customs, the turbulent loquacity and the joyous devilry of a corpulent gentleman dressed in black from head to foot, who had arrived one evening with his servant and had taken up his quarters at an inn: he had immediately unloosed his purse-strings, doling out rewards for any juicy item of information with which he was furnished. He roared with laughter when he was told that people had first mistaken him for a merchant. It was soon evident that he was no other than Messer Pietro Aretino, man of letters.

The Doge himself was informed of his arrival and bade him welcome. Even Titian received him. The entire city learnt to stand to attention for him: he was said to be a wizard as regards influence, a monster of libertinism and a master of conversation.

Aretino did not give the lie to these assertions: he lost no time in getting himself respected and feared, or in exercising his lustfulness. As to the art of conversation, native of Tuscany that he was, he could have given points to St Bernard himself. He saw to it at once that he found fine lodgings, beautiful girls for his pleasures, important connections for his new life. This life was entirely concentrated on the present, in a conjugation of immediate actions, words and intentions —all constructed to seize every practicable occasion as rapidly as could be. He did this in so sharp and authoritative a manner that it was difficult to imagine what he might have been yesterday, what he might be tomorrow. . . . He would get up in the morning, identify his own features in the mirror and remember who existed in the world simultaneously with himself—that sufficed for him to sit down and write his masterpieces, to Maria de' Medici, to the Bishop of Vasone, to the Doge, to the Duke of Mantua—letters to them all.

Among the disorder of his papers, with plucked grapes or melon-rinds lying around, he poured forth words and good humour, one foot

109

in a stocking and the other in a slipper. Ever ready to slip the other foot into the stocking, recover himself and, with a touch or two, recompose the still life of grape-stalks or fly-blown melons, he would magnanimously welcome friends, gifts and petitioners. The picturesque element in the disorder with which he was surrounded was simply love—the incessant expectation of love.

Several times a day a large part of the house had to be tidied up—here books had been dragged out to look up a quotation, there some glasses to sample a delightful drink. The floor was littered with cushions, thrown down for a hasty copulation, and especially now that the days were growing hot, books, glasses, cushions, fans, ewers and towels formed a long, entangled chain from the writer's study right down to the kitchen. A woman's work is never done, but here many women were united in harmonious collaboration.

Aretino understood Venice at once, and understood that he would never be able to tear himself away from it again. It was one of the most sensational discoveries of his life and it left him no peace until he could renew this discovery from time to time before the eyes of others—of Titian, for instance.

Titian could not always identify his own features in the mirror when he got up. Perhaps he did not even look at his reflection, knowing only too well what traces of exhaustion a new train of ideas had left on his face, a kind of neuralgia that could only be overcome by an immediate resumption of work. He was fascinated and at the same time exasperated by the face of Aretino, which seemed to appear between the lines of a note he had written on getting up, hastily and good-humouredly: the Master must come to dine with him that evening, where he would meet Jacopo Sansovino* who had only just arrived from Rome.

Aretino figured out that he would surround himself with choice, powerful friends and live in a manner befitting an artist surrounded by a court of which he would be the life and soul. Having dismissed the spiritual mourning he had assumed for the death of Giovanni dalle Bande Nere, he now prepared himself to sit laughingly, dressed

---

*Like Sansovino, who was joined in Venice by his wife and two little boys, Sebastiano del Piombo and some other artists succeeded by a miracle in escaping the Sack of Rome. Baldassarre Peruzzi actually arrived in Sienna in his shirt; Giovanni da Udine got to his home having lost almost everything, equally the eccentric Parmigianino, who had continued to work in his studio while the lancers burst into his house. That was in May 1527.

with dignified magnificence, at interminable, gluttonous banquets, sifting his company to make a definite selection of powerful and enduring friends.

For the first time Titian experienced the fascination of choice company. They talked about Rome, Michelangelo, antique sculptures and modern painting. There was sadness in his home life: his father had died, and also a baby girl who had been too brief a joy to Cecilia, having lived only just long enough to be baptized, with Francesco Zuccati acting as godfather—but these domestic sorrows found an important compensation in these new friendships, which promised to take root and become inseparable.

These friendships were to lead to practical results. Messer Pietro played the part of destiny, deciding, canalizing, arousing interest, obtaining appointments. Sansovino was bound for Paris? Whatever for? He must have a look-round him, in this paradise of Venice, and he would immediately realize that the only thing to do was to sink his roots in these waters, for no better life could flourish than from roots nourished by such abundant moisture. And thus it turned out. After a short time the overseer of San Marco, Bartolomeo Bon, died and the Republic appointed Sansovino to this office, with a decree of 7th April, 1529, and conferred on him a lodging near the Osteria del Cappello in Piazza San Marco—followed by several commissions.

Then there was a competition for the altar-piece for San Pietro Martire, to replace the slightly antiquated painting by Jacobello del Fiore: Palma, who was a companion of the School of San Pietro, together with the Gastaldo, applied to the Council of Ten asking that the competition should take place so that the work be given to the artist whose personality was the most outstanding.

'Surely they have got Vecellio!' Aretino kept repeating to all and sundry.' 'Why should there be a competition when there is an artist like Vecellio on earth?' And he insisted in his usual tone, sowing discord as he spoke, that all these applications were unnecessary—and most unnecessary of all the rivalry of so many artists.

Nevertheless the competition took place. Palma himself had taken part—in friendly rivalry with Titian, among many hostile competitors. Pordenone also competed, though he was extremely busy painting in Cremona and in Treviso, and buying land in his native province while he was working in Venice at the completion of the frescoes on the façade of the house of the well-known merchant Van Haanen.

Titian kept an eye on these younger colleagues of his; although he was merely a few years older than Pordenone and senior to his friend Palma by two years only, he had been in the habit for some time of making inexact and vague statements about his own age. He liked to make himself older—only slightly, but enough to ensure for himself the right of precedence, the formal right to precede the others on ceremonial occasions when he entered a hall together with Aretino. He also had precedence over everyone else as regards the altar-piece competition for San Pietro. His victory was certainly not due to the years he had added on to his age, but to the fact that his sketch was infinitely superior to all the others that were examined by the jury. There was none by Palma, as he had fallen ill. It had probably brought him bad luck that he had made his will that very year, Titian thought cynically, when Alvise di Serafin, Palma's houseboy, came to inform him one night of his master's death. Cynically, too, seeing that fate really seemed to be on his side, he hoped that Pordenone would be constrained to return to his own country and complete his apprenticeship on the larger altars there. Nevertheless, the façade of Casa d'Anna, where he had painted a Mercury full of movement and riders in foreshortening, pleased the idlers who were wafted past it in their gondolas with their noses in the air. Certainly Pordenone would return to Venice.

★　　★　　★　　★

While he seemed to be idling his time away and sniffing a pimpernel leaf or some other aromatic product of the garden or singing over and over again '*Inter aves turdus*', or indulging his appetite for roast thrushes until the sleeves of his wide satin gown were greasy, a flush would suddenly rise to Aretino's brow, while the wine he had drunk was transformed into pearls of sweat. Then he had need of kisses—chiefly from his mistress Angiola, called 'la Zafetta', who had a way of masking lasciviousness with seeming modesty. But from one banquet to the other, he devoured more thrushes, drank more wine, enjoyed more kisses. Zafetta kissed him, Caterina Sandella kissed him, and other women as well, all of whom had a way of revealing their charms with professional ease.

'Le Aretine' was the nickname that had been given to these courtesans. They surrounded him like the women in an Oriental harem, and Messer Pietro, lying naked on his bed in the noon-day heat of summer,

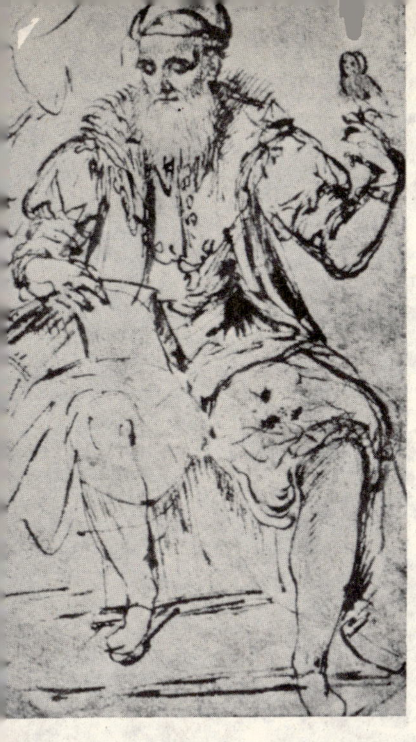

Portrait sketch of Titian (?)

(Pen-drawing in the Uffizi, Florence)

Titian's signature
on a detail from
"The Bacchanalia"

(Prado, Madrid)

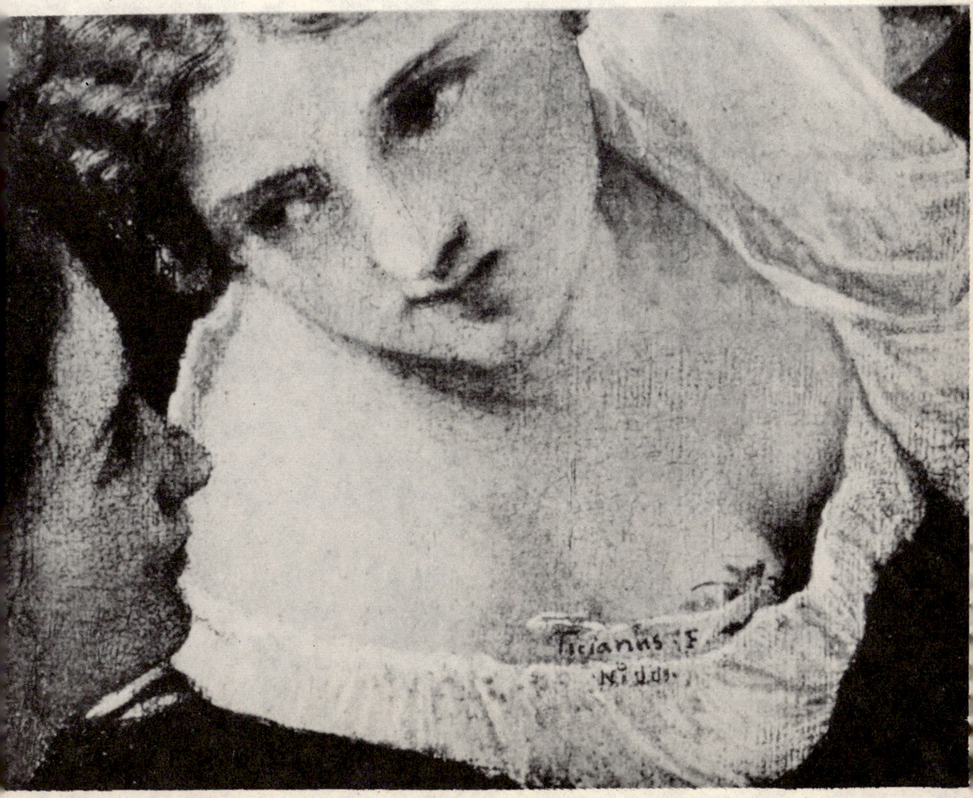

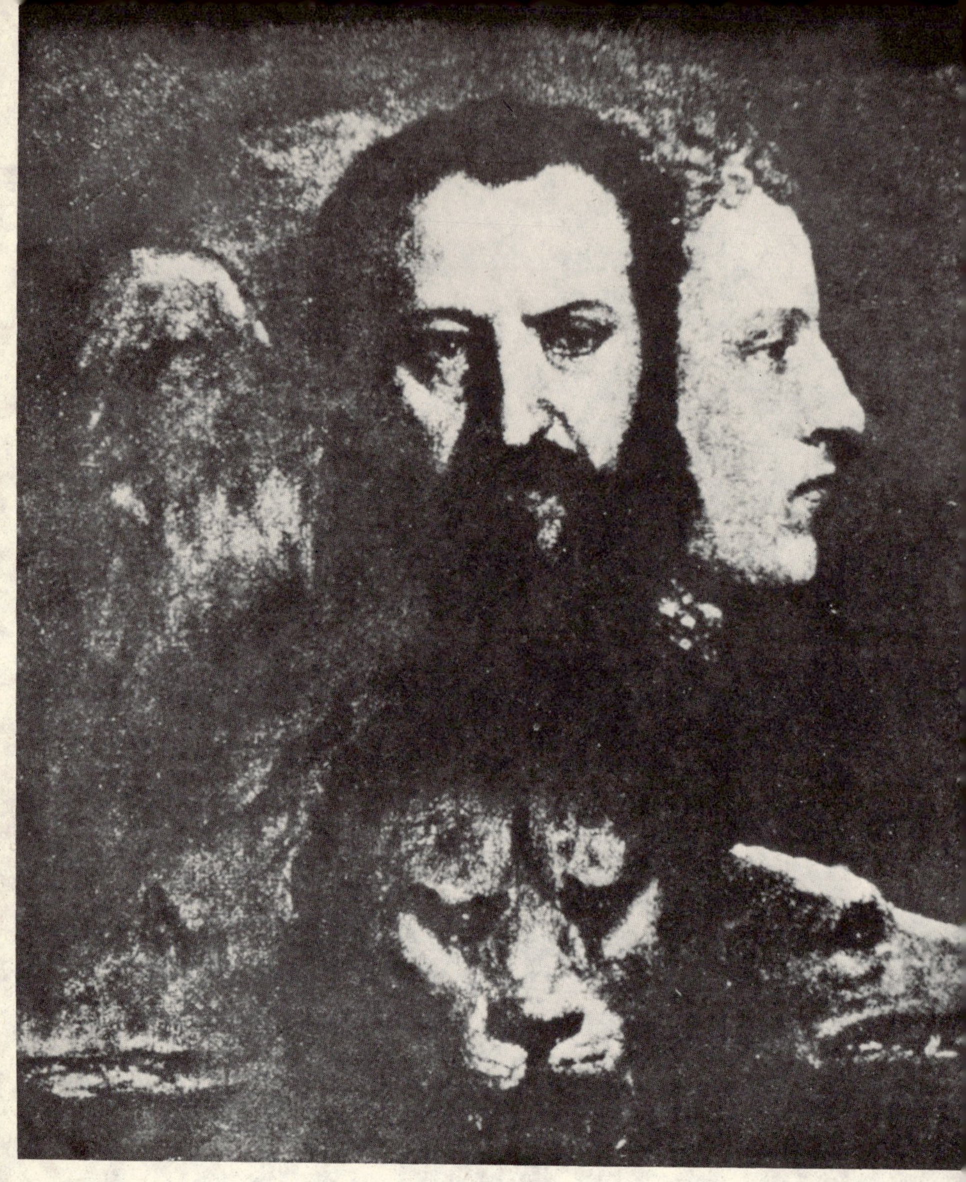

Photo: *De Antonis*

"The Three Ages of Man"

seemed truly like a corpulent nabob when he called his favourites. The girls laughed when they saw him like this, for even his beard no longer made an impression of authority as he wallowed shuddering on his bed, grunted like a boar, and dug his teeth into their tender flesh.

Unlike Sansovino, Titian preferred to ignore all this. As he had chosen for his own children names that recalled majestic memories— Lavinia for the baby girl who had died before the beauty of the world had appeared to her, Orazio, who was to become his zealous helper, and Pomponio, the black sheep of the family—he aspired, besides perpetuating it in his work, to keep alive a kind of senatorial dignity. This corresponded with his creative idea of life and eternity.

Now that he had assumed the attitude of one who has no definite age, as though he could succeed in being an Aristotle who belonged to all time, in fathering children with the austere names of ancient Rome and dominating with his works even the most ruthless minds of his contemporaries, he began to experience the splendour of a renascence fortified by the genius of those friends with whom he had decided to form an impressive artistic triumvirate. It was a creative trinity, blessed with every gift, though not without wickedness to which his personality opposed the restraint of morality.

He was in the habit of escaping from these banquets as soon as the blind instincts of his friends assumed the upper hand. They laughed at him, although deep down they understood him. They knew he was not condemning them and they realized that for him their pleasures would have demanded too great an effort. Also, Cecilia still remained his too-loving Madonna.

They would lean out of the window and shout for Luigi, his servant, who came to fetch him at the pre-arranged hour, carrying a lantern to light the way through the narrow alleys.

The Master came down and they returned to his house through the darkness, the silence, the delights and perils of the city, over which a tender veil of moisture spread, deadening the rustles, the whispers and the kisses. Walking a step behind him, Titian watched the spectral advance of his servant in the wavering light. Heavy with food and wine, he was feeling sleepy and he saw death passing all around, a tranquil death that took its time, coming towards him, rounding the corners or drawing back to let them pass.

At times he went to sleep in the gondola and Luigi had to shake him awake when they arrived. He started up and could not remember

H

where he was, feeling as though he might be in the other world. . . .
But it was Luigi, the poor servant, who was called away to the other
world, together with his faithful little lantern which threw diagonal
lights and shadows on the surrounding buildings, when he met with
a drunken patrician one night.

Titian was called for the reading of the statement to the offices of the
Signori della notte, and while it was being read out, it seemed to him
that he could see his little serving-man with his down-at-heel shoes and
his lantern, roaming silently in the darkness of the beyond. Alas! poor
Luigi, blinded in the other world—he who so often to flatter his
master had rubbed his eyes as though dazzled by the marvellous
paintings in the studio.

. . . *'The nobleman, Sir Baptista Quirino, son of the nobleman Sir Paul
Quirino, dwelling in the district of St Thomas, is accused in the month of
September, 1528, of having wounded one Aloisius de Cipro at the time
servant to Messer Titian the Painter living in the district of St Paul, by
stabbing him under the left eye. . . .'*

VIII

'ATTENTION, please, attention!' Aretino sang out: now that a king was wandering through Italy as Charles V was doing, one might expect him to sit down and rest on a throne in the dominating pose in which it would be desirable to paint him. 'Don't you agree?' he whispered into Titian's ear.

Titian had other things on his mind, but he knew that nobody in the world could advise him better than Aretino. It certainly was worth while to make an effort. However, the political situation in Italy was still rather turbulent; he hoped the king would sit down and rest for a while, providing that such a demon of energy could be expected to give a truce to himself and his opponents.

Now the turn of Florence to feel the war had come. On the 21st September, 1529, on the eve of the assault on the city, Michelangelo left in haste in the direction of France, with his pupil Mini, and Rinaldo Corsini, who had organized their precipitate flight. They stopped in Ferrara and then in Venice, where Bartolomeo Panciatichi gave them hospitality in his house near the Giudecca.

Everybody wondered whether Michelangelo would stay in Venice, and Doge Gritti found a good pretext to give him a commission, but the grim-faced, sombre genius felt ill at ease in the jewelled, complicated city. He who would design a building all in a breath—purgatory at the base and paradise at the summit—shrugged his shoulders disdainfully at all the fretwork, the squat little Oriental cupolas and the predilection for the highlights of mosaic that characterized Venice.

The Venetians waited on him, flattered him, welcomed him diplomatically and festively. He consented to draw plans for a bridge over the Canal Grande, but in the meantime he moved to another house so as to find more peace. His retreat was invaded by Aretino, who now posed as the virtual leader of Venetian society, second only to the Doge, and explained to him what artistic sensations were to be found here, under his eyes; he talked of Titian, but did not mention Sansovino, Michelangelo's enemy. The latter listened, aware of the curious dissonance between himself and this city, which was so contrary to his taste: he had no desire to pursue the argument and merely said that he was travelling to France, that he had greatly admired Titian's works in Ferrara, and that they must certainly meet again . . . but he said it in so vague and detached a manner that the meeting remained without a sequel.

Tebaldi came to bring him messages from the court of Ferrara and arrange for his visit there in mid-October. There Galeotto Giugni, the spokesman of Florence at the court of the Estes, succeeded in persuading the illustrious fugitive to return to his natal city, assuring him that he had nothing to fear once he had gone back to Florence. So it came about that after lengthy negotiations and the receipt of letters of recommendation and letters patent from Duke Alfonso guaranteeing a free conduct through his territory, Michelangelo returned to Florence early in November.

Everybody discussed the disappointment this embittered fugitive had left behind him. Sublime artist though Michelangelo undoubtedly was, he was too intractable for an angel, and too unsociable for a man: why must he complicate his own life like that? said Aretino, lying back with his arm round Zaffeta, as though he were reclining on all the gold of Venice. Michelangelo, he continued, was too interested in men and not enough in women, and so he found himself reduced to making love with his verses, an out-moded habit, a bad habit. One should make love openly, at every time of the day or night, in every season—in the house, in the gondola, behind the stove or on the terrace—and with women as beautiful as the banners of the most beautiful city in the world. . . .

'To table now! To table!' he cried, clapping his hands impatiently. At those banquets, with the bells of his gay talk and the bombardon of his great laugh sounding through his beard, Aretino presided majestically in the flickering light of the candles that were set among the fruits, surmounted by his immense shadow on the wall, like a shaking dome of gaiety.

They had come together on the eve of Titian's departure for Bologna; Cardinal Ippolito de' Medici and Federigo Gonzaga had promised to recommend Titian to Charles V, who was now going to be crowned with the Imperial crown at Bologna. Towards the end of the banquet, Zaffeta and the other girls, leaning on the table, begged the men to take pity on their ignorance and explain the politics which caused this king to be crowned with such pomp on foreign soil by the Pope in person.

'Wait a moment,' Aretino replied, in the tone of a conjuror at a fair; taking Zaffeta on his knee, he lifted a bunch of grapes from the table and placed it on one of a pair of silver dishes. 'Now watch carefully, my sweet,' he said, taking an orange which he laid on the companion dish, murmuring 'Ugh! it's like a cannon ball!' and finally he placed a nut between the fruits. The grapes, he explained, represented the Pope, the orange Charles V and the nut François I. The orange and the nut had been fighting for the right to the Duchy of Milan, which had already been conquered by Louis XII, who was related to the nut, and it happened that the latter was made prisoner and taken to Spain for a year—only regaining his freedom by signing treaties which he had no intention of fulfilling. When they had begun to make war on each other again, the orange was surprised to find that he would have to fight the grapes as well. Infuriated, he came to Rome, where he caused the grapes to be trodden under foot and put in the sack; fortunately for them, who had been pressed to the point of turning into *vin santo*, they found refuge in a fortified barrel—the Castel Sant'Angelo—and so a pact was made. Thus the grapes and the orange came to terms in a fine treaty, the Treaty of Barcelona, in the preceding year, and now with another signed in Bologna and the Coronation of the orange as Emperor.

'But how about the *vin santo*? Has the barrel not been emptied to the dregs by now?' asked Zaffeta.

'No—the grapes were too clever, their juice had not been drunk by anybody, because in the meantime they have turned into raisins,' said Aretino, lifting up the silver dish and showing the applauding, laughing listeners the sugar-sweet, withered grapes. 'Smell them— what a heavenly fragrance!' he added, handing them to Zaffeta. 'But mind you, no heresies—these are the Pope!'

'Give me France,' cried Sandella, stretching out her hand to take the nut.

'I want Spain,' said another.

'Ah, no, Marietta,' Aretino interrupted, with feigned severity. 'I am of the opinion that Charles V must be given to Master Titian . . .,' and with a cunning flash of his eyes, sparkling with devilish glee, he offered the orange symbolizing the King of Spain to the artist. 'Take it, with every good wish.'

'And your own hands remain empty,' said Titian, and the others expressed their regret that Master Pietro must remain unsatisfied. But Aretino laughed. 'Have I not got the sun and the moon right here?' he cried, slipping his hands into the opening of Zaffeta's low-cut gown, while she fell backwards, shrieking with laughter, and the others gathered round them.

This was the signal for Titian to retire. The girls, already in a state of partial disarray, accompanied him to the door, and he took leave of them with a gracious wave of his hand.

*   *   *

He left for Bologna in mid-February, 1530.

Expectation there had reached a climax. Every day there were new important arrivals from every part of Italy: the cold was bitter, and they all hastened to warm themselves in front of the fire. Naturally the conversation at these interminable gatherings turned round the Coronation ceremonies. The cortège was to enter San Petronio on the 24th February, which was the birthday of Charles V, and it had been arranged that the regal insignia should be carried by Bonifazio, Duke of Monferrato, by Duke Philip of Bavaria, by the Duke of Urbino and by Charles III of Savoy. But on the 17th, when all the others were already in Bologna, the Duke and Duchess of Savoy had not yet arrived and there was no news of them.

The gentlemen sitting warming themselves by the fires gossiped their heads off, laughing as they pictured the Savoys furbishing up their worn-out ceremonial robes. It was well-known how straitened their circumstances were, and that the Duchess had been forced long ago to pawn her jewels in Genoa and Nuremberg: the malicious fops were delighted at the idea of humiliating the young wife of that poor dwarf, Duke Charles, with their own display. In the meanwhile, they opened and shut trunks and coffers, trying on their fine clothes and beginning to test the power of their elegance, their jealousy and the possibilities of intrigue in the course of the receptions with which they allayed their impatience for the great day.

Not a word came from the ducal pair. The stories of their miserable plight assumed grotesque proportions: at the Palazzo Manzoli, where

Isabella d'Este and her court had taken up their quarters, they were already laying bets that the Savoys would not come at all.

Commissioned by Federigo Gonzaga, Titian had begun to paint the portrait of Cornelia, a lady of the Popoli family with whom Covos, the Councillor of Charles V, had fallen in love. Other patricians sought Titian out and would have been inclined to commission their portraits, but the artist had no leisure; he was already working at one of the Emperor, who had promised to sit for him on the 21st, and he was making every effort to finish it so that it could be shown on the day of the Coronation. The flood of curiosity evoked by this portrait had been cleverly kept within bounds, and the only men who were allowed to come near Titian were the Cardinal Ippolito de'Medici and, for quite special reasons, a certain sculptor known as Alfonso Ferrarese or Alfonso Lombardi. This man, who was not devoid of talent, but entirely lacking in social discretion, would come again and again and after having repeated all the gossip and poured out information, advice and opinions and bowed his way out of the door, he would re-enter with exquisite courtesy by the window. He was busy from morning to night, continually trotting from one house to the other, dressed with such exaggerated care that the ladies did not take him seriously, while in their midst he out-did himself with ever-renewed attentions, fiery compliments and *jeux d'esprit*. He arrived at Titian's lodgings out of breath to report the last items of gossip, to present him with one of the more costly colours or with one of Bologna's most delicious sweetmeats. At last he removed himself in order to go and work: he was busy directing the decoration of the portal of San Petronio, for the coronation ceremonies.

Titian had condescended to show him his sketched-in equestrian portrait of Charles V, knowing that he could find no better publicity agent than this vain fop. Alfonso stood still for a moment in admiration, and then began to combine all sorts of occupations in which the Master's participation was essential: 'Ah! what a lot of work they give us, these celebrations for the Emperor!'

'Idiot!' Titian said under his breath, from the high stool where he perched without turning round: then he stared as the intrepid Alfonso, assuming a different tone of voice, hazarded a request introduced, intermingled and followed by the most humble and pathetic appeals to his magnanimity: would the Master, who was being privileged on the morrow to paint the Emperor in person, generously consent to let him, Alfonso, accompany him in the role of his assistant? He had worked and worked at the arrangements at San Petronio, and he would never have the satisfaction to kiss the hands of His Majesty—so let him at least see him from nearby, even though he must remain anonymous and unknown to him. He would hand Titian his paints and his brushes in a manner befitting the most attentive of pupils, and then he would stand in the background and remain dumb as a fish. He would never have stopped talking if Titian, in sheer self-defence, had not agreed to fulfil his wish—at least, he told himself, he would thus get rid of him until the next day. He made him promise to be punctual, not to talk, and to wear a suit that was not too showy, as befitted a student, without decorations on the sleeves or the collar.

Alfonso kissed his hand as though he had been the Emperor himself. His voice seemed to swell and multiply as he called down the blessings of Heaven on his benefactor; in the end one might have taken him for a whole chorus about to intone the high note of the *Magnificat*. On that high note he left, chirruping ecstatically, bowing, waving, signing, bowing again. . . .

*   *   *

On the next day they met punctually at the King's residence, where the easel and the canvas, the paints and brushes had been brought beforehand.

They waited motionless, in tense silence. Titian, standing, moved the easel by a millimetre. Then suddenly, almost surprisingly, the King came in, followed by Francesco de los Covos, his secretary and adviser, Alfonso d'Avalos, his general, and other gentlemen. He immediately sat down on a chair that had been placed for him, with his face to the light, and he addressed some cordial words of greeting to the painter who was still bowing deeply. Then they looked at each other.

The King was dressed with great care. He took off his flat plumed cap and remained with his arms resting on his knees. He was wearing a short cape lined with brown fur which increased his girth. A gentleman approached attentively to take the cap from his hand; he then drew off his gloves as well and asked the painter where he wished him to look.

As His Majesty was bare-headed, the members of his suite who were standing in the background also doffed their caps which were covered with black and crimson velvet. In order that the artist, who had now begun to work, might be able to concentrate undisturbed, the King signed to Covos and d'Avalos to return to their occupations. Then he turned his face and assumed the required position.

The characteristic features of this face were sharp eyes, a sharp nose, a well-groomed, perfumed beard: traits of kindliness could be seen descending from the temples along the edge of the beard and lurking round the chin, so that the mouth was always slightly open. Possibly the King of Spain had difficulty in breathing, but this slight peculiarity gave his countenance an expression of greater humanity. For a second he turned his profile to the artist, closing his lips to swallow the saliva, and his face assumed a look of dry and cutting authority.

Titian worked with impetuous ardour. From time to time the King appeared to be watching something elsewhere, always on the same spot, then his serene gaze returned to the spot that had been arranged for the pose. He asked about the dimensions of the equestrian portrait that Titian was already painting and expressed the wish that he should continue it here, at his residence, as he was very interested to see it.

An hour had passed. The King rose to his feet and turning in the direction to which his eyes had strayed several times while he was sitting, he held out his hand asking to be allowed to look. Titian himself turned round curiously: Alfonso, highly embarrassed, was manoeuvring with a small round box which he was apparently attempting to conceal in the lining of his sleeve. He approached the King and opened the little box, stammering and embarrassed: going down on his knees, he displayed a medallion of the royal profile which he had modelled in clay.

'Do you think you could repeat this in marble?' asked the Emperor. 'Most certainly,' stammered Alfonso, sweating with excitement. He was commanded to bring it to Genoa.

Titian was stupefied and remained standing with his palette on his thumb, taking in the scene. Alfonso had the infinite audacity to kiss the Emperor's hand, then, closing the little box hastily, he turned to Titian to take the palette from him, gathered up the brushes and paint-pots, and slipped away behind the door as silently as a cat.

The King moved towards the easel to look at his image, while the painter, almost blue in the face with repressed fury, wiped his hands on a napkin. The king asked his attendants to bring him a chair so that he might sit in front of the painting and also sent for a drink of light wine. He gave orders that Covos should be called. Half closing his eyes, he considered the replica of his features—but Titian was barely aware of anything; all he wanted was to lay hands on that clown of a sculptor, who was now hiding behind the door.

The wine was brought in. While the King took little sips of it, it seemed that he was decanting in his mind the sublime simplification of his features which the artist's genius had achieved. He gave orders that they should offer the painter some wine, and told the latter that he might continue to work in that hall as long as he liked. Covos, d'Avalos and the other gentlemen were once again around him.

At last they retired. Alfonso Ferrarese now saw himself forced to come out of his hiding-place. As the servants were taking away the jugs and glasses, Titian was not able to give full vent to his feelings. He merely told the sculptor that he never wanted to see his face again and expressed the wish that the devil might take him on his journey to Genoa. . . .

IX

ON the evening of the 23rd February, the eve of the Coronation, the Duke and Duchess of Savoy, whose coming was no longer expected, arrived at last.

Everybody crowded to the half-open windows to catch a glimpse of the amazing cortège—hardly able to believe the evidence of their own eyes. Valets, grooms, secretaries, servants, maids of honour—there was simply no end to them. It was immediately trumpeted to the four winds that the Duchess was a paragon of beauty and elegance. All the ladies, who had been pondering for days on every tittle of their adornments, were dumbfounded, disheartened and nervous at the idea of having to begin all over again. They could not get over their amazement that the Savoys should arrive with such mountains of luggage and so great a following. Was the Duchess, who was the daughter of the King of Portugal, trying to impress her cousin the Emperor? She must now be trying to work miracles so that it should not become apparent that she had made such a bad marriage! A complete spy system was organized, the better to investigate the situation, which was the greatest sensation of the sojourn in Bologna. Thus it became known that on the very evening of her arrival, the Duchess, notwithstanding the fatigues of the journey, had given a reception in her apartments. She had appeared, dressed most magnificently in a wide gown of black satin split to reveal an under-skirt of crimson velvet embroidered with gold and silver thread. A golden veil covered her red-gold hair, and a small toque of black velvet, surrounded by a chaplet of large pearls, was perched on the top of her head. She sat there, calm and serene, in the triumphant flush of her twenty-two years, and her maids of honour, their tresses tied with vari-coloured ribbons, were lining up ready to dance—treading a measure so slow and grave that it took them half-an-hour to pass from one end of the hall to the other.

The Duchess had asked to be informed about the banquets and

reunions that had already taken place and those that were still to come, as well as on all other current matters. She was immediately regaled with malicious gossip; how nothing could beat the comings and goings at the Palazzo Manzoli, because the ladies of Isabella d'Este were so very generous with their favours—and at night under the portals many a Spanish and Italian gallant had been known to fight a duel.

Beatrice's twenty-two years had upset the erroneous calculations that all the rival patrician ladies had formulated while they were expecting her arrival, and now, taken thus unawares, they concentrated their malevolence on the beauty's unfortunate spouse. The next morning they laughed scoffingly as they pointed him out to each other in the royal procession: his presence was anything but impressive. One could see the Duke of Monferrato, wearing a coat of crimson velvet lined with ermine and with a little crown on his head; the Duke of Bavaria, who supplemented his lack of a crown with a cap of satin and ermine, which looked slightly frivolous; the Duke of Urbino wearing a great crimson mantle—then came little Carlo III, who was the contrary of his radiant young wife and appeared to be weighed down by the burden of his fifty years. To make matters worse, he was wearing a crown far more splendid than the one with which the Pope crowned the Emperor, while clouds of incense rose up, driving smarting tears into the eyes of the ladies.

On the square the soldiers of the King fired a salute, while the Pope, surrounded by his fifteen cardinals, twenty-two bishops and a great swarm of prelates, gave the final blessing.

That evening there was a great banquet, and on the following day the Pope gave an audience at which the Emperor assisted, wearing military accoutrements. He returned to his residence during the early hours of the afternoon and immediately sat down to table, as he had not broken his fast since the preceding evening. The people outside cheered and acclaimed him without ceasing and he had to appear on the balcony. So that he might be allowed to eat in peace, he gave orders to his gentlemen to throw copper, silver and gold coins to the crowd below. Thus it happened that for two hours there rained down on to the delirious crowd five hundred gold ducats, a thousand half-ducats, four thousand coins of half a scudo and a shower of copper coins. When darkness fell, the windows were closed, while the people on the square struggled for the ringing manna and snatched it out of each other's hands.

As all the ladies had feared, the Duchess made a great impression on the Emperor. Her husband was up to his eyes in negotiations with the Venetian legates, who suddenly departed for their city with mysterious despatch. People whispered indiscretions to each other about the claims Carlo III was alleged to have on Cyprus; this was the main topic of conversation on the evening when a ball was held with great ceremony, in the course of which Titian's painting was shown.

Ever since the preceding evening there had been heated debates, resentments and scenes because only twenty of the most high-born and lovely noblewomen had been invited. The Duchess of Savoy, who was of course among them, was charming to Titian, while the Emperor smiled contentedly as he looked at his painted effigy, mounted on his charger in an heroic pose. The lovely Beatrice seemed to vibrate like a flame, her whole soul shining out of her sparkling eyes, while sparks of blue fire flashed from the sapphires on her white hands as she moved them gently. The amaranth gown she wore made her appear paler, so that blue reflections played round her temples. There was an ardent, slightly exalted fervour in her gaze.

The Emperor was ceremoniously gallant to her and wittily affable to the artist. He asked the latter for his competent assistance in finding a definition for the lady's loveliness. She turned her head, mocking him like a knowing little girl, and a cluster of gems that fastened the knot of her hair gave a tinkling sound as it brushed against her necklace.

They were still looking at the painting, the free texture of the brush strokes, the noble horse with the star on its forehead, its nostrils breathing strength and fire. All the guests crowded round. Why not show this fine effigy of Imperial Caesar to the people, in the middle of the city, Beatrice asked. The Sovereign, without batting an eyelid, instructed Covos to have the picture displayed in an appropriate and well-protected place for a couple of days.

Cardinal de' Medici suggested that it should be put away at night so that it might not be stolen, and d'Avalos added that it must also be well guarded in daytime.

Eventually, the picture, guarded as closely as a standard, was exposed under a portico in the centre of the city. In the atmosphere of kermesse that prevailed during those days, while musicians were still playing in the streets and the citizens walked around in their Sunday best, the effigy of the Emperor, its dimensions lessened by the open space around it, united great crowds of curious spectators, who gazed at it open-mouthed.

The Emperor himself came on horseback, accompanied by a great following, to look again at his image. The Duchess Beatrice was riding in the cortège. She looked grave and held herself very straight. The people around cried 'Karolus Imperator!'—the words that were painted on the standards between the festoons.

But in the meantime the other 'Karolus, dux Sabaudiae', Beatrice's husband, had been humiliated by the Senate of Venice. His claim to Cyprus based on the fact that Ludovico, the successor of Amadeo VIII of Savoy, had married his second son to Carlotta, the heiress to the realm of Cyprus, had been refuted by the Senate as an outrageous pretension.

Beatrice must have felt that this was to be her last royal cavalcade. Charles V knew what was disturbing her, but he was at a loss for the right words with which to comfort her. An embarrassed silence reigned between them, in the midst of the frenetic applause of the crowd.

★　　★　　★

Then the beautiful clothes were folded once more, the crowns put away, the jewels wrapped up. The great retinue of the Duke and Duchess of Savoy returned to Piedmont, and the other courts as well took the road home.

The portrait Titian had painted was also placed in a packing-case and sent on the road to Genoa.

PART III

I

CECILIA was again big with child when Titian returned to Venice in March, 1530; she was already in the fifth month of her pregnancy.

She now gave him to understand in her submissive way that, though he himself might have found the right method of dealing with friends like Aretino or Messer Jacopo—to see and not to know, to know and not to see, their behaviour—their example was not beneficial for their son Pomponio. Together with Sansovino's son, Francesco, he had taken to all sorts of roguery incompatible with the practices of his religious career—getting into debt, and leading a generally dissolute life. There was the dignity of Titian's person, as the leading Master of Venice, to consider, as well as ecclesiastical discipline. It would not do for the prestige of a great name to be contaminated by the intransigence of the authorities, through the thoughtlessness of a good-for-nothing son. She laid especial stress on these arguments, knowing that Titian, since he had regularized their matrimonial situation, had become very severe about the morals of his family.

'So that is what Monsignorino is up to! Monsignorino has turned into a thorough ne'er-do-well, if I understand rightly!' Titian exclaimed, using Aretino's nickname for the graceless Pomponio.

Furiously he kicked a footstool across the studio and began to inveigh against the lewd women, that whole obscene harem surrounding Aretino: his own relations with his friends were already strained because of them. . . . He ended by saying that Pomponio must never be seen again with Francesco di Sansovino—and that was the end of it! It was not the end of it, however, for he began to shout again, working himself into a rage against Pordenone, who had spoken ill of him, and Lotto, who had returned to Venice and was working there on the quiet.

His brother Francesco calmed him down, reminding him that Pordenone was nothing but a boor; though it was true that he was once more infesting Venice with his work at San Rocco and at San Giovanni a Rialto, he had not received the high honour of being commissioned to paint the altar-piece for San Pietro Martire, which had been awarded to Titian. Lotto was as harmless as a lamb; he had immediately begun to imitate Titian in his painting for the altar of San Nicola al Carmine, so it would only add to his glory to have him as a competitor. As to 'Monsignorino', everything would come right in time.

To see and not to know, to know and not to see—Titian repeated to himself, and he made a resolution to be like those mirrors in their sculptured tabernacles which Messer Pietro, that devil, had collected, for it happened that the 'Aretine' prevented them from reflecting the embraces they accorded to their master by closing the decorated panels inscribed with the most exalted nomenclature in perfect Latin.

Yet even Titian had to admit that these females were beautiful, when he saw them standing apart while he and his friends talked to Bembo, Nicolò Franco, Sperone Speroni and other men of letters. The girls were in deep confabulation, discussing the most up-to-date ways of bleaching their hair by using a certain quantity of liquorice wood or so-and-so much safranin, or so-and-so many yolks of eggs, or the eyes from which the leaves sprout in Spring on the poplars. Or they went away and fetched Levantine spices which they boiled with all sorts of aromas, inhaling the odours and promising themselves a long session of their ritual anointings and rubbings for the next day. Their complexions rivalled the marvellous flesh tints which Titian alone could create.

'*Maistro Tucian*, do us the honour of painting these charms,' they cried, unloosening the copper-coloured torrent of their tresses that flowed down to their girdles, which were decorated with golden filigree buckles.

Titian caressed them, but his mind was occupied with other things, since for some time the eternal litanies of expectation had begun around Cecilia. 'It's sure to be a girl.' 'No, it's a boy.' 'A girl.' 'A boy.' To cut short these alternatives that exhausted his patience, he returned to Bologna during the first days of July, in order, among other things, to complete a portrait of Cornelia, a pretty daughter of the house of Pepoli, for Federigo Gonzaga. But Cornelia was convalescing after an illness and had left Bologna for a change of air. Titian wrote to Gonzaga that in any case the portrait would soon be finished, and he

made haste with his work so as to return to Venice as soon as possible.
As he placed his brush-strokes, he found himself saying: 'A boy?'
'A girl?' over and over again, like the burden of a song. He had to
keep wiping his brow, it was intensely hot.

He started once again on his journey, after having sent, with many
a curse, five hundred ducats of the thousand he had received from
Charles V to Alfonso Lombardi for that famous medallion he had so
fraudulently created. The heat of the summer was disconcerting: he
suffered from colics and insomnia.

Venice had also sunk into a torpor of heat, the water seemed to boil
in the canals. Cecilia was gasping. She embraced him, clinging to him
as though their separation had lasted an eternity of moons—moons
that for centuries had failed to hold their course in time.

'*Tucian mio*,' she murmured as she took his hand and laid
it on the palpitating burden of which she could hardly wait to be
delivered.

Poor soul, she was delivered of two burdens—that of a living girl
child and that of her own sweet white body. She died during the first
days of August, screaming in agony and exhausted by the heat.

Titian, likewise dripping with sweat and tears, supported her,
holding her by the wrists, while she drove her nails deep into his hands
during the spasms of her labour. Then suddenly he found himself
holding those quivering wrists that now contracted, the pale fingers
lay inert and all her life's blood flowed into the tiny creature of which
she had been delivered.

He turned to stone during the instant when she became motionless.
He was still clasping her wrists when, hearing the first wail of the newborn infant, he became aware that Cecilia was gone and he began to
scream hysterically, calling for Francesco, screaming, screaming. Now
they were all shouting, coming and going all through the house. He
suddenly felt an icy shudder of emotion go through him, contracting
the skin of his brow, his shoulders, his arms. He dropped Cecilia's
hands. The others came to drag him away, to take him to another room,
to make him lie down and to hold a glass to his lips. In the meantime,
the women were bathing the baby. It must be called Lavinia like that
other one, as though to reassure Cecilia that he had kept faith with
their past life together. But from now on Cicilia had no more part in
his life. . . . Now he was alone as she had been so many times during
her life, all alone by his side.

J

He begged Francesco to travel immediately to Pieve and bring their sister Orsa back with him.

*   *   *

Orsa came, accompanied by a fine young woman from Cadore, who was to act as wet-nurse. Other people came from Pieve to bring the two women their luggage.

The coming of two new inmates to the house might have been upsetting and confusing, mingling with the laments for Cecilia and her obsequies and the sad arrival in the world of little Lavinia, most desperately distressing and made more unbearable by the terrible heat, but Orsa's tact, efficiency and sensitive perception was such that Titian begged her not to forsake him. He promised to take a larger house, though it would be difficult. Orsa was still a spinster and though she might wish to take a husband—and surely they might find one— he begged her to keep house for him and to bring up Lavinia: he did not lack the means. Venice was a lovely city. God would bless her for what she was doing.

Brother and sister embraced and concealed their despair behind a smile. How could he talk like that? Orsa asked. Did they not already owe so much to him, the benefactor of all the Vecelli?—he must not have any scruples. She was prepared to stay. And as to her spinsterhood—she was a spinster, and she would die a spinster. And she was not only a spinster, she added spiritedly, she was a bachelor. That was his fault and Francesco's, too, ever since the days when they were all children and they had acquired the horrid habit of tying her to the anvils to play at being saints. Shaking her head at herself, she smiled and returned to the task of putting things back in their places, rearranging them, putting them in order, and seeing that her brothers and nephews behaved themselves.

Titian was comforted by her intrepid good humour and smiled to himself like someone recovering from a long illness. With difficulty he began to work again, taking up once more the task at the Sala del Gran Consiglio, all the commissioned pictures which ought to have been finished, the supervision of his pupils, whose number was ever increasing, and a large portrait of Doge Gritti at the feet of the Virgin. Francesco busied himself with the search for a new dwelling place.

Weeks went by. After a time Titian allowed his friends to frequent him once more. Lorenzo Lotto came to see him, but his timid placidity, his long silences benumbed their faint friendship, while the old cat curled up to sleep close to the brazier between them. Titian then sank himself entirely into a new work: for Federigo Gonzaga he painted a picture which expressed his own melancholy and his eager desire for splendour—a monumental bust of the Magdalene, with her long, wavy hair like a mantle covering the pride of her flesh, as powerful as the forces contained in the elements of nature. The flesh and hair seemed to palpitate in a dramatic light which revealed them against the dark background. He felt that this painting would never be a favourite of his, yet it was the work on which, at that time, he revealed the maximum of his hard-won technical mastery. He never wearied of elaborating and refining every effect.

'The very concentration of Beauty!' Aretino boomed, when he came to see the painting. 'The marvel of marvels!' Titian, feeling his work coming to life anew under the impact of this enthusiasm, smiled an embarrassed smile, but a smile which was beneficial, for it suddenly lifted him out of the mental convalescence which he owed to the slow completion of a work in which he had unconsciously and yet volitionally yielded up the inmost secret of his being.

He would return with Sansovino, and with all Venice at his heels, Messer Pietro continued exuberantly. In the end, as he was about to leave, he insisted that Titian must find the time to immortalize him as well, seeing what a good friend he was, and after all what a fine subject.

A year had gone by since Cecilia's death, summer was approaching its end. After long hesitation, investigations and negotiations, Titian signed a lease with Leonardo Molin for a fine house at Birri Grande in the district of San Canciano. The house had been built four years earlier for the patrician Alvise Pollani, who had left it to his daughter Bianca, the wife of Molin.

To clear a house and move to another is one of the most trying sentimental ordeals of a lifetime. To collect things and garments, rearrange them according to number and quality, destroy what is superfluous and decide what is essential to keep, equals a supreme resolution to pass judgement on the intrinsic merits of one's own world, a world built up by hours of patience, months of passions, years of effort. At a certain point, the fact of merely removing a piece of furniture from its usual place and expropriating oneself of the habits to which one has been acclimatized, transporting one's furniture to new places and oneself to new surroundings in an atmosphere which is still alien, destroys the pathetic chronicle of a whole lifetime, in the cold expectation of a life that lies in the future.

When the last load of belongings had been piled up in a long-boat and a gondola, Titian suddenly realized how many years he had spent in his old house, which now looked pitifully indifferent with its bare walls and exiled spiders: he stopped for a long time in what had been his studio, feeling that his departure was perhaps a betrayal, a flight, a desertion.

There were traces of paint and varnish on the pavement. He gazed at them, trying to remember on what occasion he had happened to stain this floor-tile with rose colour, and that other with ultramarine. Some rags, a discarded kitchen knife and a few broken receptacles of dirty glass lay in a corner. Many bygone years had imprinted each useless object, each piece of wreckage. He moved slowly towards the corner full of rubbish, as though he hoped to find something there which he might save, a secret, unexpected sign, a pin, a worthless thing which might be the treasure of his new dwelling. There seemed to be nothing except the litter left by the removal, piles of dust and clots of dried-up paint—but then, in the middle of all this, he found a sheet of paper screwed up into a ball. He picked it up, recognizing it.

He smoothed out the creases in the paper he himself had crumpled up same days ago when, together with other things connected with his work, ancient unfinished studies and juvenile composition-sketches, he had ruthlessly decided to destroy this little drawing too, the drawing he had made as a boy after a design he had found in Gentile Bellini's sketch-books: a drawing of a lion.

Venice was full of lions, but he felt that he could have found no better symbol for the vigour of his present years, not even in the Ducal Palace among the most sanctified banners in the Doge's archive of emblems. Tenderly he smoothed out the creases in the paper, folded it carefully and slipped it into his pocket as though it had been the most precious contract of his entire career.

Yes, he told himself, he would yet paint great grim lions—and he felt his eyes growing moist. Strong lions, frantic with their own barely restrained strength! Yet he could barely restrain his tears as he roamed from room to room, surrounded by solitude. Great crouching lions, roaring elements of fire, part of the incredible entirety of Nature. He sneezed, panting, unable to keep back his idiotic tears. Then he went out, closed the door, descended the stairs and slammed the portals behind him.

The two boats with their last load had already gone and Francesco was supervising their journey with the porters. Titian stepped into the gondola which was waiting for him and touched the folded sheet in his pocket.

'To *Biri magno*', he said curtly to the gondolier. The house at Birri Grande was waiting for him, breathing all the changing magic of light with the air from the sea.

II

TITIAN established the ambitious status of his new life with the new house. Now that he was alone—and it easily happens that a man living in the most dignified emotional solitude should seek every pretext to assume a tone of authority and concentrate on material possessions—he appeared to perfect the pattern of his independent behaviour. He had known examples of obstinate hegemony in Alfonso di Ferrara, lordliness in Gonzaga, of the volatile though dispersive ability to take what one wants in Aretino.

Aretino, as a good business man, who, when he acquired objects of virtue for a prince, always received a commission in money or in shirts embroidered with gold and caps of silver thread, opposed Titian's innate parsimony and encouraged him to be rather lavish in furnishing his new home. He assured him that this was good publicity, and would add to his prestige and authority: it was necessary for him to live in a place where he might even receive the visit of a king.

Therefore the furniture was partly renewed and some of the former furnishings were sent to the house at Conegliano, to which the artist occasionally returned to relax by lending a hand in the exterior and interior decorations with which he was embellishing it.

In this manner, between his work and the renewed pleasure be took in collecting precious things, Titian, like a greedy, obstinate and solitary carp, began once more to mingle a sovereign trade and heavenly inspiration while he added up expenses—and as always, effected advantageous sales of his paintings.

He sent off a painting of Charles V to Duke Alfonso, and worked at finishing a new portrait of the Duke himself. For his business and the rare barters for exceptional favours he now found an excellent agent in Messer Pietro, who would describe his work in the most fascinating manner, with ever new variants, an ever new codicil of *gloria in excelsis*.

In order to please him, Titian began to paint his portrait. Messer

Pietro came to pose at the house in Birri Grande, accompanied by his secretary, faithful friend and disciple, Nicolò Franco di Benevento, or by the beautiful Tullia d'Aragona, the courtesan and poetess who was staying in Venice for a time. Sometimes he would come with Caterina Sandella, who would remain all through the pose quietly fanning her bare shoulders with a kerchief of pure silk, or he would bring Zufolina Pistoiese, who trussed up her skirts over her clinging hose, so that she looked like a girl page or an effeminate beau attired in feminine garments. Sitting sideways on a chair, her eyes half closed—for she was slightly short-sighted—she peeled pumpkin-seeds for Monicchio, the monkey whose clever tricks Aretino was never tired of describing. And in every story he told of every situation in which he found himself, he recreated the atmosphere of a bustling bordello in which he lived at his house on the Rialto, with all the 'Aretine', busy in the midst of the joyous disorder, intent on re-discovering a most important royal edict or in remembering the exact aroma of the roast of the preceding evening.

Zufolina roamed around the studio: here a sublime order reigned; the windows could be covered with paper like those of a cloister, the brushes were laid out in a row, the little bottles numbered, the jars superscribed like those of an apothecary. But when the sitting was over, the most cloistered atmosphere could not restrain Aretino: he did his best to convince Titian that he must paint feminine nudes—Venus asleep, nymphs and satyrs, Danae under the shower of gold—the entire Olympus in the nude. . . .

'Take off your clothes, Zufolina,' he said. 'Maestro Titian does not believe that you are entirely a woman.'

She turned round, white in her prune-coloured dress, opening her short-sighted eyes wide as she began to undress. She slipped out of her bodice and her skirt and peeled off the tight hose, while the monkey helped her.

Thus a mere visit to the studio of the painter transformed it into the most 'Aretinesque' scene imaginable: the monkey, the scattered divided seeds, Messer Pietro present in the flesh and on the canvas like a commanding hero, the naked woman surrounded by her discarded masculine and feminine clothes.

'Is she not beautiful?' asked Aretino.

Slender as this nude was, it appeared absolutely harmonious, owing to the perfection of its proportions which Messer Pietro pointed out, underlining their exquisiteness, as he raised the girl's chin with the gesture of a slave-merchant.

They would speak of it again, Titian was carried away to say, confronted with all this disorder, all this unnatural naturalness. He offered his guests wine, so as to participate in the game with something that tuned in with it. But, he began to object, there was so much work to do, and a journey as well which would take him to the Emperor at Bologna, who had only just returned from Hungary. Charles V was actually still in Milan, where the treaties with the Pope, with Venice and other States were still in the making. Titian's new house could not yet be honoured by the visit of a king; he had to visit the King elsewhere.

*   *   *

When the time came, he started off on his journey accompanied by Girolamo, his pupil. This was during the first days of January, 1533; it was cold, and again they sat drinking mulled wine in the evenings by great braziers and open fires that crackled like petards. But the city was different, everything looked grey: it was no longer as it had been during the days of the Coronation. There was nothing in the streets of the town to remind one of the gay floating banners of those days, but, on the contrary, a bustling activity, an atmosphere of curious combinations and controls. In front of the Residence, there was a coming and going of officialdom with ceremonies, tricks, inexorable barriers and corruption.

Since the last time, Señor de los Covos had acquired a louder voice and a heavier jaw—a sign that his affairs were going well. Cardinal Ippolito del Medici had brought back an extraordinary costume from Hungary, in which he wished to be painted by Titian, and d'Avalos had ordered a chiselled suit of armour so fine that it also had to be immortalized by the brushes of the celebrated Master. But first of all, Titian had to arrange for a new portrait of the Emperor. He went to see los Covos to ask him to procure an audience for him.

The Spaniard immediately proposed that Titian should paint a portrait, not of himself, but of the graces and beauties of Cornelia, the lovely daughter of the house of Pepoli. He let it be clearly understood that he was deeply interested in these charms. Titian consented to begin the painting at once, for he felt sure that the lady would in no way object to seeing herself immortalized once again by the same artist who had already portrayed her loveliness. But first of all, of course, he insisted on having an audience with the Emperor.

He should have it the next day, without fail, Covos assured him. And immediately he shouted:

'Don Brujo!'

A kind of grunt was heard from behind a damask curtain.

De los Covos informed Titian that his first portrait of the Emperor had achieved an unparalleled success: several copies had been made of it in Spain. Then he began to shout for Brujo again.

Cornelia's portrait must be as good, he insisted: then, with the blood mounting to his head, he hit the table with his fist and roared: 'Brujo!'

At last the secretary appeared between the folds of the damask curtain—it was not quite clear whether he was pulling them apart or trying to pull on his own trousers. However, as though to prove that the practice of good living was not being neglected in this ministry, he was preceded by the smell of good wine.

After Covos had consulted the list of the audiences, it was arranged that the painter should be received the next day, in the middle of the forenoon.

Titian took his leave. In the corridor he came up against the agitated and impatient envoys of the Duke of Ferrara. They had been besieging the Residence for days, waiting in the ante-chambers, sending memorials right and left; like ship-wrecked mariners who at last discover a firm rock among the waves, they were overjoyed at the mere sight of him.

Jacopo Alvarotti and Matteo Casella, clutching the minutes of their memorials, lists, notes and codicils, rushed towards the Master, fawning on him and invoking the sacred name of Este, doing their utmost to obtain advice, explanations and support from him. Was he going to portray de los Covos, they asked, or perhaps paint another picture of the Emperor? Would he be able, with a few words, to recommend the affairs of the Duke to His Majesty?

Titian walked on slowly with his senatorial gait, and the two excited men accompanied him, keeping an eye on the movements in the ante-chamber even while they were going away from de los Covos's door: they informed him that the Duke desired to obtain the restitution of the city of Modena and of Reggio—a mere trifle.

The first thing they must do was to ingratiate themselves with de los Covos, Titian explained; they knew him already, so there was no need to say more than that Duke Alfonso lacked neither the means nor the initiative to support his petitions with certain attentions.

Now the door of the *Commendator mayor* opened and the two gentlemen, hastily murmuring words of gratitude and excuses, flew off in that direction, while Titian, continuing his senatorial progress, asked to be announced to d'Avalos. With him he sat down to enjoy the comfort of a great open fire into which a stout page was throwing handfuls of aromatic salts which turned the flames green.

III

IN Bologna Titian realized that his painting represented an excellent international currency. It was not Aretino alone who stunned all Venice with his talk, and every foreign country with his letters about it: the mere fact that Titian had become the favourite painter of Charles V stabilized the gold standard of his art.

The first question the Emperor asked was whether he had brought any paintings with him. Titian had no wish to justify himself with many words, supplications and demonstrations, even though his interlocutor was not only a king, but a king accustomed to the declamations of Spanish ceremonial. A new portrait was discussed, about which both parties were in complete agreement—this time the clothes were to be less ceremonious, in a light colour—and the time for the sitting was arranged.

Covos took the painter aside: he told him that as he had not brought any paintings with him as the King had wished, there was a way by which he might produce some, and with the utmost dispatch. Those two busy individuals, Alvarotti and Casella, the legates of the Duke of Ferrara, had described to him at length all the art treasures in the possession of their master: there was a large choice that could be offered in exchange for the favours they were asking, and he, Titian, would do well to give him some impartial advice as to the choice. These two gentlemen had mentioned, among the works of Titian, a fine portrait of His Imperial Majesty, one of the Duke himself and one of his eldest son Ercole—what did Titian think? The Master, wishing to act correctly towards his patron, proposed that he should advise the Duke himself. Covos referred this to the envoys of Ferrara, not without stressing his own wish for the gift of the two portraits in question. In an incredibly short time, they brought a formal answer to their master, who delegated Titian to effect the choice, but there was no mention on the ducal list of the portrait of Charles V.

'I demand the portrait of the King!' bawled Covos, angrily

139

and leaving his antechambers crowded with pontifical and Venetian legates, he rushed off to Cornelia, to find Titian, who was intent on his work. The painter could not do much about it, but having realized that the resentment voiced by Covos was mainly a pretext to show off before his lady, he put down his brushes and his palette, promising to draw up at once an exact inventory of the pictures to be collected from the Duke.

Poor Duke Alfonso! It would have been possible to relieve him of a fine haul, but Titian had no desire whatever to bring a windfall of too many of his own paintings to the Imperial collection. He informed Covos that many of these pictures were part of the irremovable collection in the celebrated alabaster cabinet, for it seemed to him it would be the lesser of two evils to stress the fact that the Duke also possessed many precious works by other artists.

Covos, with the inventory in his hand, called for the two Legates the next day and dictated to them the list of the paintings he wished to have: among them was Titian's portrait of the Emperor and that of Duke Alfonso. Casella interrupted him to remark that the portrait of the Emperor, painted in a stylized manner, was actually less like the original than any other portrait painted from life, besides being already rather out of date.

'No!' roared Covos, and this 'No' of his could not be ignored—he wanted this picture, and this he insisted on having. Let them send the portrait to Bologna, and without delay. The other paintings, a Madonna, a Judith and a Saint Michael might go to Genoa to the Imperial residence.

The two gentlemen went to find Titian; he sent a message to say that he could not receive them, but he charged Girolamo to reassure them because, except for the portraits of the Emperor and the Duke, on which Covos had now set his heart, he had suggested other works which their master would not really mind parting with.

The two envoys left. In the meantime, the portrait of Cornelia was almost finished, and Titian applied himself with all the more zeal to that of the King and that of the Cardinal de' Medici.

The portrait of His Majesty was already arousing much admiration. Instead of the classical three-quarter-length in which he had painted the portraits of the Cardinal and Cornelia di Pepoli, this vertical painting represented the entire standing figure and reminded one of the firm elegance of an image in bas-relief. But the greatest sensation of the time was the affair of the Duke of Ferrara's pictures—an affair which had roused arrogance and resentment to the point of appearing like a race towards a precipice.

When seven days had gone by, Covos, seeing nothing appear on the horizon, lost patience and rudely demanded the consignment from Ferrara. On the 23rd January, Alvarotti and Casella arrived, bringing the two portraits and a letter from the Duke, confirming that the other works had been sent to Genoa.

Covos smiled. He would be delighted, he declared shamelessly, to make further demands on the Duke in future if he should learn that the latter possessed other objects of interest. Then he dismissed the legates.

The unfortunate gentlemen picked up their papers and their caps and sat down again to wait in the antechamber, exhausted and humiliated. As usual, there was a continual coming and going of postulants, deputies, dealers, commissions of envoys from every part of Italy. The ushers and guards standing before the doors filled their pockets with ever-increasing bribes. The two Ferrarese, whose eyes were starting out of their heads with impatience, hardly dared to breathe: they saw Titian approaching, walking with precise though hurried steps, no longer with the senatorially measured gait he had assumed in former days. They sprang to their feet as he passed them, to remind him that they were still there, and he stopped for a moment to excuse himself for not having received them when they had sought him out, owing to pressing work. He was terribly busy, he could hardly find time for anything, not even for meals. Then he hurried away, resuming his unceremonious gait—and he immediately obtained an audience with the Imperial Councillor.

The latter was always ready to receive him now, since the brilliant success of Cornelia's portrait, and even Brujo did not grunt any more. Titian despised the three of them in his heart and looked upon Brujo as a domesticated swine, Cornelia as an aristocratic opportunist and Covos as an amorous boor, but he had plenty of opportunities to indicate to Covos, with studied negligence, what reward he expected for his artistic work and his personal intervention in the affair with the Duke—the bestowal of an honour which would prove the esteem in which the Emperor held his art and his person.

Even an amorous boor, adoring an aristocratic opportunist and served by a domesticated swine, can possess a certain discernment of true values and genuine respect for superior natures. Covos, though he was impervious to the deeper subtleties of life, knew only too well what great store the Emperor set on this taciturn artist who was so sure of himself—and he did his best.

The Emperor showed himself magnanimous. When Titian took his departure he was given the formal assurance that, in the course of the next few months, he would receive from Spain the charter nominating him Knight of the Golden Spur and Count of the Sacred Palace of the Lateran, as though he were descended from four paternal and four maternal ancestors of most noble lineage. And furthermore, he was awarded an annual pension of three hundred scudos.

*　　*　　*

In his studio at Birri Grande there was another painting of the Magdalene, languid and monumental, waiting for him. He had made the sketch when he sent the first one to Federigo Gonzaga. For a moment it seemed as though he were seeing Cecilia again. In the vaguely suggested forms under their tender covering of flowing hair which was like a warm and wavy sea, she seemed to float in a liquid paradise.

'Cecilia,' he murmured softly.

In the silence he could barely recall the feeling of her own living silence in bygone times. They had already forgotten each other—she in her paradise, immersed in the waters of time, he in his unending struggle to venture, to succeed and to conquer the world. She had now become a mere image, a thing transformed by his genius. The young lives of her children growing up around him absorbed the last traces of remembrance: there was Pomponio, already twenty, eighteen-year old Orazio, who was always holding a paintbrush between his teeth, and little Lavinia, peering in at every open door and searching every room with sparkling eyes and inquisitive fingers. . . .

'Cecilia,' he said again. But now she was no more than an image, a thing transformed by his genius.

IV

'C*AROLUS Quintus divina favente Clementia Romanorum Imperator Augustus, ac Rex Germaniae, Hungariae, Dalmatiae, Croatiae, Insularum Balearium, Sardiniae, Fortunatorum et Indiarum. . . .*' Orazio was reading out aloud, '. . . *spectabili nostro, et Imperi sacri fedeli dilecto Titiano de Vecelliis, sive equite aurato, ac sacri Lateranensis Palatii, aulaeque nostrae et Imperialis consistori comiti gratiam nostram cesaream, et omne bonum. . . .*'

Orazio could not wait to read through the entire charter written out on a fine sheet of parchment with illuminated initials and many pendant seals attached to it. Holding it in his hand, he embraced his father with deep emotion, as they stood in the middle of the studio, surrounded by the cheering apprentices, who collected round him until he had finished reading out the aulic phrases of the document in which the august names of Apelles, Alexander the Great and Octavian were also quoted.

'And what are the emblems?'

'Golden spurs and a chain.'

'Golden spurs?'

'And a chain.'

The boys stood there, sticking their chins into the air as they tried to imagine the great master wearing spurs. Then they went back to grinding their colours, but they continued to chatter about this event which made them feel as insignificant as a swarm of flies.

The latest neophyte who had come to busy himself in this workshop, smeared with white chalk from head to foot, now came up to have a look at the charter: he was like a white fly with two black, burning, aggressive eyes.

'Don't you dare touch the parchment, you mudlark!' hissed the others. 'Do your father's apprentices all cover themselves with dye like you do with chalk?'

'Hi! Tintoretto, snowman, we're in May now, not in winter!'

Though the boy was always ready to kick even the biggest of his comrades when they provoked him, he now controlled his temper faced with the sacred document, but he only had time to read the date before Orazio had rolled it up again. The only remark he made was that it was amazing that messengers could travel fast enough to bring letters from Barcelona to Venice in a few days. The master would have liked to shake him, but he left him to his daubing.

Now he decided to employ the authority he had acquired through his new title for the good of his beloved Pieve. In the meanwhile, his friends came to tell him with delight that Pordenone was now moving heaven and earth to obtain a title for himself. 'He might be made Count of bad painting,' they sniggered. 'Knight of scrawls! Duke of vulgar colours!'

Titian passed over the matter with a disagreeable smile. He was looking through the proofs of *La Cortigiana* with Aretino, at a sideboard raised on a dais, so that he seemed to be raised on to the platform of a throne.

At that time Michelangelo had just left Florence in order to go to Rome, where Pope Clement VII had commissioned him to execute a gigantic work which was to complete the decoration of the Sistine Chapel—a great fresco of the Last Judgment, people said. But hardly had the news got around when it was followed by that of the Pope's death. 'Michelangelo finished him off,' they said maliciously. Titian's meetings with Messer Pietro and Sansovino were regulated by the arrival of news of the outside world, and therefore they came together even more frequently than usual: at the end of the year 1534, they had so many events to discuss that they chattered like a trio of formidable village gossips. On the 25th September, Clement VII had died: on the 13th October, Pope Paul III Farnese had been elected, and on the 31st October, Alfonso, the great Duke of Ferrara, had also departed this life.

It seemed to them as though they were living outside time, in the fortress of their security, invulnerable thanks to their genius, immune thanks to their prosperity.

Yet Titian, the grave Count Palatine, the supreme artist, was peremptorily drawn back into the rhythm of his time. He could not resist his vexation when his friends came to inform him that Pordenone was once again in Venice and had even intruded into the Ducal Palace in the confraternity. Like a couple of gossips,

Messer Pietro and Sansovino returned again and again, to hem him around with their plenipotentiary meetings, where their ingeniously exacerbated tittle-tattle composed of judgments, condemnations and metaphorical death-sentences. Owing to these conventicles, they began to be known as the triumvirate of Venice.

Sansovino's red beard was beginning to turn white, but he still carried himself erect, his gait remained the same and his features lean. Messer Pietro, however, suffered from a slow digestion which at times dimmed the sparkle of his eyes. Titian sat between them, stroking the red velvet carpet covering the chair from which he presided over these meetings. Here were three gentlemen, who, forgetting the broad-mindedness which their professions imposed on them, delighted themselves by flaying their neighbours. At times, they communicated only by broken sentences, like beasts of prey who understand each other by a sniff, a twitching of the shoulders or a side-long glance.

They dropped fragmentary hints, seeming to stress that they were just crumbs of information, merely to conclude the arguments about some tiresome person. They remarked that one of these days, Pordenone, also known as *il Sacchiense*, was marrying his daughter Graziosa to one of his pupils, Pomponio Amalteo. Aretino had often told Titian laughingly that it was not worthy of his genius to be annoyed by this personage, who was a mere dauber compared to him. And still laughing, he turned the conversation to Michelangelo, knowing only too well how Sansovino reacted to this subject.

His reactions were violent, typical of the red-haired natives of Toscana. It once happened during a dinner at Birri Grande that he let himself go on the subject of 'that devil's limb Michelangelo', so that everybody round the table was stricken dumb with embarrassment. Their reaction was the result of seeing certain of Michelangelo's drawings for the Medici tombs, which Vasari had sent to Aretino in Venice, so that he might present them to Cardinal Domenico Grimani, who had asked for a painting by Buonarroti ten years ago and was still waiting for it. Titian had remained silent, and in silence Sansovino was now listening and Aretino looking. It was something entirely new for him to keep silent. Then they separated. For a time they did not see each other, merely sending each other messages like great gentlemen living in the lap of luxury. But at night Messer Pietro and Sansovino, brought together by their irrepressible instincts, would

K

find each other, like shadows lit up with laughter, near the women in that militant brothel which was the harem of Aretino's house. They fondled the girls, who hastened to serve them, and called in handsome boys from the lagoon who fetched and carried for them in daytime, but were like bronzed, unclothed demi-gods at night. Monicchio, the monkey, also played its part, crumpling the velvets and the muslins, retiring to a corner to watch, and coming to introduce itself into the charming confusion. They caressed and kissed it as though it were the most important and pleasing creature there. Finally, they fell asleep, half undressed as they were, heated by wine and lethargic with high living. Sansovino remembered that he had an appointment for the next morning to work at the Scuola della Misericordia, but he did not move. Half asleep, he began to re-evoke ancient memories and started to tell Benedetto Varchi about the theatricals twenty years ago in Florence, when he took part with Andrea del Sarto and Giovanni Rustichi in a performance of *Tantalo all' Inferno*, for which he had prepared such ingenious fires. But Varchi was more interested in the handsome, semi-nude youths than in these sleepy stories. Aretino was already snoring. He half-opened one eye, stretched, gathered the folds of his gown and blew out the candles from which wax was dripping slowly, like thick honey: then, yawning, he prepared to go to sleep.

The handsome youths of the lagoon, silent and slender, were quietly slipping into their clothes: impeccably discreet, they appeared to have seen nothing and heard nothing, not even to have undressed. They crept away on tiptoe, but not before they had emptied the drips of wine that remained at the bottom of the cups.

*   *   *

As always, Titian's nights were very different.

He had not given up the habit of keeping a little lamp burning behind the limpid belly of a jug filled with water, and now he had begun to work once more with greater serenity, after a silent pause in his activity had imposed itself on him. Though at first he had hardly been aware of it, a feeling of slight feverishness had put him on his guard. He had looked around him; there was Bonifacio de' Pitati, Veronese, who seemed to impart a chill to everything he painted; Paris Bordone, who was introducing a silly mannerism into his finest compositions; Andrea Schiavone, il Medola, distraught and as poor as a church mouse, who, having agreed to decorate chests and coffers, was now adopting the manner of Parmigianino—and Tintoretto, bursting with restless talent, who had gone to learn the technique of fresco painting. A brief crisis. . . .

Titian knew what people accused him of: not that he shirked the boredom of teaching others, but that he was afraid of creating a rival for himself. They said that he had been too severe with Paris Bordone, because he had desired to equal him, that he had driven Tintoretto out of his workshop, forced his own brother Francesco to concentrate on business rather than on painting, and allowed his son Orazio to occupy himself chiefly with alchemy. That he was hostile to Lorenzo Lotto, to Pordenone—what else could they say about him?

They said that he was an excellent portrait painter.

He had stopped working. 'An excellent portrait painter'—as he might have said of Moroni! For a time he painted nothing.

Now, by the light of his nocturnal lamp, he had begun once more to work with zeal, conceiving the sketch of a composition and attempting to reduce as far as possible the chromatic range of his palette. He succeeded in making a deep brown suffice to evoke the forms, suggesting the relief with white, and using the red earth colours to give the right degree of warmth to the solidity of his harmonies.

In the refuge of these solitary hours that could not be contaminated, he reassembled all his energies in the integrity of his loneliness and created new themes, which he put by jealously and concealed for the time being. He concentrated on drawing and meditated on the sufficiency of the few colours he was using. He wanted to advance to a point where no one could possibly imitate him.

In the life of a man there are dispositions which present him anew with the eternity of his ideas. Now that he was again applying himself to the anxious custody of his own work, clinging to every instant of a vast, infinite time, he found himself again in such a simple attitude, concentrating so tenaciously on his work that he was liberated as by limitless time, living the present so intensely that it miraculously became the future.

The break, that brief relaxation of his industry had not meant anything. Many, many years would yet be consumed under the light of his lamp. In the course of the seasons, seasons of heat and cold and rain, the silence, the typical isolation of one who watches through the night, created in him a wakeful, continual train of thought. At times, the fact of sitting there beside the everlasting light of his patience appeared to him to be absurd and mad—and yet so natural, profoundly human and sweetly intoxicating.

Alone, free of all human ties, at that hour when he was not even father to his children, sleeping serenely in another part of the house, he gave rein to his imagination, inventing compositions outside himself and the physiognomy of the period in which he lived. He pondered over the canvases which were prepared for sketches: his hands moved almost involuntarily, putting in touches of colour. He laid his brushes down.

He would have liked to dispense with the artifices common to all—so that his compositions might transcend the formal resemblance to the objects and rise above it, laden with the full mysterious essence of art.

In that state of sharply conscious intoxication, stimulated by the watches of the night, which added to it a flavour of greatness, he would happen to recall shreds of his life, names and faces of people who had surrounded him or still did so. But it was disenchanting and wearisome to try and discover the whereabouts of these recollections in his memory, and he would sigh and drive them away with a contemptuous 'Who is that?', as though they were appearing to him for the first time or as though, in the deceptive unbalance of these abstracted hours, he had been thinking of someone who did not yet belong to his life but might have to play a part in it in the future.

It was late. With an effort, he detached himself from his work.

He could not ask himself 'Who is that?' when his memory brought back to him a poignant recollection of Giorgione. But with a certain coldness, he dwelt on the memories of those years and not of the person who had dominated them. Time was serving as a defence. They seemed to have been years in a different life, so entirely did they belong to the past. He was now living in his *own* time, that absolute time of his most recent work of art, or in that of the next one or of one that lay entirely in the future.

Those were years, these were moments. Two by two, in processions moving in musical intervals, the twofold coming and going in timelessness of such echoes went to his heart with a poignancy he had never felt before. Faces appeared before his inner eye, memories returned, and then everything faded away in a consuming void, because he invariably ended by having devised an ultimate artistic theme which surpassed his stature and his ideas. Greedily he stretched out his hands towards that which was creating itself, robbing the moments of his past and giving them to the interminable years of his present.

In the fixed ritual of nights and moments, years passed by—and they were not only moments and nights.

In the midst of composition, he turned again to portraits—portraits of the Duke and Duchess of Urbino, his new patrons. The Duke's armour, which had been left with him to serve as a model after the Duke had worn it in Venice when he was invested with the title of Generalissimo, acquired a frightening splendour as the light played over it in the studio. More portraits: the picture of the twelve Caesars for the Court of Mantua; sketches for the great work in the Albergo della Carità; the Presentation of the Virgin at the Temple: and finally, certain attempts to which he returned from time to time: beautiful women asleep, sleeping naked in the open air, in an atmosphere of serene mythology. It was his ancient, celebrated theme of poetry in painting.

Now Giorgione came back to his mind. It was late: he rose from his chair in order to go to bed. He took a taper, lighted it and extinguished the lamp that had presided over his patient industry. Dragging his feet, he crossed the studio.

Giorgione . . . how many years had gone by since then! The armour of the Duke of Urbino was mounted on a padded pivot and tied up in the pose the sitter took for the painting; now Titian peered at the breast-plate which reflected the bright orange flame of the taper. He saw his own reflection, transformed by the uncertain light and the convex surface of the metal: where the heart should have been in that curved breast of iron, he saw his own ageing face. It had aged, that face of his. For a second, he imagined the ageing rhythm of his own life between his fleshless ribs: a dry heart, a careworn countenance.

It was late. He went to bed.

The rhythm of his life was now slowing down. While he was slowly undressing, he began to take account of himself. The year was 1538, and everything was in order. His meetings with the Emperor during the last two years had brought him a patent for a pension on Naples. As to the patent of the Senseria, which the Great Council had withdrawn because of his delay in completing the 'Battle of Cadore', he would certainly get that back: he had worked so much for it, and besides, Pordenone had received a commission for the Sala dei Pregai.

The devil take the fellow—he was setting up to be his rival! In Santa Maria degli Angioli at Murano, they were now hanging an 'Annunciation' he had painted because Titian had not agreed to let them have one of his for five hundred scudos. He would not mind letting the Emperor have it for two thousand, he grumbled, as he stretched himself out on the bed and pulled up the coverlets. Leaning forward, he blew out the light and went to sleep.

V

MICHELANGELO had been working for two years at the 'Last Judgement', when Aretino wrote him a letter full of presumption, although couched in terms of respectful esteem, in which he offered his suggestions for the work. He had promised himself to be not only the mentor of the great Imperial painter Titian, but also of the great papal painter of the Sistina.

There can be little doubt that Michelangelo, on receiving this letter, asked himself what that limb of Satan wanted of him. Possibly, as rumours had got around that he was portraying well-known contemporaries in the guise of the damned or the saved, Aretino was attempting to escape being devoured by a demon of the infernal regions.

'Magnifico Messer Pietro, my lord and brother,' Michelangelo wrote. 'In receiving your letter, I felt joy and pain together. I was greatly gladdened to hear from you, whose virtue is unique in the world, and also I was very grieved because, having completed a considerable part of the picture, I cannot carry out your idea which is such that, if the Judgement had taken place, and you had been there in person to see it, your words could not have described it better. . . .'

It was a correct but tepid response to the verbosity of Aretino's suggestions and the impetuous expressions of his admiration.*

It is certain that he did not take it too much to heart, for even if he had been straight to Hell in the 'Last Judgement', he was at that time in the seventh heaven, as he dandled little Adria, the delightful little daughter that Caterina Sandella had borne him. He would hold her

---

*This is established by a letter he wrote in June, 1537, to Nicolò Franco, who was first his secretary and disciple but later his embittered enemy: here he says that 'Michelangelo has employed both nature and art to such an extent that one hardly knows whether they are his masters or his disciples.' This is also proved by a letter published by Gaye in the original text in his *Carteggio inedito di artisti*, II, 332. A letter similar in tone was written by Aretino to Messer Alessandro Corvino in July, 1546. Connoisseur that he was, Aretino always had the greatest admiration for Michelangelo, which he declared in several letters: in the one already mentioned, with suggestions for the 'Last Judgement', dated 15th September, 1536; in one to Giorgio Vasari (from Venice, 15th July, 1538); to the Duke of Urbino (from Venice, 1542); and to Michelangelo himself (from Venice, April, 1545), etc.

on his knee and show her a fine medallion that the sculptor Leone
Leoni, his adoring disciple and good friend, had done of him, or he
would let her turn the pages of a little Book of Hours, a beautifully
bound and illuminated little volume, which had been a gift to the
child from Battistino da Parma. Crowing and making inarticulate
sounds, the baby sat in the golden sunlight, while all around her
flocked the 'Aretine', one bringing an embroidered chemise, another a
little necklace, one a coral, another a tiny bell.

Michelangelo's letter brought about a truce between Aretino and
the Tuscan aesthetic world, to which he had formerly belonged with
body and soul. Afterwards he could do not other than identify his
taste and his theories with Venice and foster in himself and the artists
of his inner circle the Venetian colour-sense.

At that time Titian was painting a picture that expressed these
theories and tenets—a 'Nude Woman', which was to be sent to
Guidobaldo, Duke di Camerino.* Aretino came to the studio and
declared that it gave him a new kind of emotion. For, although the
artist had taken up once more the theme of Giorgione's 'Sleeping
Venus' which he had completed long ago, he had created around it an
atmosphere of such subtle intimacy that he achieved an amazing
degree of realism.

In a work of art one can discover either the constructive silence of
the design or the fascinating eloquence of the colour. The design
composes itself on the plane of meditation and suggestion; colour is
incorporated in the fundamental freedom of plastic contacts from
which arise pacified and eloquent vibrations. A silent nude, twin sister
to the richly dressed figure, such as he had painted years ago by the
fountain of love, untouched in a *silentium* which was still evidently
courtly, was, therefore, an entirely different thing to this modern
invention of simply painting bare flesh against the linen of a bed.
The new Venus born at Birri Grande, whose only clothing consisted
of an armlet, two drop pearls in her ears and a ring on her little finger,
was not merely a figure in a picture, but an entire situation in which
she participated with her gentle breath, and even the women in the
background, busy taking out clothes from a coffer or putting them
away, formed an integral part of the story of that beautiful nude.

*Guidobaldo II was to be the successor of Duke Francesco Maria d'Urbino. Not having
money enough to pay for the painting of the 'Nude Woman' (the 'Reclining Venus' of
the Uffizi), he had to borrow it from his own mother.

She was not nude—she was naked. The first naked female figure in the history of painting, said Aretino. Giorgione's Venus had been mythologically nude, and so had Titian's twin sister by the fountain of love, even though she had been partially draped with the red cloth. They were nude, their skin was neither warm nor cold. But this one was naked, delightful and soothing as only the human temperature could make her.

'Titian! Imperial, divine Titian!' Messer Pietro exclaimed, as he found one formulation after the other for the ideas that crowded in on him. That figure, he maintained, was no longer an object: it had become a necessary element, formed with consummate mastery in the representation of real life transfigured in art and the extraordinary truth of art which is transfigured by the emotions of life.

*　*　*

Another year was about to die, and again there was that familiar, bitter savour of death around the fatal disappearance of beloved, respectable and powerful personalities. The triumphant triumvirate of Venice, reunited again for their conversations, came together this time to enumerate on their calendar the passing of the Duke of Urbino on the 20th October, that of the greatly beloved Doge Gritti on the 28th December. But they little expected, when the year 1539 had begun, to learn not only of the death of Isabella d'Este, but also of the sudden and mysterious death of Pordenone.

They heard about it one evening, surrounded by other people, who all involuntarily looked at Titian, perplexity written large over their faces, as though no one better than he could have told them the story of that death. Titian was standing beside Aretino and Sansovino, and together with them he sustained the concentrated attack of those accusing eyes. At last he asked them to tell him what had happened. Someone began again: *as Titian must know*, when Duke Ercole of Ferrara returned from Germany, he had brought master weavers with him, but as there were no good designers for fanciful figures in Ferrara, he had sent for Pordenone. *As everybody knew*, Pordenone had accepted, but had delayed his departure for a month. At last he had travelled to Ferrara and lodged himself at the Osteria dell' Angiolo, the inn which he, Master Titian, *must have known very well* during his sojourn in that town. The story ended with the rhythmical recurrence of the expressions 'as he knew' and 'as he must know'. Pordenone had immediately gone to work on compositions inspired by the Odyssey and the Labours of Hercules: after a few days, he was suddenly seized by a mysterious illness, and in less time than it took to relate he was found dead by the same physician who had hurried to save him. There could be no doubt that he had been poisoned.

Orazio noticed the concealed snare which was being laid for his father and was about to speak, but Titian remained motionless and faced the looks turned on him; before his son could make an impulsive remark which might have been bad policy or in bad taste, he himself commented briefly on the pitiful plight of poor Madonna Elisabetta, the painter's widow, who, as he said, repaying his interlocutors in their own coin, 'as they must certainly know' now remained alone with children to support. 'Three girls, a boy, and an unborn child,' the others said all together, and then they all fell silent.

The malevolent rumour that Titian had taken some part in the mystery of Pordenone's death circulated all through Venice and was on the tip of every gossiping tongue. Aretino, wearing the celebrated golden chain given him by François I, consisting of intertwining tongues enamelled in red and with an inscription on the clasp which ran '*Lingua eius loquetur mendacium*', went round pompously denying this foolish nonsense. He added laughingly that '*Prodonon*', as he had always called Pordenone, had been destroyed by Master Titian a long time ago—did they not all know it?

It happened that they spoke of it again one day at Titian's house, when Tebaldi was present, as well as Don Lope de Soria, Charles V's ambassador to Venice, and d'Avalos, who had just arrived for the enthronement of the new Doge Pietro Lando. Jacopo Tebaldi had returned to the case of the widow, which was more pitiful than ever. Duke Ercole had sent her a gift of fifty gold scudos, but the poor woman could not get over her husband's mysterious death: Pordenone had always been in robust good health, which was also proved by the alacrity of his activities and the great number of pupils he had trained— words that remained suspended in the air, quivering with hesitation, but capable of raining down on the head of a guilty man who was yet unknown. Titian was sitting down and made a boy turn his last picture to the light; involuntarily he was reassuring himself of his own immortality, faced with these fragments of life and lives. Truly, life flees away, he said: there is nothing enduring except one's own work.

Faced with the concrete vitality of Titian's paintings, Aretino, as though to lay around him devastatingly with his scimitar and send legions of heads devoid of brains rolling in the dust, decided that there was no time to lose. The appellations he was known by suited him well—the *divine* Aretino, the 'scourge of all princes', the 'secretary of the whole world'. As to the other two, his companions, Titian was the triumvirate genius and so was Sansovino. And as they had already assumed a position of supreme authority on aesthetics in Venice, they would stand by each other so that the entire world should get that fact into its head. With a volley of belches, he rose to drink yet another cup of the wine which Master Meo Franci had sent him from Lucca, blessing the grapes of Tuscany. As Franci had been generous enough to present him with more than one barrel, the toasts consolidating the academy of their triumvirate became a ceremonial which was repeated over and over again, until almost every corner of the civilized world had learnt to re-echo it.

What matter if people thought that their august verdict had sent an artist of debatable merit like Pordenone to enjoy a better world? On the rare occasions when they were united near the Osteria del Cappello in Piazza San Marco with Priscianese, the well-known philologist, Marcolini, the editor, and Benedetto Varchi, they appeared like the members of a modern academy, intent on definitive discussions such as Aretino had described in his recent dialogues about princely courts.* Count Titian, the Painter, had already received the patent of the Senseria. He gazed at the clear sky above the crowded square, where the sun was now setting. Among those who passed by, appearing to watch their conventicle, were Andrea Sciavone and Paris Bordone—and at that moment Aretino was just holding forth on the fanciful pictorial possibilities of a certain absurd theme for a wager, but which only the man at his elbow, Titian, could have realized for the delight of humanity. Lodovico Dolce came over and joined the group—and Aretino suddenly, though with all necessary *punctilio*, resumed the offensive against Nicolò Franco, 'that filthy fellow.'† Then Don Lope de Soria's secretary came up to them, in

---

Dialogo o Ragionamento delle Corti, published in 1538, conversations between Aretino, Lodovico Dolce, Piccardo and Giustiniano, which were held in the garden of Casa Marcolini.

†Nicolò Franco had first been an assiduous admirer and superficial imitator of Aretino and then became his ruthless enemy. He initiated a series of defamatory rhymed accusations against the 'Scourge of Scourges'. Naturally he also hated Gian Ambrogio degli Eusebi, follower and secretary of Messer Pietro and husband of the beautiful Marietta dell'Oro. In the end Ambrogio left on his face the eternal memory of the blade of his dagger. . .

order to transmit the greetings and respects of the ambassador, who was taking a walk in the neighbourhood—and immediately Aretino gave orders to place a seat in their midst for Don Lope, who sat down and was soon discussing with him beauties they had both admired, eternal love and fugitive passion.

Others passed across the square; some of them could stay. Her hair severely veiled, but recognizable by her open smile, the poetess Veronica Gambara from Brescia, accompanied her husband, the fresco painter Giuseppe Porta, known as il Salviati,* the brothers Zuccato, some noblemen of the Vendramin family, and, following them or accompanying them, many others. Only the Doge himself was missing in the Parnassus, Orazio whispered to his father, while Aretino played the host, as he would have done at the gates of hell itself, with all the devils standing round in respectful silence. Titian looked around with the air of someone profoundly absorbed in his own thoughts. Yet it did not escape him that in the distance, passing hurriedly through the crowd, young Tintoretto went by: the latter had left his workshop long ago and now, after having hung around Bonifacio Veronese for a time, he was busy establishing an independent reputation.

Everything went towards the exhibitionist consolidation of this academy. Aretino, comfortably installed at home to pose for his portrait by Francesco Salviati, sprinkled the world around him with his praise and blame, putting it down in black and white in a thousand letters. To Titian he addressed the words. . . . 'My only friend, fame takes delight in publishing the miracle wrought by your brush. . . .' Or, returning to the argument about Nicolò Franco, he wrote to Master Lodovico Dolce: '. . . the poor creature resembles a dog which everybody chases away.' In a letter to Don Lope di Soria: '. . . consequently, and always in love, we remain apprentices for ever. . . .' And to another he wrote describing a Parnassus with Apollo and the Muses which he had seen in a dream. . . . 'As I sat down between them (the Muses) I felt as though I were in my own house, for the face of

---

as Aretino wrote on 7th October, 1539. The case was brought before the courts, but Ambrogio got off with the minimum fine. Franco left Venice, and eventually found favour in a little provincial court. Finally, in 1570, he ended in Rome on the gallows, condemned for illicit profits, through intrigues at the Papal court.

*A native of Tuscany, but educated in Rome by Francesco Salviati, accompanied him to Venice in 1539, where he decorated the façades of several palaces with frescoes and worked for the editor Marcolini, for whom he did copious illustrations, most of which were designed or suggested by Marcolini himself.

History and that of Comedy was smirking at me and caressing me. . . .'

Titian felt that Aretino, sharp-sighted and expert as he was in matters of art, was always ready to divulge emotions and intuitions with the marvellous impetuosity of his vocabulary, but not always to go to the bottom of a matter and evolve critical ideas. Bah—it was all right as it was, the painter thought to himself; these things were too difficult and complicated. And he turned his attention to Orazio who, with a couple of apprentices, was busy with sponges and brushes attending to the preparation of canvases, absorbed in the spreading of gesso and sweet glue as though it were a most complicated alchemistical operation. On the other canvas, which had been dry for some time, Titian was 'preparing the bed' for the painting, sketching it in with a few warm earth colours and nut oil. Then he put this pictorial preparation to dry as well.

He paused. The apprentices were spreading white on the fine, immaculate canvases. Yes, he thought to himself, too many debates and dialogues, too much idle talk was reeled off in the modern academy. How much more alive, even though youthfully romantic, had been the ferment of thirty years ago, when he and Giorgione had believed that they could understand and conquer the inexpressible. Fewer books had been published then. A sudden emotion drove the blood right into the pale skin stretched over his temples: it now seemed to him that all had been contained in that extraordinary voice of Zorsi's, Zorsi who was now singing in his memory, simply, like a shepherd of the golden age, from a far-away world which was moving even further—a world which had ceased to exist.

He continued vigilantly to watch the young men busy with the canvases. The nape of Orazio's neck, with its youthful taut skin, as he bent down against the white canvas, reminded him of that song: which he began to hum softly to himself:

> *Tanto avrebbe potuto essere amore*
> *Che la bellezza mai sarebbe morta. . . .* *

The two apprentices turned in amazement and cast sidelong glances at the Master who was behaving in so unaccustomed a manner. He noticed it and thought how these moving lines must seem like some ancient tuneless complaint to those boys who would whistle like chaffinches for hours as they worked. And he fell silent.

---

*'Love could have been so great
That Beauty never could have died.'

VI

IT was due to Aunt Orsa, to Orazio and to Fabrizio and Cesare Vecellio, second cousin of Titian's, because they were the sons of Ettore, who was Master Gregorio's first cousin, both of whom had been staying and painting for some time with him at Birri Grande, that a frequent intercourse between Titian and the people of Pieve was maintained. Whenever relations, friends of relations, and relations of friends came to Venice, they would spend the greater part of their time in his house. Titian would keep out of the way, but he could not avoid long conversations with his nearest kinsfolk and, in any case, he met them at table. Besides, it was a bit of Pieve which had come to his studio, and it pleased him to gather information on this or that part of the forest or on a certain hamlet.

Swelling with pride, his relations stood in front of his pictures; they did not understand the first thing about them, but they were delighted to breathe art as deeply as they breathed the morning air of their mountains. And seeing the nude, reclining goddess, they thought secretly that the painter who assumed so awkward a dignity, as he shuffled round in his shabby slippers, must nevertheless enjoy a wonderful love-life with the most sophisticated, exigent and voluptuous mistresses.

They looked around, amazed at the luxury of the chiselled basins that spread light around them like stars.

Lavinia was now ten years old. Her aunt Orsa had taught her everything that a little girl as graceful as she was could learn. First and foremost she proved herself useful in the garden behind the house, for Orsa, poor woman, since she lived in Venice, had been plagued by terrible pains in her legs, and now she was not even able to stoop down and pick a leaf of mint.

Titian loved the child tenderly with an assiduous anxiety, almost as though he were continually aware of her miraculous escape from the shadow of death which had robbed her of her mother when she was born. Orsa, now a confirmed old maid, had installed herself quietly in the role of mother and housewife and played it to perfection. She ran the house wonderfully well: the man and maid lacked nothing. And on the occasions when Aretino announced that he was coming to dinner, they would line up in the kitchen as though to celebrate a solemn rite: religiously they laid out knives for pastry, for tarts, knives for scraping and beating, and all the available spits. The pheasants that finally appeared at table might have been purified, blessed and sanctified by sacred fires, divine odours and heavenly sauces.

Both aunt and niece, like all the women in Venetian houses, led a very secluded life, in the midst of the cauldron of masterpieces at Birri Grande, where at any time of the day pupils, functionaries, purveyors, ambassadors or noblemen would arrive, men who had a great deal to say about the imperial and the papal court, about the picture gallery of some splendid prince, or that of some scoundrelly one.

Then Titian and Orazio had to leave all of a sudden: cases large and small, coffers, rolls of canvas and piles of linen had to be packed: everybody was bustling around and panting. These enterprises were the result of Titian's relations with the princely courts. Now, during the great heat, he and his son had gone to Milan. They were to return in October.

Orazio delighted in the most minute descriptions, no matter how many times he had heard them. The first might be the enumeration of certain luxurious articles for daily use seen in the rooms of Luigi Davila or Gonzalo Perez, the secretaries and confidants of Covos, the *Comendator Mayor*. Or a perfect description of the Emperor's suits of armour, chiselled in Milan; one known as 'il Negrelo' and signed by '*Iac. Philippus Negrolus Mediolani faciebat*', had a gilded coif, mouth, ears and nose; another showed the allegory of Tunis on the summit of the helmet, like a monument ready to move. Titian for his part was only interested in repeating to himself the best of his Milanese stories: it pleased him to add the catalogue of these riches to the exact notes he kept of his revenues, which were now increased by the pension he had acquired on the Treasure of Milan.

Once again, he took up the threads of his work. But it was anything but easy for him to keep himself in a good mood, knowing that on the 1st November of that year, 1541, the doors of the Sistine Chapel in Rome would be opened wide and the last, enormous 'Judgement' of Michelangelo revealed to the amazed and bewildered number of those who succeeded in gaining admission. As yet the scaffolding at the bottom had not been removed, and it was only towards Christmas that the Chapel was finally cleared and hundreds of visitors were admitted.

Bewilderment gave way to enthusiasm, amazement to resentful criticism. The public formed two frenetically divided parties. On one side, letters were sent to the four quarters of the globe, and in order to boost the work even more in the *salons*, sonnets and even Latin epigrams were composed in great haste, while legions of copyists were labouring furiously to reproduce the fresco in oils, in drawings and in copperplates. From the other side, an embittered censure was released; all that shameless nakedness in so sacred a place . . . it was simply nauseating! One could see nothing but bare legs and buttocks! The most acidulous critics pointed to the artist's most arbitrary whims —which others called his most sublime ideas—for instance, that he had represented the Christ without a beard. Even in Venice, where until now not even an engraving of the 'Judgement' could be found, one could hear echoes of the opinions of Michelangelo's most ardent admirers who, though they defended the work, could not help admitting that he had really exaggerated his liking for nudities. In this atmosphere of scandal, the Holy Nativity was celebrated.

The 'divine' Michelangelo had spent a sensational Christmas in Rome, and now the 'divine' Messer Pietro wanted the Carnival in Venice to be equally sensational. The patricians of the 'Calza' had decided to have his comedy *Talanta* performed; as it was customary to turn to non-Venetian artists for the scenic decorations of these carnival performances, Aretino, who had been working himself up to a pitch of excitement about this event for quite a time, selected Giorgio Vasari.

He arrived at the end of the year, preceded by two paintings he had sent to Messer Pietro, one representing Venus, the other Leda, both of them after Michelangelesque designs. This was a pretext for the endless discussions about Buonarroti to be resumed among the intellectuals, and at the same time to give great publicity to Master Giorgio. Naturally Aretino acted as his tout, and as always he had the last word, he pointed out, exalting the merits of the Venus, the goddess who vouchsafed her gifts to both sexes, how the beautiful feminine body was audaciously composed with masculine proportions and muscles.

Titian had begun to paint a tender portrait of a little girl—Clarice, the daughter of Roberto Strozzi. A tiny, curly-headed mite of two years of age, adorned with pearls and chains studded with precious stones, who was holding a valuable rattle and bending towards a good-tempered little dog. As though to prepare his reply to the challenge of the mountain-overthrowing giant of the Sistine Chapel, he lingered to play with a straw.

Not only was Vasari preceded by the two paintings, which were sold for two hundred gold scudos, but also by his two assistants, Cristofano Gherardi and Battista Cungi. But as they travelled by sea, their ship ran into a storm and was driven off its course and they did not arrive in Venice until their master had already taken up the plans for the scenery and for the arrangement of the hall of Cannaregio.

Messer Pietro was beside himself with impatience. When the two arrived at last, he seemed to breathe again and immediately sent them to work with a thousand recommendations; darting to and fro in his gondola, peppering the actors who were rehearsing the comedy, while they shivered with cold, then returning to the work in the hall, and finally going to see Titian and confide to him certain doubts that assailed him about Vasari's decorations. He returned home in a state of exhaustion. But soon he had recovered once more and sent his manservant to tell the actors that they could come and rehearse in his own warm house, with the encouragement of good wine. Thus he would be in a better position to supervise the progress of the performance.

The entire city was in a turmoil. True, every year at Carnival time there were frenzied preparations for mummeries and complicated processions representing a variety of subjects, but this time the preparations for the comedy *Talanta* began to assume the proportions of a ducal investment.

There was a continual coming and going of cloth-merchants who showed peacock-blue velvets, black satins and gilded cloths with applications. Aretino, who was not satisfied with everything, had insisted on visiting the store-rooms and the antique shops personally, though it was actually only a pretext to show Venice to Vasari, introducing him to a certain antique dealer or some other merchant. Finally they went to dine on soles prepared with a bitter-sweet sauce, a dish which anticipated the customary Carnival fare. Titian had come to join them and sat eating in silence, while Messer Pietro continued to importune Vasari to enrich every recess and square of the theatre with allegories.

The house was topsy-turvy, the rehearsals were started all over again. The 'Aretine' crowded round to see the comedians trying on their costumes—the courtesan Talanta, her four lovers and her two slaves, one a man who was a woman, the other a woman who was a man, according to the classical canons of those comedies with complicated intrigues. They laughed madly. The lamps were lighted, and the rain beat against the window-panes so that it sounded like a burst of applause.

On the night of the performance the applause really sounded like a cloud-burst, and the clapping went on interminably. Vasari had decorated the hall profusely with mythologies of the sea, the sky, the woods, the Virtues, Victory overcoming War, and finally Charity driving them out. Hundreds of lights were suspended from the ceiling, shining through globes of glass filled with water and illuminating the ladies who were admiring the painted figures of the Hours and chariots of Dawn and Night, drawn by cocks and owls. Titian stood apart, the tacit observation of his watchful eyes reducing all this exuberance to its proper proportion.

The comedy amused the audience, though many among them would have preferred to see one of Plautus' plays again. But the ladies, who maliciously as their husbands insinuated, did not care whether the author had only begun to write books because he had been apprenticed to a bookbinder at the age of thirteen, decreed that the evening was a success. They threw back their fur-lined capes, looked each other up and down and arranged their golden hair with a few deft touches: going out to take refreshments, they held themselves very straight and affected an indifferent mien, but they had to restrain themselves from rushing towards Aretino and crowding round him.

As they repressed their enthusiasm and passed along, spreading out their skirts as they walked, they seemed like beautiful ships followed by a breakwater of satin and golden roses, with flags flying on the masts, the prow and the stern, signalling with the bright flashes of their eyes, a fleet in festive array. The admirals, the pilots, even the simple, intrepid cabin-boys of these superb craft—that is to say the husbands, the lovers, the beaux and fops, cast vigilant, authoritarian, thrilling and melting looks at them. But the adorable fleet was not easily intimidated: it was prepared to weather any storm, to weigh anchor and sail out into the open sea, or to glide softly through the waves preparing complicated landing-manoeuvres.

Now, with the unerring prow of their foot that parted the ornamented bands of the over-skirts, they were advancing towards the exit. The wretched pilots helped them to wrap themselves up—shivers went through them as they stood near the door, but that made them laugh even more: they pulled their cloaks tightly round their shoulders and adjusted the black veils which made them look paler.

Outside, joyous masked revellers were shouting. A few drunkards stopped and stood there motionless like posts, watching the ladies pass as, one after the other, they descended into the black gondolas swaying on the black water.

VII

VASARI came to see Titian in his studio and converse with him—it was obvious that he had come to pick his brains. Slowly and indifferently, Titian displayed his paintings.

Just because the great *memento mori* Michelangelo had created in the Sistine Chapel was the topic of the day, he gave his visitor to understand, though in silence, as he showed his portraits and his portable compositions which were now ready to travel round the world, that the modern attitude towards art was not in favour of gigantic works. The application to a varied series of canvases favoured a variety of tone, mood and inspiration and helped the artist to concentrate on the beauty of the surface.

However, he did not explain all this in so many words. Instead, he asked his visitor how he was progressing with his work at the Palazzo Corner and which compositions he had thought out. But before Master Giorgio could open his mouth to enumerate the subjects, he had already, with a yawn, foreseen in every detail the tedious and inevitable traditional array: Charity, Hope, Faith, Justice. . . .

Michelangelo was right to depict Christ without a beard, was the final liberal judgement. Aretino, who hoped to get rid of his paunch, was now frequenting the *stufe*, the hot-air baths: he had hit on the most pungent definition of Michelangelo's great work, saying that the Valley of Josaphat in the Sistine Chapel must truly resemble a *stufa* crowded with nudes. Besides, it was well known that Michelangelo often went to the Roman *stufa* in order to seek fine models among the ephebes who sold their favours there.

Vasari failed to penetrate deeply into the modernity of Titian's painting. Although, like Francesco and Giuseppe Salviati, he enjoyed being in Venice to study the methods of good colourists. When he was asked to say which he preferred among the fine works of art in the city, he pointed out the octagonal 'Psyche' which Cecchin Salviati had painted during the preceding year for Grimani. This painting was a prototype of the Tuscan style, influenced by Michelangelo and tending, without manieristic relief, towards the Venetian chromatic phenomenon —in the manner that Andrea del Sarto had initiated.

The painter-critic struck his tents in August. He had not achieved a single success in Venice, with the exception of the Carnival decorations.

In the meantime Arentino had had other worries: in the interests of the good name of the triumvirate, he had advised Vasari to remain in the background. His troubles had begun with Marietta dell 'Oro; while her husband Gian Ambrogio, who was Messer Pietro's secretary, was in France, she had bundled up all she could lay hands on in the house of the king of the 'Aretine', and had run away with her lover. Her husband did not remain empty-handed: while he was in France he had been able to lay hands as co-signatory on a large sum which François I had offered as a gift to the 'divine' Aretino, and without a second thought, he had lost it at cards in the house of Cardinal Gaddi.

People were already beginning to jeer. But worse was to come: Gian Antonio Serena, so as not to be recognized as the cuckold he actually was, gave vent to his suppressed resentment and accused Aretino of sodomy.

The Magistrates of the Republic conducted the affair tactfully. The *sbirri* had orders to look for the divine black sheep, but not to find him. Titian, greatly incensed by the stupidity of the whole business, went to see his friend and insisted that he should be more careful in future and see to it that his house on the Rialto was not open to too mixed a company.

Obstinately Messer Pietro still attempted to be funny, describing how the stairs of his house were being worn down by the coming and going, like the pavement of the Capitol by the wheels of the triumphal cars. But he realized that it was too inconvenient and expensive to keep open house for the needs and curiosity of all the world. People came to ask him for the cast-off clothes of Adria or for help in cash, to bring him petitions for the release of a prisoner or to scrounge a meal. It even happened that a wounded young man had himself transported to one of his rooms one night, merely because he knew one of the girl friends of one of the 'Aretine' of his eccentric harem.

Titian felt that he could never thank the Lord enough for the distance that lay between his house and Aretino's, and for the fact that their connection was usually concealed in missives carried to and fro by their servants. He also had his worries at that time: consultations with his cousin Toma Tito, who was now a well-known barrister, about a dispute he was having with the Canon of St Spirito concerning an altar-piece he had painted months ago, and his profound disappointment when he received the news of Charles V's defeat at Algiers where the Imperial fleet had suffered grave losses.

He discussed it with Gian Francesco Leoni, the tutor of Ranuccio Farnese, the beautiful little boy who was sitting for his portrait, swinging his legs from a high chair where he was perched, because he was unable to stand still on his feet. To obviate the restlessness of his high-born pupil, Leoni was at pains to inform the painter about a meeting that the Pope, Paul III Farnese intended to arrange as soon as the Emperor should have crossed Italy in order to return to Germany.

Titian sent for Lavinia, so that she should be introduced and make her curtsey, and also in the hopes that she might keep young Ranuccio from yawning all the time. Dressed in her best gown, she moved gracefully between the canvases and came to admire the painted image of the model, looking up at the picture on the easel.

At other times there would be deep silence in the studio. The beautiful Lina was posing for the Master in the nude; she was then at the zenith of her splendour, with her flaming hair and her milk-white skin, and the air of one who walks on clouds between the sun and the moon. In ordinary life she was a sensible girl who, when the pose was over and she had dropped her role of Venus, went home to cook her supper. And if it happened that the maids of the Vecellio house, seeing her go out, pursed their lips and looked askance at her, she would go straight on with supreme self-confidence, holding a purse which contained the money she had earned for the pose, or a bundle of two yards of crimson satin from which she was going to fashion a bodice. Her lover might be angry and Heaven alone knows what stories she told him, but he had to be convinced that art was great and needed her beauty, the effulgent magic of her hair and the milky whiteness of her skin.

Sometimes she fell asleep while she was posing. The painter would pause to watch her breast rising and falling and attempt with his paint-stained fingers to create an echo of that peaceful breath on the canvas.

Time passed. He travelled to Ferrara, then to Busseto to join Pope Paul III, who was in the midst of great discussions with the Emperor. Titian painted a portrait of the Pope, and the Emperor commissioned him to do one of his deceased consort Isabella. When he returned to Birri Grande, he saw his works again and sent for Lina.

She arrived, as beautiful as ever, with her magnificent air, but she immediately informed him that if he wanted her to pose in the nude he would have to paint her back only—she was engaged to be married. He laughed at her—surely he was old enough to be her father! But there was nothing to be done, and he had to be content with painting a few studies for a Venus turning away and clinging to Adonis. A few weeks later, Lina came again because he wished to elaborate the final composition based on these studies, but this time she would only condescend to pose fully clothed. She told him that she was going to be married in two months' time, and she needed some more money in order to complete her outfit.

She stayed motionless under her flowing draperies, which were striped black and white and fell in pleats, forming a continuous narrow zig-zag, gazing gravely into the void from under the mass of her golden-red hair. The nearer her wedding came, the more sure she felt of herself. During the pose, she barely moved so as not to disarrange the folds. Her gaze seemed to traverse a ten-fold barrier of silence which isolated her in a voiceless world, and it was as though she were begging permission to sing softly, under her breath. At other times, she posed for the portrait of Queen Isabella, one hand lying on a drape of velvet, the other holding a tiny, open, illuminated book.

Then it happened that she missed a pose or arrived late, and finally she disappeared and nothing more was heard of her.

*　　*　　*

Charles V used to say that princes should imitate Alexander, and lend their features only to Apelles or his peers. Old Paul III obviously thought the same. Titian was soon to go to Rome, for after he had painted his first, much-admired portrait of His Holiness, he knew that he would be received at the papal court with honours to equal those which were lavished on Michelangelo.

In the meantime, Aretino, shuffling the fine hand-painted playing cards which had been made for him by Padovan, had finished his *Dialogue of the Speaking Cards.*[*]

He could not tear his eyes away from Titian's picture of himself as Pilate in the great 'Ecce Homo', painted for the merchant Van Hannen:

---

[*]Published in 1543 with the title 'Dialogo del divino Pietro Aretino nel quale si parla con moralita piacevole'. The protagonists are various types of card-players—nobles, courtesans, porters, inn-keepers, galley-slaves, ruffians, the Pope and the Emperor.

now, after his conversation with Charles V in the environs of Verona, he wrote a letter of congratulation to his divine painter, dotting all the i's of the latter's refusal to accept the office offered to him by the Pope.

The Master laid the letter down. In the vitiated air of his studio, he sat looking at the sketched-in canvases, the unfinished works, the drawings. He looked at the shining shoulders of the girl who had lent her hands to the Queen, living hands in that image inspired so indirectly, soft hands, sweet as the splendour of springtime.

Once again he re-created her image in his mind. It lasted a moment only, but while he allowed himself to be disarmed by that slight, tender sensation, emerging from the abysmal demands of his pride to survey all his egotism concentrated in the transparent diamond cone which was now his heart, he was suddenly overcome by the realization of his utter solitude.

He let himself go and sank down on a seat, dropping his palette and his brushes. Now that he was soon to reach the seventy-sixth year of his age, he realized how careful he had been, as careful as an old prisoner who was now permitted to open the doors of his prison for a moment and rediscover, in the blinding light of day, the unrecognizable examples of human life and relish once again their fascination.

He looked at his work as though he hoped it would help him, but he felt nothing but hostility and resentment towards it. He pulled himself together and went up to his canvases: taking a palette-knife, he scraped off the sketched-in figure of Lina with its halo of narrow white and black rays, and it seemed as though flashes of lightning were sparking away from it.

Ordering Cesare to close the shutters and bolt the doors of the studio, he sent for Lavinia. He told her to pack her things; they would be leaving for Pieve tomorrow.

He was longing to have a rest there—up among those hills of his, summer was a delight, not a trial as in Venice. He went for walks with Lavinia, saying that she was dressed up as though it were always Sunday, but her aunt Orsa maintained that her clothes were those befitting the daughter of the titled gentleman he now was.

In a few days the girl would be thirteen years old. Picking up her overskirts of brocade, she went into the stables to look at the mules. The peasants bowed to her as though she were the Dogaressa in person, saying among themselves that she was the living image of her poor mother, Master Alò's Cecilia.

Several times it happened of an evening that Titian would take out a letter that Aretino had sent him two months earlier, reading it again and showing it to the others. It was a calm letter which, in a wonderful way, evoked the atmosphere of a sunset on the Rialto, such as the Master had distilled into his paintings by the magic of his colours. 'O, my Titian, where are you now?' ended the letter, which seemed diffused with the glow of minium and the fading tints of green and azure. Though it appeared to be merely an affectionate, nostalgic homage to the painter, and a feat of epistolary *bravura*, the letter gave him to understand in a subtle manner that the things which he, the artist, had seen and transfigured, could not have been found in reality until he had pointed them out.

A reminder of such emotional precision was just what he had needed during this period of recollection and solitude. He remembered his frequent discontent, because a kind of mannerism had seized even him and he felt that the poetic zest and restrained force, such as had filled his youthful works, the *Bacchanalia* for Duke Alfonso, might have carried him onto a far more superb development than that attained in his recent *Ecce Homo* for Van Haanen.

He would begin again, he told himself, and he kept the letter like a precise memorandum, a relic. Yes, he would begin again to recapture the best that was in him, with all the impetus of conscious defiance. Besides, every new work always represented an unknown adventure, as though the enemy most difficult to overcome were within himself, in his own bowels. Suddenly, he could not bear to stay in Pieve any longer; he was already longing to return to the chase of himself in his studio at Birri Grande.

With every possible pretext and the fondest invitations, he was held back by Count Adriano, the Lord of Spilimbergo, and his wife, Giulia, who were good friends to him and often came to Venice. During the trips he undertook to see things and places and to increase his personal popularity, he pushed forward as far as their residence, and accepted their hospitality.

Now that the days were so long, they lingered in the loggias to admire the sunsets. The Lord of Spilimbergo disclosed his fine teeth in a serene smile which was always renewed: he was a noble intellectual who delighted in the pleasures of the mind. His wife would join them after having said good-night to their two little girls, Irene and Emilia, and would relate the last innocent tricks they had been up to. Then she would call a maid and ask her to bring the velvet cape with which she enveloped her slight harmonious figure. She could hardly wait for her daughters to be old enough to have their portraits done by the Master. . . . Then all three would fall silent and allow that immortal hour to nourish their spirits with all the beauty shining down from the sky over the darkening depths of the valleys.

'O! my Titian, where are you now?' a voice was asking him softly. He settled back in his chair and gazed into space, like one who is waiting for a revelation.

Soon he found himself back in his studio at Birri Grande, confronted with wonderful unsullied light canvases, ready to sail to worlds of greater mastery. He painted, he wrote letters: Guidobaldo, the Duke of Urbino, invited him to come to his court, and Cardinal Farnese asked him to Rome. Now that etched copies of Michelangelo's 'Last Judgement' were arriving in Venice, he felt eager to go to Rome, to take up his work there and face that monster of *bravura*.

In the meantime, Guidobaldo came to Venice and sat to Titian for his portrait. The duke insisted that he should come to his court, and the artist obeyed and was welcomed there by his friend Sperone, who received him with open arms.

It was not till the following summer, the summer of 1545, that Titian, after reaching an agreement with Cardinal Farnese, left Venice and, after staying for a considerable time at Pesaro with Guidobaldo II, finally arrived in Rome at the beginning of September.

VIII

IN the Belvedere, Titian was given an apartment fit for a Pope. At first he slept prodigiously, but Sebastiano del Piombo assured him that Rome had this effect on people who came from the North —to them it was like the Orient. Yet as soon as he had become used to the Roman climate, he went to visit the antiquities and the palaces in the company of Sebastiano and of Bembo, and at the same time he painted several pictures which could spread his fame rapidly through the the city.

He was a great worker, they said in the palace, lumping together the Master's initial long sleeps with his present periods of retirement which lasted many hours: these were already beginning to bear fruit lavishly: there was the portrait of the Pope, together with his nephews Alessandro and Ottaviano, the portrait of Pierluigi Farnese and of two ladies of the same family, and finally the sketch for a superb Danae.

Michelangelo was sick and lived in deep seclusion in the house of his friend Luigi Riccio. He had experienced nothing but sadness for months: during the last year Riccio's nephew, Cecchino Bracci, a boy of marvellous beauty, whom Michelangelo had called '*l'idolo nostro*' —'our idol'—had died. His uncle then wrote heart-broken sonnets, invoking him as 'my idol'. It was a consolation to him when the famous sculptor declared himself ready to model a bust of Cecchino to complete the tomb he had designed—but then Michelangelo was stricken by a serious illness. Riccio took him into his own house, for Michelangelo's house at Macel de' Corvi offered no comfort and he was continually having disagreements with servants who cared only to feather their own nests.

Sebastiano del Piombo, who kept Titian informed about all the events of the day, accompanied him when he went to see the Sistine Chapel in the bright light of noon. The Master stood looking at those hundreds of figures in violent movement, involuntarily shrinking back from their terrible impact like someone who dreads the explosion of a

171

fuse. Truly, this was a disquieting, anguished world. . . . What could the cardinals and the burghers see in it, he wondered, those people who looked at a work of art with the same bovine, respectful lack of comprehension with which they admired a sacred, venerable relic?

In the 'Last Judgement', he recognized Aretino at the feet of the Almighty—looking more like a St Bartholomew intent on flaying others than one who has been flayed: he also recognized immediately, among the folds of the saint's flayed skin, the contracted face of Michelangelo himself. Sebastiano del Piombo was stealthily watching Titian's reactions.

Impassively, he lifted his head to look at parts of the ceiling, at Jonah and the magnificent Sybils, and then his eyes strayed back to that detail with its bitter jest, and he smiled.

'Aretino must have seen an etching of the Last Judgement by now —a very fine print carried out by Enea Vico from Parma,' Sebastiano remarked, but Titian knew nothing about it. But a few weeks later, in November, Sebastiano came hurrying to tell him that Michelangelo had received an unpleasant letter from Messer Pietro—a flaming philippic in defence of modesty and sacred things. He had committed whole passages of it to memory and now recited them, including Aretino's felicitous suggestion that the sex of the damned should be covered with flames, and that of the saved with rays of light!

Titian was disconcerted, foreseeing that the resentment which Michelangelo was bound to feel towards his friend and fellow-member of the triumvirate might be extended to his own person. In his heart he actually wished the indefatigable busybody to Hades, with his constant interference, but he felt bound to explain the real reason of Aretino's pique to Sebastiano: Messer Pietro had asked Michelangelo over and over again to let him have a sketch or some outline of the plans for his work in the Sistine Chapel, but he had never received anything. This was the result of his disappointment.

Sebastiano often visited the Master of the Sistine Chapel and accompanied Titian when he went sight-seeing in Rome, so he was able to ply a shuttle-service, repeating items of news, impressions, judgements and comments. From time to time, in the corridors of the Vatican, they would meet the Flemish composer Jacob Arkadelt, maestro in the Papal Chapel, who had set two madrigals of Michelangelo's to music. Sebastiano and he asked each other for news of the sick man or enquired when one or the other had been to see him last.

'Arcadente, this is Messer Tiziano from Cadore,' said Sebastiano.

The musician bowed, and notwithstanding his faulty Italian, he described very wittily how he with some others had been the victim that very morning of a curious mistake which did great honour to the artist. As he was walking through the garden, he happened to look up and saw His Holiness sitting on a balcony, in conversation with two of his nephews. Thereupon he bowed deeply, thinking that it was rather strange and very imprudent for a person as old as the Pope to sit out of doors in the December sunshine. His companion also remarked on this fact, and after they had all bowed once more, they went to make sure whether they had not been mistaken. Of course it had not been His Holiness in the flesh, but the now celebrated portrait by Titian, which had been placed on the balcony to dry in the sun!

This anecdote circulated through all the apartments of the Vatican and eventually reached his Holiness: it made the rounds of Rome, penetrated into all the palaces where the rich Christmas fare was being consumed, and finally arrived in Venice. But the news that came back from Venice was anything but good, in fact it was highly embarrassing: the Library, erected by Sansovino in the Piazetta, had collapsed, and the unfortunate architect had been thrown into jail.

Titian could not have felt more acutely mortified if the news that his own daughter had been dishonoured had been spread in Rome: it was a mercy that he at least was upholding the good name of the triumvirate with his portraits, which were so lifelike that people bowed to them! Whatever were the other two doing in Venice? One wrote insulting letters to Michelangelo, and the other allowed his buildings to collapse like a pack of cards and let himself be put into prison. Truly, Michelangelo had every reason to rejoice!

Titian read Aretino's letter from beginning to end, over and over again. When Bembo came to see him, he felt incapable of telling him what had happened and simply gave him the letter to read:

'. . . When I came home about four o'clock, I received at the same time your letter and the news of the collapse of Sansovino's building, together with that of his arrest; therefore the joy I had in receiving your news was turned into affliction and sorrow at the disaster that has befallen him. Indeed, I can barely restrain my tears as I write to you. . . . All night long, instead of sleeping, I had to think of the terrible, ignominious end fate has reserved for so talented and honest a man; it is indeed a cruel trick of destiny that this work, which is the tabernacle of our brother's fame, should have become the grave-yard of this fame. . . .'

However, the end of the letter did not sound so bad; there were certain extenuating circumstances:

'. . . people put the blame on the furious haste with which the building was erected, on the lack of skill of the workmen and on the severe winter, also on the damage which was done when the fabric was shaken by the firing of the artillery on the arrival of certain ships. . . .'

Messer Pietro also wrote to that effect to Bembo. The latter, together with Titian, used all his influence and wrote letters to all the powerful men in power. They succeeded in persuading the authorities to liberate Sansovino, though the unfortunate triumvir was condemned to pay a thousand ducats to compensate for the damage.

* * *

The portrait of Paul III with his nephews seemed to fix a given situation with the maximum of historical authority, and the living modernity of the painting left the stiff papal portraits by Raphael far behind. After this, Titian wished to show that he could put as much of the modern spirit into the depiction of the beauty of the classical world, which Rome had revealed to him, and he resumed work at his 'Danae'.

Dear old Bembo came to visit him. Now that they had brought off the affair of Sansovino, they relaxed serenely. How many years had passed since those days of long ago when he had created his first poems in paint! Had he done some more and were they even more beautiful, Bembo asked. And Titian, just as in days gone by, silently turned a canvas towards him—for his latest work, the 'Danae', was very nearly completed.

Then they looked at each other, both of them grey-haired and wrinkled now, and Titian grumbled that he was no longer as young as he had been in those days: he worked far more slowly and Rome, with all the marvels one had to see, tired him out. Bembo could only click his tongue in amazement, saying that Titian was younger now than in those long past years if he had the power to paint a great epic poem like this monumental Danae, so sensuously feminine, so volup-tuous. Truly, she could only be possessed by gold—gold alone could illuminate her skin. Impetuously, as though to award him the highest secret premium by imparting joyful news in advance, he told Titian that the Pope had decided to honour him at the same time as Michelangelo, now that the latter had almost recovered from his sickness. Soon they would both be awarded Roman citizenship.

How would this take place, Titian asked, and when, and with what ceremonies?

On the Capitol, without a doubt, in the presence of the highest authorities of Rome, the foreign embassies and all the intellectuals, and early in March, Bembo said, adding that this ceremony meant much more than merely giving them the citizenship of Rome: it signified that they had been chosen as the highest exponents of art in Europe.

The news spread very rapidly. Bembo, Sebastiano, Vasari and others among their friends held confabulations as to whether it would be a good thing to bring about a meeting of the two artists before the event, or whether it would be best to let them meet face to face for the first time on the Capitol on the 19th March. They left it at that, for Michelangelo was still keeping to himself and never went out.

Thus it happened that the two great men met on the Capitol. They were both in their seventies: frowning yet calm, absent-minded, they looked up like two fighting cocks recovering their resolution.

They liked each other, scrutinizing the traces the years had left on them. They looked at each other's hands.

Perhaps, for a single moment, in the proud impassibility of their glances, they understood each other in the hint of a smile they exchanged, an unspoken comment on this family festivity flavoured by Latinizing harangues—for they were both inwardly miles away from it all, wrapped in the mantle of their supernal solitude.

A few days later, at the Belvedere, Titian was occupied with the final touching up of his 'Danae' when Michelangelo was announced. He had come with Sebastiano and Vasari, and it was obvious that both of them could hardly wait to witness a meeting between the two artists which must be more intimate than the official one on the Capitol.

There were brief silences, which Sebastiano and Messer Giorgio made solicitous attempts to break by bringing about a general conversation, but it was an arduous enterprise, for it would have been hard to find two men less talkative than these two, or at least less inclined to talk in front of third persons.

Once again Michelangelo and Titian scrutinized each other. And once again, perhaps for the fraction of a second only, the watchful Vasari thought he saw a look of mutual understanding flashing up from the depths of their eyes, which seemed to express nothing but impassibility. Vasari was burning with impatience for Titian to bring out his 'Danae' and he arranged that the latter should be in the advantageous position of letting his work speak for itself, turning to the Master and asking him to tell Orazio to have the picture brought into the light.

Michelangelo was not the man to express conventional praise in order to make himself pleasant, as one could see by one look at his face with its deep furrows of stoically endured pain and deep thought that seemed engraved into the stone of time.

He rose to his feet and went right up to the picture, his nose close to the painted flesh as though he hoped to surprise the breath of its colour. He looked and looked again, like one who seeks to capture a thought or a phrase. Then, in silence, he turned round and signified his complete approval.

It was a wordless colloquy between two champions who were mute, though not speechless; because they were both drugged with the same fierce passion for their art, all they needed was a single whiff in order to recognize the intrinsic quality of that rare, secret essence of which they both partook, though under vastly different forms. There could be no doubt that Michelangelo felt slightly repelled by the advanced modernity of this work, the pulsating life which was sweeping away the severe design to which he was accustomed. The figures he painted were like architectural constructions—cupolas, supporting vaults or architraves. But Titian devoted himself to depicting the amorous ecstasy of a woman overcome by the sonorous, impalpable glitter of gold.

'It's his self-portrait,' Vasari suggested maliciously to all who asked about the picture. Titian could not possibly have found a more accurate symbolical definition of his own nature than this unconscious representation of his notorious cupidity and avarice, transmuted into supreme pictorial sensuality.

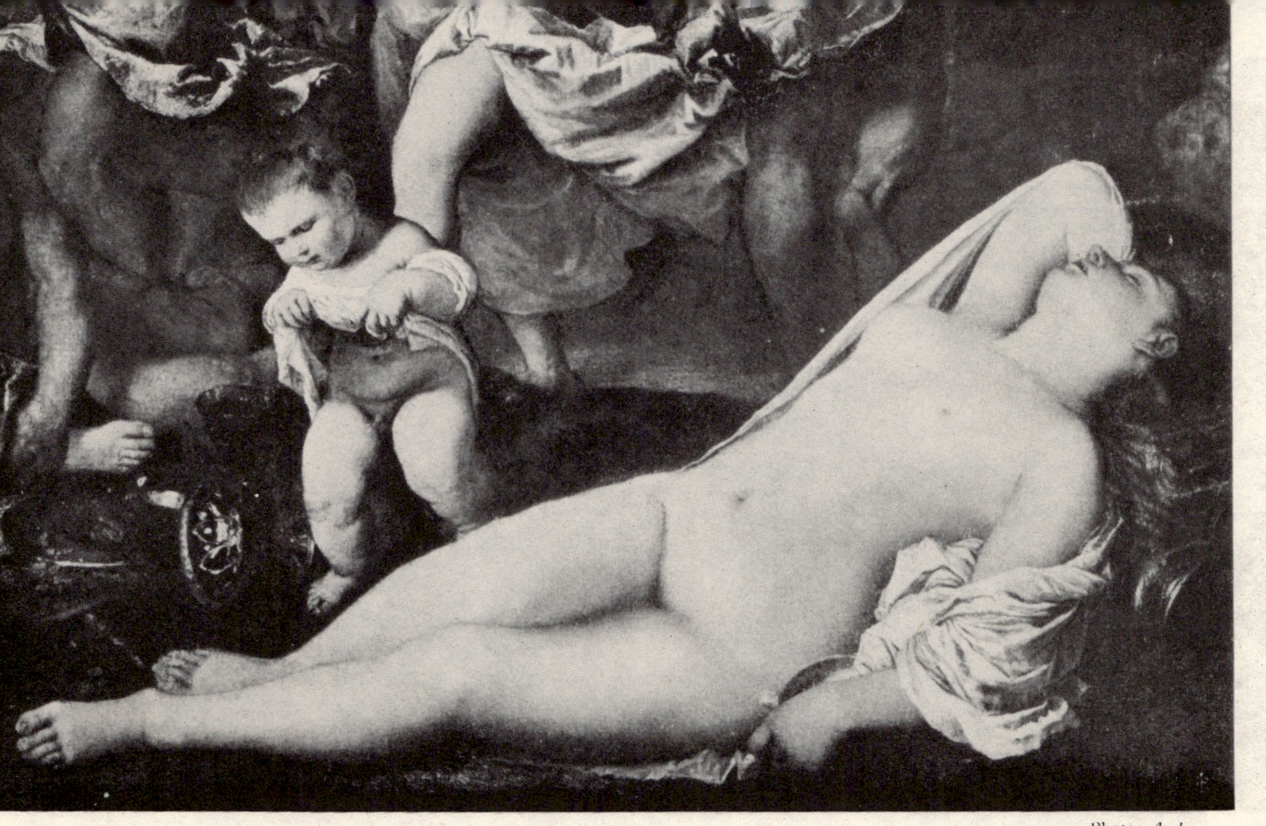

Photo: *Anderson*

Ariadne slumbering
Detail from "The Bacchanalia"
(Prado, Madrid)

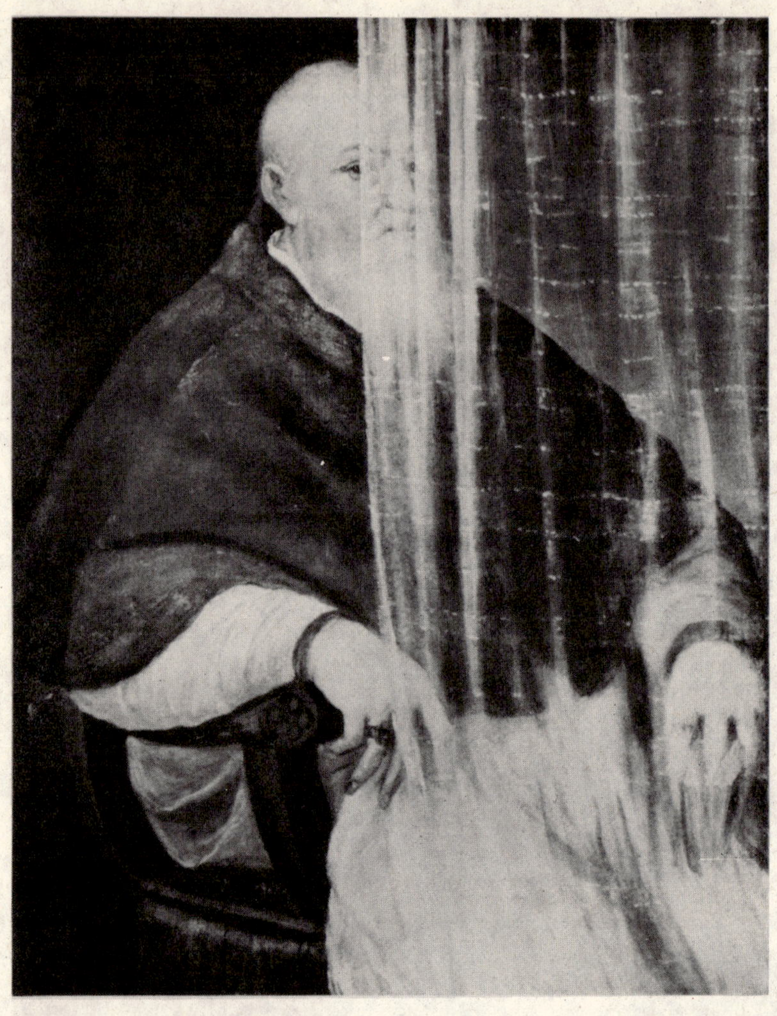

Photo: *John E. Johnson Art Collection*

Portrait of Filippo Archiuto
(Johnson Collection, Philadelphia)

IX

ON his way back to Venice, he stopped in Florence. He remained there alone with two apprentices, for Orazio, who had joined him in Rome, went straight on to Venice. Orazio was in love and could not bear to stay away long from Lucrezia, who was soon to be his wife.

The Master walked through the streets of Florence, under the calm sky, and it seemed to him that the entire city was filled with the sound of fear-inspiring, antique bronze: the bells that sounded the hours might have been brown bodies, created by a divine sculptor, swinging in the void, until even their form disintegrated. Even the nude figures in the paintings of Bronzino or Pontormo looked hard, as if they had been incised into metal, cold as if they had been hewn out of marble.

One evening, as he was admiring their jewel-like strength in the hall of a patrician prince, he heard the bells of the whole city ringing vespers: his heart sank at the haunting sound of the great bronze bodies that he imagined floating in the air. Servants came to escort him down the stairs, carrying lighted candles: as they moved, the little flames were blown backwards and, for a moment, he thought of death.

He went down the stairs and, as he stood below, he paused for a moment to wrap himself tightly in his cloak.

'Messer Ticiano,' a woman's voice called out from the dark spaces of the night. He started, looked round and saw, coming down the stairs he had just descended, and accompanied by servants carrying lights, a lady he failed to recognize. She was no longer young, but despite her slightly dishevelled appearance, she still showed traces of former beauty. She came up to him, took both his hands between her own and exclaimed: 'Maestro!'

The flickering light of the candles wavered in the draught under the portals.

'I am Tullia; do you remember?'

177

Tullia d'Aragona, the great beauty he had known long ago—now he recognized her. How many years had gone by since she used to come to his studio with Aretino!

'*Titian is not merely a painter and what he achieves is not art, it is a miracle,*' she recited. '*And all his portraits have a quality I cannot describe, a quality of divinity; as in heaven, in the paradise of souls, it would appear that God has concealed the paradise of our bodies, not painted, but . . .*' Here she stopped short, betrayed by her failing memory.

Yes, Titian remembered now: Sperone Speroni and his '*Dialogo d'amore*' between Tullia and Bernardo Tasso.

'*Not painted, but sanctified and glorified by his hands,*' she resumed, pressing his hands once more with an almost despairing fervour. Then she lifted them towards the light and said: 'God bless you.'

They went out together. Darkness was falling. She held herself very straight, re-arranging her hair from time to time, as she walked on, talking agitatedly. She told him that she had come to Florence a short time ago. She had left Sienna and her husband, Silvestro Guicciardi. She was now working hard. She had intended to send her *Dialogue on the Infinity of Love* to the printers, but now something had occurred that had upset her terribly. Duke Cosimo had decreed that very severe measures should be taken in Florence against the courtesans, ordering them to wear the infamous yellow stripe on their veils. She had never dreamt that she would have to submit to this ruling, and suddenly she found herself summoned before the magistrate's court. Thereupon she had addressed a petition to the Duchess Eleonora, asking to be spared this indignity—was she not a woman of letters and a married woman as well? She had just been to the palace of the Medici to solicit a favourable reception of her petition. What a world! she exclaimed —to cut the matter short, she now refused, as the Master could see for himself, to wear a veil like a stupid bashful housewife; she preferred to go around bare-headed! She was certainly not going to pretend to him that her past, with its legions of lovers, did not exist, but in what way did that diminish the value of her literary work?

Titian patted her arm kindly.

In her anger she looked beautiful again and the deepening twilight nearly effaced the traces that the years had left on her countenance. He remembered her young and gay, many years ago, when she described how she had posed as Salome for Moretta da Brescia, her fair hair contrasting against a dark background of laurels; and when

Bernardo Tasso had been her lover; and when Benedetto Varchi corrected her verses and the poet Muzio sang her praises, calling her 'Talìa'. And now that she was forty, and her bitter mouth was signed by the kisses of all her lovers, all those who saw her in the street were to have the right to call her a harlot!

She pulled herself together and continued to talk with dignity, for some noblemen from the Medici palace had come up to greet Titian. He had the wit to stop, making it appear a matter of urgency, and ask for information, about the courier service with Rome and Venice, at the same time excusing himself for this interruption to his companion, whose name must surely be known to them: Tullia d'Aragona, the poetess. . . . Their eyes popping out of their heads, they bowed.

The next day, when Tullia accompanied the Master to a picture gallery, she was able to acknowledge further salutes addressed to this literary celebrity of hers which he had underlined. The fact that the famous artist, who had never been suspected of libertinism, should show himself in public with the unfortunate woman who had reached the stage of having to defend herself with her back to the wall, was not to be without influence on the outcome of her petition. Three days later, Tullia saw it in the hands of the magistrates: Duke Cosimo himself had written on the margin: 'Granted in view of her being a poetess.

Titian was getting ready to leave the next day: joyous boys were singing in the streets, and he had ceased to hear the clangour of the bronze from the bell-towers. In the shop of a merchant who sold silks and embroideries, he listened to the songs the young boys improvised as they went along—about the maid-servants going about their duties, the cobbler sitting outside on his stool, and everyone who passed down the street.

From a pile of fine silk, he chose a present for Lavinia and bargained for a magnificent embroidered veil which he wanted to take home for his future daughter-in-law Lucrezia.

'It is worthy of a bride!' said the merchant, draping the veil over his shoulder and showing it off with his hand on his hip.

> *'Bellinchero tu sei*
> *Donzello del mio cuore! . . .'*

sang out the little boys who had been watching from outside, making off as swiftly as a swarm of bees.

To hell with economy, Titian thought, and he agreed to acquire the beautiful veil, although it cost the earth.

When Tullia came to say goodbye to him, he laid it over her head. It was almost too ostentatious for her, for by this time she had dared to go out with her head bare, breaking all the rules. At first she smiled, as every woman smiles whenever she receives a bizarre present selected for her by a man—but then a spasm contracted her thin face as she held back her tears.

He begged her to accept his gift and to be calm and serene. It hurt him to see how the first signs of suffering and misfortune had marked with humiliation the beautiful face he had known in the splendour of youth. She must be serene once more, he repeated. She was an artist herself. Would she do him a favour and not leave him with so sad a memory? He wanted her to go down into the streets and walk away proudly, wearing his veil. That would be the best farewell greeting: he would watch her from his window.

Tullia understood: this was to be the sudden cutting short of an unbearably pathetic situation. She walked away towards the sun with swift steps, her head bent a little—possibly to hide her tears.

People turned to look at her and look at the resplendent diaphanous drapery that floated around her like the mantle of the Madonna. Seeing her so alone, so disturbed and agitated, they imagined her surrounded by mysteries, excitements and disasters.

She disappeared in a side street: Titian thought that he would never meet her again in the difficult and complicated time to come.

*　　*　　*

At Birri Grande, all his family and the apprentices crowded round to welcome him in the happy spirit of Biblical personages welcoming a jovial patriarch.

Later, in his own room, Orazio regaled him with all the latest news. First and foremost, was his own decision to marry Lucrezia as soon as his father consented. It would be very soon, he hoped, and it would not bring about any change in their manner of living, as he was prepared to follow him and serve him wherever and whenever he desired. Then the young man described the stay in Venice of Leone Leoni, a well-known medallist much favoured by the Emperor and Messer Pietro, but anything but a pleasing personality, about whom one had heard very curious things. He had come to Venice accompanied by

one Martino, an honest youth who, when he returned to Milan, did
not want to go back with him; he had made contact with Venetian
artists, made friends with Orazio and admired Sansovino, and he
could not bear the idea of being bound again to that intriguer of a
medallist. The latter, by return of post, so to say, sent a ruffian to
Milan to murder the unfortunate youth. But Martino had been
fortunate enough to get away with a stab in the back and had succeeded
in slashing his assailant's face and having him put into prison.

'And what has Monsignorino been up to?' Titian asked in the end.
As a matter of fact, Monsignorino Pomponio had incurred a heavy
debt, but Orazio took good care not to say a word about it: with the
help of his aunt Orsa, he had succeeded in raising the sum to pay it off
by booking it under the heading of household expenses, carpenters'
work which had been necessary, and 'etceteras'.

Titian saw through the ruse, and every time he was charged with
'etceteras' in connection with household expenses, he thought that
Pomponio had been up to his tricks again.

What other news was there? he asked. Orazio informed him that
Caterina Sandella had left the house by the Canal Grande, the 'Aretine'
and their pasha: she had married that Messer Bartolo who had been
in love with her for a long time already. But someone who had not
succeeded in getting married was Lina, who had sat for the Venus:
Orazio had met her and she had begged him to think of her in case
his father should need a model. Don Lope da Soria was waiting
impatiently for Titian's return in connection with an important
commission but, as usual, the most impatient of all was Messer Pietro.

Soon the latter arrived with open arms, preceded by a little letter of
a few lines which were as many welcoming salvos. Once again Venice
was all around him, as always. But Titian, as always, desired only to
to get on with his work and to rid himself of the bitter savour of
human decadence—too swiftly the days, the months, the years were
slipping away. . . .

Hastily he sent for Lina.

X

THE new year of 1547 brought forth many fine new paintings and
many new events—weddings, deaths, births. The wedding of
Orazio, his dear son and faithful companion; the death of
François I, the King of France and Aretino's protector; the death of
Sebastiano del Piombo. But in the meantime a new birth was expected
in Messer Pietro's house: Angiola Zaffetta was pregnant and the
'divine Aretino' looked upon his belated paternity as a most auspicious
and fortunate omen. Then there was little Marco, the two-year-old
son of Titian's dear Toma Tito, who was continually being asked by
his doting parents whether he wanted to be an artist or a barrister.

'Say artist,' Lavinia gaily whispered into his ear, Lavinia who was
already sweetened by the flowering of her sixteen years.

They sang, they whimpered, they laughed all round him, these
members of the new generation who were thrusting their way joyfully
into the bitter-sweet sadness of life. Titian barred the way to their
restless energy, shutting himself up in the limbo of his studio. Two
enormous braziers filled with glowing firebrands warmed the milk-
white body of the beautiful Lina posing for a new series of paintings of
Venus reclining, and of Danae, in which he resumed in a more grandiose
manner the theme of the painting he had done in Rome the year
before.

Then the clement season returned, the braziers disappeared, towards
evening the gondolas returned to lie below the garden of the house
and the lovers reclined in them, kissing each other until nightfall.
Other gondolas moored at the entrance and discharged clients,
amateurs of the arts, but when they were not preceded by a marvellous
reputation, they had to be content with being received by Orazio.
The young man, courteous and diplomatic, reminded them that his
father's artistic production was monopolized by the Imperial Court,
the Papal Court and a few chosen clients such as the Duke of Urbino.
Nevertheless, he gave them to understand, there was some hope that

between commissions the Master might find the time to paint a portrait: some people were prepared to wait many months.

These manoeuvres were perfectly timed, so that the clients should not be distracted—for Tintoretto was beginning to acquire a reputation and to snatch all sorts of commissions and orders for portraits from his colleagues by accommodating the clients in every possible way. This popularity of his young rival might become a veritable inflation: Titian, who was always on his guard to defend his interests and the sale of his work, clenched his teeth angrily, so preventing himself from cursing. The devil take Tintoretto—that fellow would supplant him in the favour of the Emperor himself, if he could! And every time Titian went to Aretino's house, he could not help casting a sidelong glance at the decorations Tintoretto had carried out there. Messer Pietro always asked him into another room, for he knew that his old friend's temper became frayed when he had to sit under Tintoretto's Apollo and Marsyas, Argus and Mercury. 'Come, come over here,' he would say, giving him the softest cushions and the most comfortable chair in another room.

Aretino passed over the subject of Tintoretto, but the presence of the decoration with its skilfully painted figures revealed the good understanding between them, which was all the more surprising to Titian when he remembered the famous anecdote which had amused all Venice. Messer Pietro, loyal to the triumvirate in his allegiance to Titian, had directed a string of abuse against Tintoretto, but the latter, who was no fool, had flattered him with the request for a sitting. Then, while Messer Pietro, who was sitting in all his glory in the middle of the young artist's studio, looked round, preparing to lay down the law in lapidary sentences, he suddenly saw right under his nose a two-edged dagger and behind it, Tintoretto's hallucinated eyes. He very nearly died of fright. The artist then half-closed his eyes and stepped backwards slowly, grinning at his terrified sitter, who had grown mortally pale, as he announced that there was no need for him to fear this instrument, which he always used to take the measures, and, as he said after a calculated pause, the divine Messer Pietro was two-and-a-half daggers high. It had been a rather drastic and primitive way of gaining his friendship.

Poor Messer Pietro lost an ounce of his boastful dignity whenever this incident returned to his mind or was mentioned by one of his gossiping acquaintances. Titian, restraining his disapproval, succeeded in making him understand that he had never heard the story. It was something he could shrug off lightly, now that he was sealing his last letter to the Emperor. He had been invited to Augsburg, to join Charles V there—and he had accepted. The news spread immediately.

'His Majesty forces him to join him, furnishing him with the money and all other things necessary for the journey: Caesar Imperator demands the presence of his Apelles,' they wrote from Birri Grande.

The old Apelles let them chatter away. It was certainly useful to begin soon with the exploration of new places; Venice was no longer what it used to be, the financial situation might decline, lesser men were being admitted to the Serene Republic, the combinations with bankers and merchants had become listless.

But in the meanwhile, he shut himself up in his studio and continued to paint the beautiful Lina. Aunt Orsa was not too happy about it; she was afraid her brother might become too fond of the model. He was now well over seventy, and the company of far younger people could lead to morbid attachments. The wise spinster, whenever she had a chance, went through the family title-deeds to make sure that none were missing—it would not be difficult to tell whether, in an excess of generosity, her brother had used the income from the mill at Ansogne, or from a certain field or a certain wood in favour of his Venus, who remained stretched out so patiently hour after hour to help him create the series of masterpieces of the new art.

Titian was not without domestic psychology: he never indulged in his usual scrupulous precision when it was a question of entering the sums with which he rewarded his muse for her priceless presence in his studio.

Assuming an air of indifference, Orsa would try and question Orazio: had Lina not been wearing a new gown today? And yesterday, had she not arrived in a gondola—very nearly like a patrician lady? At the time when she knew the sitting would be over, she would linger in the garden, ordering the rearrangement of certain jars, once near the garden gate, another time near the stairs, and keep her eye on the studio door. At last the lovely Lina would emerge, wearing her everyday gown, and without a gondola waiting at the landing-stage; she would curtsey to the Master's sister, inquire about her rheumatic pains, which Orsa exhibited like a halo, and take her leave with another curtsey and a look as though butter would not melt in her mouth.

'She's too pale,' Orsa would then say to Orazio—adding that she would not be surprised if the girl turned out to be pregnant. Heaven knows by whom—but it was to be expected that, in the sacred name of art, she would play a shabby trick on her protector and introduce another baby to the house at Birri Grande. What else was one to think, considering that Aretino had become a father a second time in the first days of September? It was a lovely little girl, called Austria, she had been told, bonny and chubby, a real credit to her father's renewed youth. The best thing would be for Titian to go to Augsburg as soon as possible. Yet the departure had to be delayed to the first days of March in the coming year, as it would not be wise to travel in the rigours of winter.

*   *   *

'A brace of pheasants, no more, is waiting for you at dinner together with the Signora Angiola Zafetta and myself; you must come, so that, seeing us continually devoting ourselves to having our fun, old age, that spy of death, may never tell the latter that we are old. . . .' With this little letter, Messer Pietro indicated to Titian the best manner of preparing for the Nativity—in the intimacy of good company.

Before the board loaded with delicacies they opened their hearts to each other again. Aretino emptied one goblet of wine after the other —drinking to Angiola, to Titian, to Cupid, to Life, to Poetry, to Painting—ah! he only needed a lute to sing his joy aloud! And actually, on New Year's Day, 1548, the lute arrived, a present from Buonconte di Carpegna. Roaring like Orpheus with a sore throat, strumming a verse on the strings, he improvised good wishes for the journey that Titian would now undertake to join Caesar Imperator. A member of the Fugger family was with them, the famous family of rich merchants whose headquarters were in Augsburg, but who also had a sumptuous dwelling in Venice. Titian tried to find out all he could about the journey, and the kind of weather he might expect to find when he arrived. He felt as though he were already due to leave the next morning.

XI

TITIAN immediately felt at home in Augsburg, the august city. It was a home that was in every respect dissimilar from everything he was accustomed to, but yet it seemed to be home, in a way a place seems home which one finds in a dream, feeling one has always known it.

Everywhere there was a coming and going of orderly and cordial crowds. He felt that at any moment he might happen to recognize one of the passers-by, who would turn out to be a familiar friend, an inseparable companion. But it was obvious that he could not recognize any of these people, who were not the lean, loud-voiced eye-flashing Italians of the lagoon. They were blond, northern stallions with almost invisible eyes, strong and stout, either walking on a pair of great legs like pillars, or riding real stallions whose powerful pacing struck sparks from the cobblestones.

It was a coming and going of well-disciplined crowds, as befitted a city elected as the Imperial residence. Through the narrow streets they walked as quietly as contented artisans or serene conspirators— or as one does in a house when one is afraid of disturbing an important visitor.

This visitor, with a few of his companions, was to be the only really familiar face that Titian recognized—the Emperor.

It was a great relief to install himself at Court. And once again the King expressed the always welcome, now almost habitual wish to have another portrait of himself. This was the first stimulating event which shook Titian out of the dream-atmosphere of his arrival, or at least the first event which gave him a concrete reason for waking up completely. Never before had he felt dreams and reality melting into each other so easily. The quality of illusion which had characterized the atmosphere of his arrival was now assuming the physiognomy of everyday life, and everyday life seemed about to be transfigured into a consoling sense of well-being. With his cousin Cesare and his assistant Lamberto

Sustris, the Master was leading a relatively social life as was his custom, but he now tried to explain to himself that the dream-atmosphere which was still surrounding him was a feeling he had acquired through the passing of the years—one of the more sensitive moods of senility. Was it old age that made everything around him appear like a dream? Or was it the fact that he was in a strange country and had not many connections with the others?

Now, however, he woke up entirely, though he did not know what the cause of his disturbance had been. In any case, he realized he was not at home, but in a place where all the languages of Europe could be heard, where formal courtesy was at its height, and where it was possible to meet the most interesting personalities of the moment.

The Emperor showed himself only rarely in public. People said his character was becoming increasingly sombre, but the real reason for his lack of mobility was an acute attack of gout. Ferdinand, his brother, was as different from him as possible. He had now come back from Innsbruck, and immediately started organising hunts, banquets, reunions and concerts. Their sister, Maria of Hungary, joined in with her placid and unshakable determination to sustain a conversation on every possible and impossible subject under the sun.

Titian had a magnificent programme of portraits to carry out: the cousins Maximilian and Ferdinand; the councillor Nicholas Perrenot de Grenvella and his son Anthony, Bishop of Arras; Johann Friedrich, the Elector of Saxony; the entire family of the Duke of Bavaria; Emanuele Filiberto of Savoy and the Duke of Alba.

The ladies here, though more modest than those of Italy, were nevertheless unconstrainedly at ease and amiable. More than once the celebrated old artist, when he was introduced with great ceremony, was saluted by the ladies with a profound curtsey and the kissing of hands. They smiled like children, their eyebrows had not been plucked, their fresh faces were not smothered with unguents, but their skins looked clearer still against the dark fur of their collars as they rose from their curtseys, their left hands holding the gilded chains that sparkled on the sombre amaranth of their dark robes. . . . The Duchess of Lorraine, the Princess of Orange, Dorothea, Jacobina. . . . It was more than he could do to remember all the names.

In the second place came the families of Augsburg's great merchants and patrons—the Fuggers, naturally, and the Welsers. They had magnificent houses with façades painted by Burkmair, Breu, Ulrich

Apt. Titian made his cousin remind him of the names of these artists and pulled a long face when he was confronted by the fleshless Nordic art; in the old churches as well as in the halls of the palaces he was always seeing pitiful statues, drowning in their ample draperies like consumptive creatures covered with mattresses. Their art was really not up to much; he noticed it by the way in which Emanuel Amberger, the artist, and others pressed around him as though attempting to snatch some of his ardent energy.

There were pleasing features among the decoration of the Fugger house—but naturally they were the work of Italian artists, Antonio Ponzano and others; by and large the great house was like a vast cabinet of curiosities, an emporium filled with nereids, tritons, Roman emperors, red and black marble, vases, masks, stucco work, lilies, Moorish queens. Every visit to these splendours ended with an admiring inspection of the most luxurious bathroom, with an adjoining grotto. Cousin Cesare nudged Sustris in the ribs, giggling at this display of wealth by the owners of so exaggerated a temple of hygiene; it was obvious that if they had possessed a finer picture-gallery, they would not have had to boast about the courtly surroundings in which they were wont to perform their ablutions! The masters of the house did not take long to understand this. Immediately the canvases Titian had brought with him appeared on their walls, following a recompense of three thousand crowns, and marking an important date in the family history. A date after which the new masterpieces of the Latin world were shown with greater pride than the stuccoed latinizing comforts of the bathroom.

*　　*　　*

Titian arrived at the actual residence of the Emperor by traversing two quiet, narrow streets where, as always, people walked with the soundless steps of conspirators—conspiracies of beer, he thought to himself as he restrained a regurgitation, promising himself once again not to touch that beverage any more. He went to work, without breaking the sad silence in which the Emperor's features appeared fined down and very pale. Titian concentrated on his work, but the intense seriousness of his sitter, the indefinably neuralgic tone of everything that surrounded him, made it possible to guess at the weight of his problems and anxieties. His Majesty was very tired; he had to assist at intermin-

able meetings devoted to theological examinations in which the
greatest experts ordered the clerks to cover sheet after sheet with
comments on Luther's theories. There was much talk about this all
over the town, and also much confusion. Queen Maria was past-mistress
of the latter; during the sittings for the portrait that Titian had now
begun of her, she pretended to foresee conclusions and discussed the
minutiae of possible and impossible arguments. Ah! she sighed, the
Great Reformation! And Luther and Calvin, the Jesuit missions to
the Far East, all the ups and downs of the Council of Trent, and Adam
and Eve themselves had to pass muster. Even her maids of honour
could talk of little else. No wonder that the Emperor had attached
to his person an illiterate valet, who could not understand the first
thing about all these matters, but was very zealous in serving his master,
and had no interests outside his duties, except in eating, drinking,
sleeping and making love.

Titian also began the portraits of Johann Friedrich, the Elector of
Saxony, and Moritz, the leader of the Lutherans, who were calmly
imprisoned in the adiposity of their well-being; they talked of nothing
but horses and jousts held in the fine Hippodrome in the residence. The
Granvellas, father and son, who were also sitting for Titian, were the
only people there capable of understanding the Latin quality of the
taciturn Master, and they succeeded, with subtlety and intelligence, in
winning his sympathies and his consideration.

He now went back to working at the Emperor's equestrian portrait.
Charles V was beginning to have a mute, fond devotion for this
picture. It contained certain mysteries, such as the frailty of human-
kind, even though it is armoured with the steel of morality, while all
around the light of the sun is going out, in those lovely fading colours
which Titian had made his own. And by the height of ingenuity,
instead of making his severe Caesar ride a solemn, heavy quadruped,
he had sat him on a small, fiery black horse, young in muscle and
hocks, young of eye—like Prince Philip, the Emperor's son and heir.

Yes, Charles was beginning to have a strange devotion for this
picture. But the fact that he wanted another portrait done immediately,
revealed that there was something about this equestrian portrait,
which had only just been completed, that saddened him when he
contemplated it.

Instead of making further comments, the Emperor limited himself
to smiling affectionately at the spirited little black horse that was

bearing him away, then he made a gesture, pointing to his poor legs that were tormented by the gout. He sat down.

This was the age when so many things came to torment the heart. Titian painted him thus, sitting in his chair, sitting still and looking at the world.

XII

WHAT might be happening in Venice while he was so busy, he frequently stopped to ask himself. And although he was receiving news all the time, he wrote very often to Orazio, to Messer Pietro informing him of the possibility that the Emperor might grant an annuity to Austria, and asking him to charge Lorenzetto, the courier, to furnish him with half a pound of lacquer; he wrote to Toma Tito, telling him to remind his brother Francesco of certain interests at Pieve and other business, and to have good care of Orsa's health, for she had been ailing of late. Then he wrote once again to Messer Pietro asking him to give greetings to this one and the other, also the ill-used Lorenzo Lotto, about whose unceasing misfortunes he had been informed. At the moment he was having a law-suit with a pair of Venetian clients, whose portraits he had painted, and Paris Bordone had been called in to value the pictures. Yes, he could really afford to send a greeting to Lotto now, from the bottom of the Imperial cornucopia, well away from everything, and through the shameless mouth of Aretino. If he could have imagined how he, Titian, was honoured here, how deeply people bowed when he came to Court with his golden chain round his neck, and what toasts they proposed to him, and how many golden crowns came jingling into his purse—poor old Lotto!

The month of May went by, and Titian, in excellent form, was now completing the portrait. In June, Charles V signed a decree doubling his pension, which he drew on the treasury of Milan; in July he received more portrait orders. In August, the Emperor left for Ulm, to continue his struggle against the Lutherans; in September Titian left as well, but first he stayed in Innsbruck, where he received from King Ferdinand the concession of a large stretch of timbered land. Thereupon he returned to Venice.

Never before had Toma Tito been seen so often at the house in private confabulation with Titian. Whatever was the matter with them? asked Aunt Orsa, who was now bent double with arthritis,

191

but more inquisitive than ever. They were discussing business, Lavinia said soothingly; now that Francesco had settled down in Pieve and Orazio had his own family to think about, the 'signor padre' had no one he could trust except his well-beloved cousin Toma.

Nevertheless, there was something mysterious afoot. Lavinia had noticed it: she was a girl with subtle intuitions. Her father would be in a gloomy mood for days, he would go out in a gondola with Toma Tito, come home and shut himself up in his studio. But it was not as though he were doing much work. Lavinia, between her aunt, who grumbled all day long about her pains, and the black depression of her father, resolved to take an active initiative in the affairs of the family. Aunt Orsa, from her chair, would still send for the man and poke her nose into all the supplies, finding fault with everything and telling her niece to be on her guard. But Lavinia was a Vecellio, one could not teach her much on the question of domestic economy—and she believed that every ducat she managed to save must go to increase her dowry. This hoarding instinct of hers pleased Titian. Well done, he said, she was a true Vecellio; And as though this fresh energy had encouraged him, and because his voyage to Augsburg had been so profitable, he devoted himself to schemes for the employment of his newly acquired capital: he now bought the freehold of the ground surrounding his house. Now, when he walked in the garden, wrapped in his fur cape, he looked around him as though his property extended as far as Burano, embracing all the frozen waters. Later, in April, he bought various precious objects: then he fell in love with an organ, but he could not make up his mind to acquire so expensive a toy and combined an exchange for a portrait of the ambitious purveyor, Allesandro dagli Organi.

'An organ!' Aunt Orsa cried, shocked and amazed. 'What does he want to do with it?' She could think of nothing but her brother's impending ruin through such extravagance.

They would acquire it without spending a penny—in exchange for a portrait, Lavinia shouted into her ear, for now she was becoming increasingly deaf from day to day. 'It's an exchange for a portrait,' was what she told her aunt about many other things that were being acquired, chiefly so as not to have to account to her about everything. She took care to have the new crystal table-glass well polished, for the old set was chipped, no longer complete, only good for the servants, or for the house at Pieve.

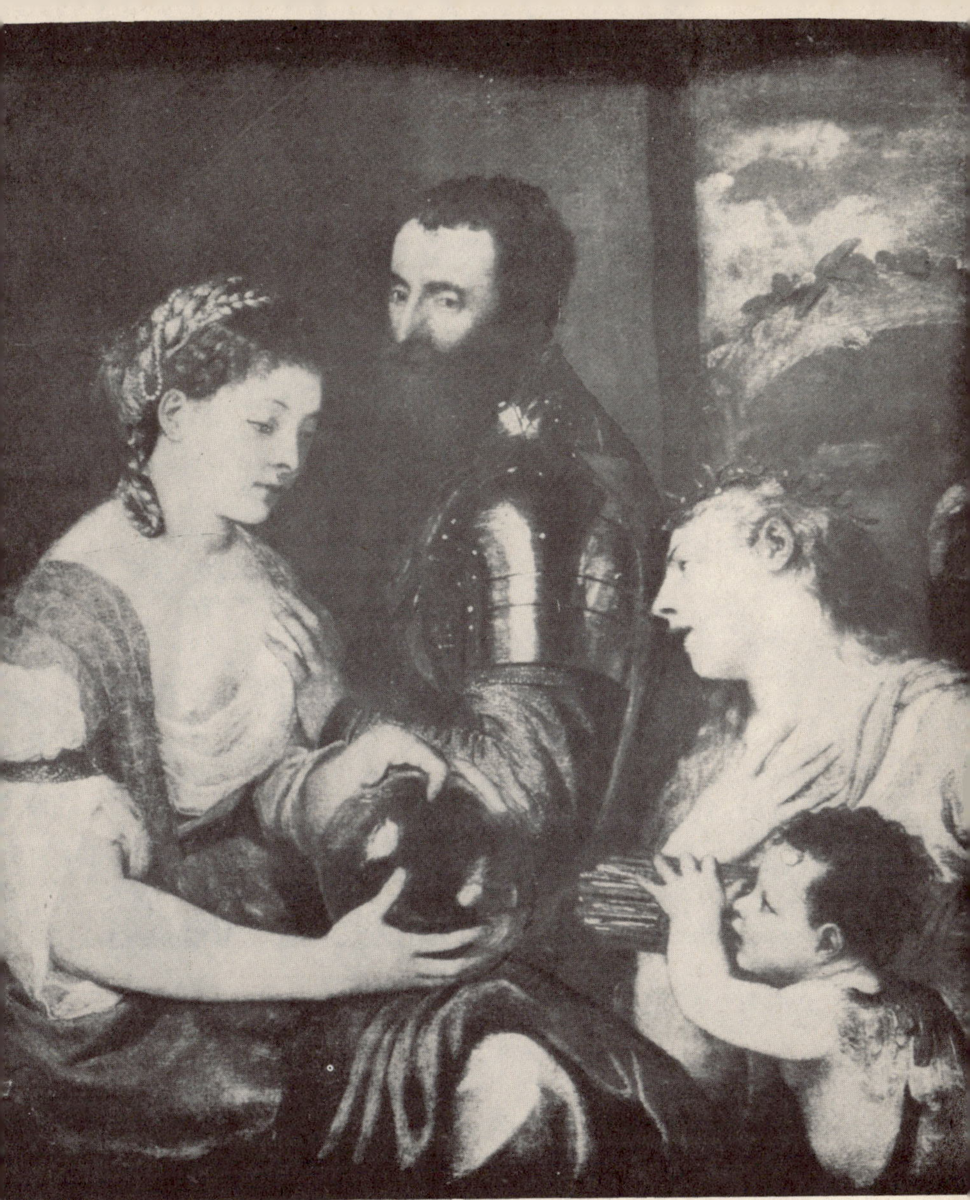

Allegory
(Louvre, Paris)

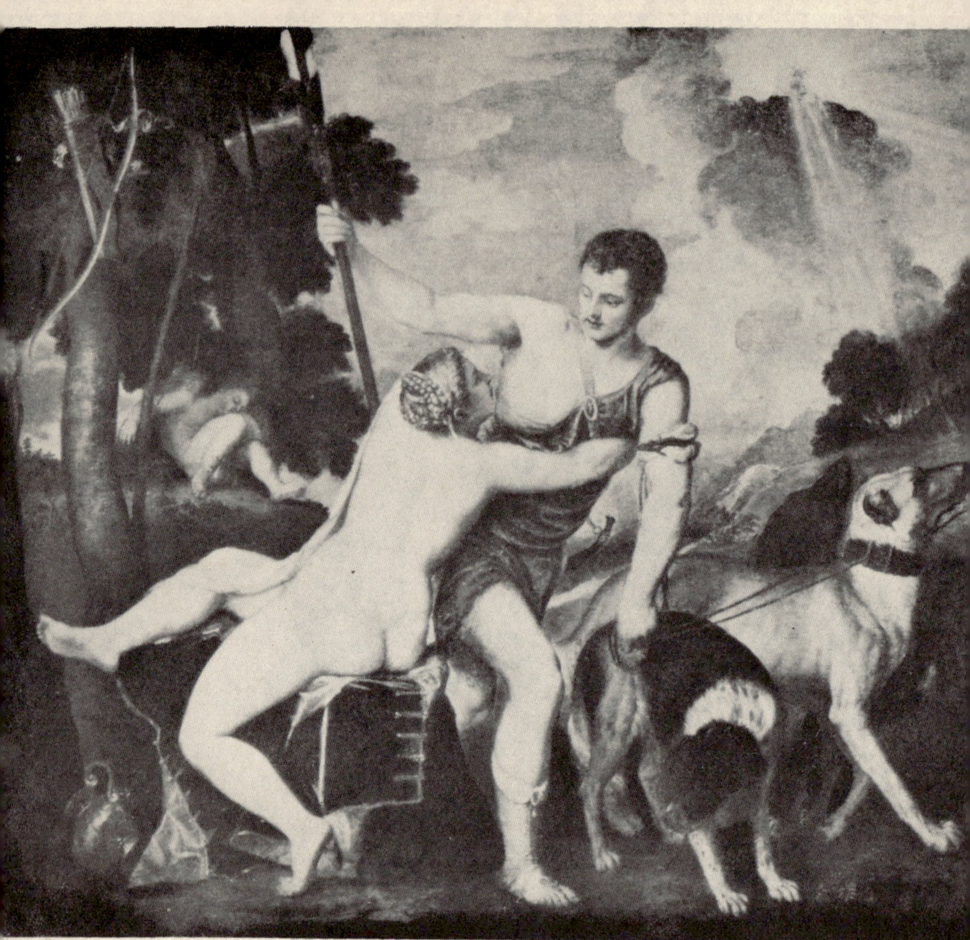

Venus and Adonis
(Prado, Madrid)

This slight euphoria of well-being which was cheering Lavinia was also beginning to put her father into a better mood: he began to work again, concentrating on the portrait of Alessandro dagli Organi, of Elisabetta Quirini, the sister of Girolamo, the Patriarch of Venice; and on the replica of a portrait of Charles V, which was to be sent to Ferrante Gonzaga, so that there should be no difficulties or unpleasant surprises concerning the pension on Milan, which had now been doubled. Those blessed pensions were his cross: the Emperor signed the decrees, but before these paper promises turned into actual cash, there were a thousand complications, delays, and endless solicitations. He would have wished the gold to roll in, more than all the cabinets and padlocked chests could contain, great bags filled with coins as in a miser's dream. And while poor Lorenzo Lotto left Venice to go to Ancona and left some of his paintings with Sansovino, Titian was planning new financial undertakings: he must now return to Augsburg, give His Majesty a rest and begin working at a portrait of his son Philip.

★ ★ ★

After his arrival, he immediately went to pay his respects to the Emperor and he realized at once that it really was necessary to give him a rest; it was the son's turn to be painted.

The Emperor looked extremely ill; in a short time he had aged by ten years. He was as pale as wax, and it seemed as though even the effort of smiling was too much for him. But as always, he seemed to enjoy talking to his favourite artist. He thanked him affably for the print Titian had brought him as a present, one of the few works he had carried out during the last months of idleness. It was entitled 'The Submersion of Pharaoh', etched by the pupil Domenico delle Grache after a drawing 'by the hand of the great and immortal Titian'.

As he sat looking at the print, the sovereign looked even more cadaverous. 'And Aretino, what is he up to now?' he asked, as though hoping that the very fact of hearing about that gay and merry person-age would bring the colour of life back to his own cheeks.

Titian reported that he had seen Messer Pietro frequently of late, at farewell banquets; now the possibility of his receiving a cardinal's hat was being much discussed.

'Messer Pietro a Cardinal?' the Emperor said with a smile. Then he made an allusion to a composition which he wanted to discuss with

N

Titian, a picture that he had wished to have him paint for a long time already. He would talk to him about it at length another time. While they were talking, Titian could feel Philip's eyes fixed on him intently, as though he were some rare animal.

He was to see father and son again many times. While the life of the one seemed about to be extinguished in solitary recollection, the other's life was pulsating feverishly in the blue veins of his temples: the sensual mouth moved to give orders, short and sharp as stabs, while his white hands—almost feminine hands—caressed his small chestnut-coloured beard: the hands were sensual too, the hands of an irascible person.

He would have been very handsome, in spite of his moods, if the legs that sustained his twenty-four year old frame had been more sinewy. Whenever he forgot to don thick hose, it was obvious that they were really far too lean. Nevertheless, the portrait that Titian began to paint of his new young master was the best reply art could give to his ambitions. Philip was represented standing and armed, the expression of his face made more gentle, the delicacy of his pale skin stressed. The ladies thrilled at the mere sight of that mouth, imagining the cruel kisses it could give. In his exquisitely chiselled armour, the prince resembled a rare little fighting cock, as he rested one hand on the hilt of his sword and the other on the helmet which was laid down beside the steel gloves.

One after the other they came to inspect the picture: the prince's aunt, Queen Maria of Hungary, the princes, the Fuggers, Lukas Cranach the painter, and other colleagues. Philip, whose pride was as firm as a nail in the centre of an anvil, warmed towards this beautiful image of himself. His father had the old Apelles brought to his rooms and congratulated him. Then he began to discuss the composition to which he had already referred several times. Now he spoke of it again, with pathos: he wanted it to be the most lovely thing on earth. And just because he found himself lingering so long on earth, he wanted the painting to represent heaven.

Heaven—and he himself in heaven.

Titian was thinking of life, of so many little things belonging to life: how necessary it was for him to return to Venice, to adjust his affairs with the Great Council, to look after his household at Birri Grande— for even Orsa was no longer there, she had passed away a short time ago.

Heaven, the Emperor repeated, as though he himself were already passing on. It would have to be a vast composition, he said, where among rays of light one would see the Trinity, the Evangelists, the Saints, his own image with Isabella, his sister Maria, his son Philip: a glorious apotheosis of his religious struggles, the expression of his great longing for the peace of the spirit.

He was already beginning to think about his own abdication in favour of his son. Heaven . . . peace . . . he kept on murmuring.

*   *   *

Titian appeared to have found peace in luxury, surrounded by all the cosmopolitan celebrities. His frequent journeys to and fro between Venice and Augsburg, between the meetings of the triumvirate at Aretino's table and the society of the Imperial city, seemed to act on him like a tonic.

In Venice, the Doge himself inquired about his sojourns abroad. Orazio informed him in detail about all the commissions snatched by the celebrated Tintoretto, who was all out to become ever more celebrated. There was a '*pictor celer*' in Augsburg as well, Titian wrote to Aretino and to Messer Jacopo: this was Lukas Cranach, the Protestant painter of Wittemberg, who was in the service of the Elector Johann Friedrich, himself a prisoner in Augsburg. The Elector, who was known to be extremely adverse to physical exertion, would send every morning, after he had finished his regular reading, for his painter and would make him paint something until it was time to go to table, where he proceeded every day to augment his already impressive weight. The girth of the enormous Elector of Saxony increased from day to day, and so did the number of pictures executed with such celerity by his artist. Thus it happened that when they both had to leave for Innsbruck in February, 1551, it seemed as though all the tribes of the Holy Bible were engaged on an exodus, what with the vast person of the prince and the cases, rolls and parcels of the painter. Among these pictures there was even a little portrait Cranach had done of Titian.

But many, many pictures by 'Thucia', as the Germans called the Venetian painter, had come into being in Augsburg.

Now Venice was again taking from him the patent of the *Senseria*, owing to his frequent absences. But in Augsburg, Philip gave him the commission to paint a Saint Margaret for him, who was to be a splendid martyr as well as a beautiful woman. The prince's treasurer paid the fee—two hundred and thirty ducats. He also received further compensations from Maria of Hungary for the figures of Sisyphus, Tantalus, Prometheus and Ixias he had painted for her.

When he got back to Venice, he began the much discussed composition for the Emperor. This was to be his farewell to his great patron— a glorious parting gift, a last offering. However, he began to feel pessimistic about his future when his new pension of five hundred scudos was granted at Innsbruck.

Now he settled definitely in Venice and once again he sat at table with Aretino, though this time in the latter's new house, on the Riva del Carbon at San Luca, into which he had moved with all the books, the musical instruments, the roasting-spits, the cut glass. . . .

There they sat once again, at table, round a turkey stuffed with three different kinds of meat. Tirelessly, they fêted their unceasing friendship, the restitution of Titian's patent and the imminent betrothal of Lavinia to Cornelio Sarcinelli.

It was March, 1552.

PART IV

I

DURING one of Titian's absences from Venice, while he was in
Augsburg, a pedantic examiner of the Serene Republic, accompanied by an even more pedantic clerk armed with pen
and paper, presented himself at Birri Grande. They wished to compile
dates for the register, the civil status of the illustrious artist, etcetera,
etcetera. Orazio furnished them with all the dates he knew, and asked
them to make further enquiries from Don Paolo, the parish priest of
San Giovanni Novo.

The toothless old man was delighted to prove how excellent his
memory remained. He testified to having blessed the marriage between
Titian and Cecilia, and added; 'The said Cecilia lying in bed and there
were present the goldsmith Nicolò, Geronimo the apprentice, Silvestro
the stone-mason and Francesco Vecelli, and very joyfully we all dined
together that evening.'

Toma Tito was informed of these rectifications and registrations and
Orazio could not help telling him of his vague suspicion about the
existence of a natural son of his father's, saying that there was probably
some sort of legitimation or some baptismal document to be registered.
Toma, as the expert barrister and advocate that he was, displayed a
great inclination to doubt this. He promised to talk to Titian about it
when he returned, but it was not mentioned again.

All sorts of rumours were circulating—people said the Master had
died suddenly, without even receiving the holy oils, nobody knew
where, possibly on a journey. Others again affirmed that the artist had
been seen several times at a place on the outskirts of the city, visiting
a nurse who was bringing up a little daughter of his, who was only a
few years old. It was the least one would expect of so assiduous a visitor
to Aretino's house. But Messer Pietro himself denied that Titian
possessed these fiery attributes—naturally it gave him another pretext
for yet another letter. After having confessed to Sansovino that he
could not succeed in liberating himself of the brothel, the great letter-

writer ended his missive, dated January, 1553, with the words:

'. . . Titian never does this. What amazes me in him is that whoever he sees, and wherever he may find himself, he will fondle them and kiss them, and he will entertain them with similar youthful pranks without going any further. Truly, we should follow his example and correct our behaviour.'

But when he wrote in February of the same year, he had again lost his head about a new beauty.

'. . . Donata, whose appearance is rather that of a Goddess than of a human woman, and who is thus made that a thousand subtle tongues could not express the excellence of her shapely person. . . .'

He had Donata on the brain, but at the same time, he delighted in describing how he loved to play with his beloved little daughter Austria; now he would buy a golden string for her hair, another time silken slippers and many-coloured gowns. He asked Titian to do a painting of her as a little angel, with his delicate magical touch. Then he suddenly left everything and went to Rome in the suite of Guido-baldo d'Urbino for the inauguration of Pope Julius III, so as to see what could be done about his cardinal's hat.

Titian had taken up work again with a will. He had painted two replicas with variants of the portrait of Philip, because the one he had done in Augsburg had been sent to England with the treaties about the marriage of this prince to Mary Tudor: furthermore he had finished the Saint Margaret, a Venus and Adonis, and now he had promised to execute a new work for the same patron—a new 'poem' representing Perseus and Andromeda. He was finishing the 'Gloria' for Charles V, as well as a portrait of the Doge Trevisan, and on the 15th August, 1554, he signed a contract to paint an apotheosis of the Doge kneeling between the Saints.

While Philip was celebrating his nuptials with the English Queen, it seemed to him that he was holding a parallel festivity in conceding Lavinia's hand to Sarcinelli. Aretino had returned from Rome: he had to be content with having been dubbed a Knight of Saint Peter's, with a benefice of only eighty scudos. While he was giving directions to Lodovico Dolci about a projected dialogue the latter was preparing to write, he sent Titian his good wishes for Lavinia in a letter which was a masterpiece of affectionate spontaneity. The Master read it aloud to his daughter as she was posing for her portrait in his studio: she, how-ever, was trying to persuade the 'signor padre', appealing to his generosity to let her have such and such a piece of furniture, or such and such a roll of cloth out of the storeroom for her dowry. She was to receive a great deal, thanks to her father's affection, about two thousand ducats to be paid to her in the course of the next two years, as well as jewellery and silver-plate. In view of this agreement he succeeded through his future son-in-law, who was from Ceneda, in obtaining the last instalment of his fee for an altar-piece he had painted in 1547 for the Cathedral of Serravalle, which was in the neighbourhood of Ceneda. He solicited the payment of other sums which were owing to him as well. Then, furious about some new debts Pomponio had incurred and wishing to prove the impeccability of his behaviour without losing too much, he wrote to the Duke of Mantua asking him to transfer to one of his nephews the benefice of Medole, which that rogue of a Monsignorino was enjoying.

Lavinia interceded and begged her father to forgive him—she did not want her wedding to take place under such gloomy auspices. But he was adamant.

Philip II's marriage did not seem to be taking place under very fortunate auspices either. Ottavio Farnese had put himself under the protection of the King of France after the occupation of Parma by the Spaniards, and this had led to new hostilities between the two great powers. Charles V had retired to the Monastery of Saint Juste, while Philip had been elected as ruler of the Netherlands. So new brawls and struggles ensued. Titian grumbled and cursed, foreseeing all the complications and delays which would befall his work at the Imperial Court, now that he had almost bled himself white to prepare a happy wedding for his daughter. Dear, sweet Lavinia—if only she would really be happy! And he caressed her as though he were giving her his benediction

II

Wᴴᴬᵀ the world was saying was true: they had given out that he was dead, had they? Yes, he was ill, and had only come back to life because he had promised to paint an altar-piece for the church of Santa Maria di Medole. And he was alive because he was painting. They said he had illegitimate children? Yes, he had a lovely little girl, Emilia, eight years old. Her mother had died at her birth.

Now that he was more lonely than ever before, now that Lavinia was happily married and the Emperor had abdicated at Juste, where he too was alone, and would never again meet the artist who had painted him in all his glory, if not in Heaven—now, Titian sent from time to time for his little daughter. He would play with her: it grieved him that she had not yet got accustomed to his white grandfather beard, and then he sent her to run around in the garden, and gave her fruit and toys. She stayed with him for a few days before going back to Pieve, and he watched her from the window, while she played games with the maid or occupied herself alone by throwing stones into the lagoon.

Dear God, everybody round him was dying, and this little mouse aged eight was the most living spark of life he knew. Aretino had told him that poor Tullia d'Aragona had died in Rome a short time ago—and she was still young. Gaspara Stampa had died two years earlier. The Doge Trevisan had died, and hardly had he painted the portrait of his successor, Venier, when the latter died as well. One could say that his Emperor was also dead, in his retreat at Juste.

It was obvious that new lives must be born, new phenomena must appear—and one of these was the little mouse in her long skirts, who ran in and out of the plants at Birri Grande, the most charming novelty he had known in his old age. Others were getting inured to the work which he directed: the Dutchman Sustris was making excellent progress, the pupil who had worked so much with him and with Cesare at Augsburg. But others were still pushing their way to the fore in the world of art which he had created—Tintoretto, whose activities never ceased, and recently Paolo da Verona who, at Titian's instigation, had received a premium for a decoration a year ago.

Yet in all the novelties that were now appearing, there was more of the old left than in the continuous inventiveness of his own work. And he began to design figures on the canvas with the light of his penetrating genius.

What did they mean by painting, design, colour and composition when they wrote about it—Aretino, Vasari, Domenichino, il Dolce? He had noticed that when they were faced with his works, with the indefinable vibration with which he constructed figures and objects, they lagged on behind, pursuing uneven, worn-out ideas and indulging in partisan dialogues. He remained unattainable, his youth continually renewed in the antiquity of his new inventions. Like a cat seeking the warmth, he coiled up on the glowing cinders of the vital, serious, eternal themes he loved: Venus, Venus over and over again, women in the woods, Diana, myths. . . .

In the evening he washed his eyes with distilled water and rested with care. And then he would begin to work again.

At times he noticed that Messer Pietro's humour was declining, and he would be reminded of life and death—the thought of death came back as it had come quite suddenly in Florence, when he had heard the great bronze bodies of the bells agonizing in the evening air.

Then he would look at his things—his property. For his painting was his property, like the gold of Lavinia's dowry, like everything there was in his house, secured by bolts and bars.

As he was struggling against these thoughts, tensed up to resist discouragement, the first to betray him was none other than Aretino himself.

At dawn they came panting to Birri Grande, calling out excitedly before the door. Titian was still in bed and Orazio went down to find out the reason of the commotion.

'He has gone! He has gone, struck down by the apoplexy!'

'Who has gone?'

'The divine Messer Pietro, poor soul. Hurry, hurry!'

Titian had to make an effort to take in the news. It changed everything, and seemed to turn the whole of his world and his time upside down; he suddenly felt as though he had entered a barricaded limbo, obtuse and numb, and yet full of passionate grief.

With many others he went to his friend's house: like many others he saw him stretched out inert under the coverings of the bed. But even before he entered the room, hearing the laments of the women and the friends who were gathered round, talking or praying, he stopped for a moment on the threshold, knowing only too well what he would see. He, too, was old, nearly eighty, and tears now came only too easily. He was leaning on Orazio's arm, but now he moved away from him. He gave his hand to Sansovino, who came towards him weeping vehemently, as Tuscans do when they give way to a passion of grief.

He disliked these ceremonies, but when he saw the dead man's face, so absurdly transformed, he felt that his own heart was breaking. For a long time he stared at the unrecognizable epidermis of dusty leather that covered the shrunken cranium. It seemed that there was dust everywhere, in the hollows of the eye-sockets, on the hands, even on the rich robe.

He stared at the corpse for a long time, and then looked round at the chorus of wailing women, united in their mourning so that they seemed one single widow. Messer Pietro had used their poor bodies for his pleasure, flattered them with fanfares of his idle talk, made love to them and slapped them by turns, and now it seemed as though he could never have had any connection with them, and was scoffing at their distress. . . .

The presence of Aretino's daughter Adria finally saved the situation. The chorus of mourning women gradually diminished their wailing and, under the pretext of informing such and such a person, they all went out together, passing first into the kitchen to refresh themselves before they scattered through the alleys and across the squares.

Messer Pietro died during the night of the 21st October, 1556, a short time after the abdication of the Emperor Charles V.

The curate Demetrio officiated at the funeral of the 'divine Aretino' at San Luca. Many friends had come, as well as important personages and people who were there out of curiosity. It was painful to assist at the requiem Mass for this extraordinary person, whose originality recalled nothing else, and everybody felt the need of some living trace, a sign, some memory that could prolong his rare energy. But the sign was given: as the rite drew to an end, Adria, enveloped in her dark cape, made a sign to a sacristan, who came forward carrying on a large dish the chain consisting of golden tongues that King François I had given to Messer Pietro.

Now the '*Lingua eius loquetur mendacium*' was broken up into many separate golden tongues, and one of them was laid into the outstretched dirty palm of every poor person who happened to be present at the ceremony.

People who had come to the funeral stood in groups outside the church. They called the gondoliers to take them home, and stayed discussing whether Aretino's death had really been due to apoplexy or, as others maintained, whether he had cracked his skull falling backwards in a fit of laughter during a banquet. They went on gossiping like the true Venetians they were: so-and-so said so . . . the cousin of so-and-so was there. . . . Tizio had got the priest out of bed to give him extreme unction . . . and Cajo had told everybody what Aretino had said after he had received the last sacraments! Had they not heard? Really not? They moved closer together and their noses seemed more pointed, their chins more protruding, as they repeated amid gusts of laughter: 'Save me from the rats, now that I have been greased!'

III

CALMLY, Titian settled down to re-read his tattered copy of Dolce's 'Dialogue' between Aretino and the grammarian Fabrini—the Dialogue on Painting.

The discussions he had had with Messer Pietro and the latter's suggestions came back to his mind. But in these pages, although they praised him, Titian, to the skies and cast aspersions on the other, on Buonarroti, he found again the weariness that had come over him so many times when he had listened to them pontificating on the method of colour-mixtures, which should be soft and united and should represent nature, and that nothing should remain to offend the eye like visible outlines and the firmness of bold, disunited shadows.

'Soft and united,' he read again, 'bold and disunited.' Ah, poor Aretino, so far away already. He laid down the book and picked up the portrait which had been executed years ago on a medallion by that strange, bitter man, Leone Leoni, a compatriot of the deceased, who now lived in Milan.

Round as a jovial sun, the fine bronze coin revolved between his fingers. Adria had sent it to him in memory of her father. He turned the medallion this way and that—with the profile looking up, as though Aretino was throwing back his head in a burst of laughter— then down, as though he were meditating. He weighed the coin bearing his friend's profile in his hand, then, with a sudden movement, he dropped it on to the crimson damask cover of the table. The arabesques of the cloth seemed to open up in a series of unending rings round it, like the surface of water into which one has thrown a stone.

Milan, he remembered suddenly—there was something he had to see about there! He called Orazio and together they looked at the dates of their copies of the petitions they had written in connection with the pension of the Duchy of Lombardy. They had insisted with every available argument, taking advantage of the truce that followed Charles V's abdication in favour of Philip. Titian had sent him his picture of 'Perseus and Andromeda', but for some time now the only coin that had arrived at Birri Grande had been the bronze coin bearing Aretino's effigy, which his daughter had sent. They turned over the pages. Titian crushed a pair of useless sheets into a ball and threw it away impatiently. Orazio made plans to leave for Milan immediately.

Then the '*signor padre*' sat down again. Once more he touched the bronze profile of Aretino, as though desiring to consume it with the affection of his eager fingers. Orazio lingered, toying with the crumpled paper which he pushed around with the toe of his shoe. The bronze coin between the fingers of the old man, the ball of paper under the young one's foot—and, between them, time and silence.

They represented two ages, two epochs, though now the distance between them was diminishing. Orazio was over forty, and once one has reached that age it is as though one were on equal terms with an octogenarian. He has already caught me up, thought Titian, he has caught up with me.

During the silences between father and son there was always a certain complicity, a tacit approach, a loyal attempt to make the father younger and invigorate the son, to change their roles or to equalize them.

Orazio had caught up with him, even down to the many white threads in his hair. It seemed like yesterday that he had been toddling around, making his first steps and falling to the ground. Now his father looked at him placidly: he would have liked to leave rich treasures to him and to the others, for it appeased his mind to do all he could for the well-being of his children. At last he had made peace with Pomponio, and had obtained for him the living of S. Andrea del Fabbro near Mestre from Cardinal Trivulzi, the Papal Legate to Venice. He made a mental inventory of the paintings, the furniture, the house, the acres of timber—yes, and there was the whole of Birri Grande, and sometimes he counted the rooms one by one, like precious acres which added up to a great estate.

Orazio now said that it would be better to wait a little longer before settling the affair at Milan. He would go there in three months time, towards the end of the year. In the meantime, he would manoeuvre, writing further petitions to his 'very mighty lord'.

And, as he had done so many times before, he began: 'Most Sacred Caesarian Majesty', and ended: 'Of the most high and most mighty Lord kisses the feet, Yr Highness humble

TITIAN.'

★   ★   ★

Finally Orazio suggested that Aretino's disciple Leone Leoni, who was also working for the Imperial Court, might be putting the '*signor padre's*' affairs in a bad light. In the meantime, the tidings came that Charles V had expired at Juste, on the 21st September, 1558. His failing eyes had remained fixed until his last moment on the saints in the beautiful heaven of Titian's apotheosis, which hung on a wall beside the regal death-bed.

They had sent off new petitions. Then the Master returned to his occupation of passing in review the most recent works of Sustris, of Girolamo, and of the haggard, passionate El Greco.* Or he would grant short sittings to the artists who had asked him insistently for permission to paint him, though his image could now be found in every corner of Venice, like that of a titular saint, and they should really be able to portray him from memory. Several times Sansovino had represented him in marble as an Olympian Saint Jerome, with a heavy body over which the turgid veins meandered. Alessandro Vittoria had made of him a naked saint, powerful, desolate and venerable. El Greco had portrayed him together with Giulio Clovio, Michelangelo and Raphael in one of his religious compositions.

Titian considered these followers of his, these apprentices, pupils or colour grinders, looking at them with his penetrating eyes, whose light could be almost deadly. In terse phrases he attempted to explain to them what no manual or 'dialogue' and none of Vasari's lengthy elucidations could tell them; the art of not abusing one's own style. What Tintoretto had already begun to do, for example. What Michelangelo had already done, he might have added, but he let it pass.

He travelled to Pieve and visited the Lords of Spilimbergo. Little Irene's father was dead, and she was now a young girl burning with ardour to paint and to write poetry. She ran to meet him with all the eagerness of her youth, tall and straight on long legs under a simple skirt which she would raise a little to go up and down the stairs or to run. With joyous exuberance, she showed him drawings and studies. She told him that she did not want to go on vegetating up there among the hills; she longed to go to Venice; she begged the Master to make a real artist of her. And she said all this as though she were singing madrigals, gay little songs welling up from her heart.

Titian was suddenly reminded of Beatrice of Savoy, that time in

*Domenico delle Greche or Greco ('El Greco'), whose real name was Domenico Theotocopuli. Before going to Spain, he had stayed in Italy up to the year 1576.

Bologna at the coronation of the Emperor, when she had gazed at the great portrait of Charles V, smiling and dazzled. The Lady of Spilimbergo had now married again, and as they had a house in Venice as well, there was no reason why the girl should not go to stay there with her grandfather, Gian Paolo da Ponte, whom Titian knew well, and come to work at the Master's studio at Birri Grande. Irene danced with joy when this was decided, and taking her sister by the hand, she dragged her along with her to run down the slope of the meadows.

Titian began to sketch both girls, preparatory to painting their portraits. Irene adored him; he was her ideal, a patriarch of infinite wisdom, a father in whose heart all the loves of heaven and earth had taken their abode. With burning eagerness, she leant forward to demand knowledge, asking questions, smiling at him, obsessed. It was an effort for her to sit still and hold the pose. She got up to open the window wide over the beautiful valleys below, and turned round, her gaze as wide as the vast spaces of the sky which she introduced into the silent room.

Perhaps she was predestined to fall into a decline, suffocated by the fever that excites and consumes its victims, Titian thought to himself. And he laid a caressing hand on the young head. His touch soothed her with sudden calm, and she resumed the pose like a musical heroine.

Soon she was asking questions again; about the late lamented Emperor, about Philip II, about Sofonisba Anguissola, and about Titian's pupils, whose names she had memorized as though they had already been her companions at work. And finally she said:

'Are there swallows in Venice?'

* * *

On the 25th December, 1558, after pressure had been brought to bear on Garcia Hernandez, the ambassador of Spain to Venice, Philip II wrote ordering the Governor of Milan to pay Titian the arrears of his pension. Orazio left for Milan, where he lodged at the inn of the Falcon. He presented himself to the Duke and obtained letters by which the accounts were to be settled immediately.

In the meanwhile Titian began a portrait of the nobleman Alberigo di Lodron, His Majesty's colonel in the German infantry.

IV

As luck would have it, Orazio came up against Leone Leoni. His experience in Milan was almost incredible.

As he lay on the bed, a doctor was disinfecting his wounds on one side and on the other the notary Zoppa, assisted by his clerk, was taking down Orazio's statement. The poor fellow had barely recovered from his amazement as he described his vicissitudes.

'Take it slowly,' said the clerk, tapping his goose-quill against the paper and putting out the tip of his tongue, as he indicated the rhythm for the plaintiff's deposition. 'Now, let us begin.'

'A few days after I had come to Milan, where I took lodgings, there came the Signor Cavaliere Leoni Aretino, my friend, and like a father, he took me with him and brought me to his house with my horses and servants, and I stayed with him about a month. As I had then arranged with His Excellency for work at some portraits, it seemed to me that discretion was necessary, and so I withdrew to a room which I took there at Sant' Andrea, for I must work at the portraits chiefly in the morning, which I could not do easily, as Signor Leoni is a late riser.

Yesterday evening, at the time of the Ave Maria, I went to remove them, and with two of my servants, I went to sit down with Signor Leoni in the place where one dines, and as my said servants passed with the pictures, the thrush which was in the said place began to beat its wings. I got up and took off my cloak, spreading it over the cage, so that the thrush did not need to be frightened as they passed . . .' and here Orazio began to curse, remembering the attentions of his host and feeling his wounds burning again under the disinfectant.

'Let us proceed,' said the notary, raising his hand; for a moment he got up to have a look at his moaning client's riddled back, then he returned to his seat and repeated: 'Let us proceed.'

'While I was thus occupied, the said Signor Leoni, without a word, with the dagger with which he had armed himself, stabbed me, wounding me on the right side of the jaw and on my forehead with two wounds. Then, so as to escape from him before he killed me, I ran to the door and, warding him off, I fell; and he, with Alessandro his step-son, armed with a sword, leapt at me shouting: "Give it to him, kill him, kill him!" and they wounded me with two other wounds in the right shoulder and in the arm, and many other stabs. I went as best I could to the house of Signor Cademosto, physician, near here, although I was still being followed by them and by another of the house, and there I was rescued by the said physician and other gentlemen who happened to be there; and that is how things are.'

'Interrogated for what reason this was done,' the notary now dictated to his clerk, 'or whether he could infer the same, the plaintiff replied:

' "I cannot think of any reason except that it was caused by jealousy, because I was liked by His Excellency, whom we all serve. If I had not believed that Signor Leoni looked upon me as his own son, certainly it could not have happened in such a way." '

Pages and pages were covered with 'Interrogations' and 'Replies'. Then, while the doctor finished bandaging him up like a Lazarus, Orazio broke out into a string of imprecations; 'A scoundrel! A prince of scoundrels! A villain! That Leoni!' The whole of Europe knew it; in Rome, where he would have been in gaol for ever if Andrea Doria had not managed to get him out; in Spain, from where he had been expelled as a Lutheran; in Venice, where he had caused one of his unfortunate pupils to be stabbed. But let him not venture to take advantage of Imperial favour, for this time he had a hard nut to crack. He had come up against the divine Titian, *Cavaliere Cesareo, gran Conte Aurato, Spron d'Oro.* . . .

They had to calm him with a soothing potion.

*   *   *

Leoni also produced an entire fascicle of gossip, entitled: 'The Quarrels of Lion.' Here he maintained that Orazio had had dealings with a rogue in his house. But it was no good, he had to go to gaol, accused of attempted homicide and attempted theft, having tried to rob Orazio of two thousand ducats.

The Master began his campaign with a letter dated 12th June, 1558, to King Philip, a veritable rhapsody of fulminations:

'Invincible Catholic King,

The malevolence of Leone *aretino* your servant, unworthy of the honoured name of cavalier and of Imperial sculptor, is to blame that, although I would write to Your Most Sacred Majesty merely pleasing things, today I must dispense my pen of its duty by writing of his wicked operations and my quarrels. . . .' Then he embarked on a detailed account of Orazio's Milanese adventure, begging the King to intervene with inexorable justice. Thereupon he turned to Garcia Hernandez, the Imperial ambassador, making recommendations, petitions, precisions and pouring forth streams of invective. After a month he wrote to Philip again and included with some paintings that were being sent to Genoa, a little crucifix painted by his dear *Horatio*.

And indeed, Leone Leoni had to pay young Vecelli two thousand ducats compensation: a sum as round as the sun! The affair occupied half Venice for weeks, and from time to time Lucrezia, Lavinia, Madonna Caliopa, her sister-in-law, and heaps of relations came together and went over the whole story once again from beginning to end. And whenever Titian, with Irene or another of his disciples, went to visit the collections of pictures and antiques in Casa Contarini, or at the house of the Marcello or the Loredano family or at the Palazzo Cornaro, all those present raised their eyes to Heaven in horror that such an offence had been perpetrated against the person of the venerated Master, and once again they recited the litany of invectives. Even the medallion with the profile of poor Messer Pietro was relegated to the bottom of a casket as though it were something malefic and execrable —and it did not come to the light again.

V

HIS work as a teacher, in the midst of the crowd of his collaborators and pupils, often gave him intense pleasure, although he had always been accused of being so jealous that he was unwilling to help anyone else to attain proficiency. In his studio, Cort and Boldrini, the etchers, El Greco, de las Ruelas, Muziano, Irene and Giovan Maria Verdezzotti, all of them fervent disciples, came and went, flew off and returned. Toma Tito's fourteen-year-old son, Marco, had now come to him to learn drawing. Girolamo Dente, that Giro or Gironimo di Tiziano who was held by many to be the Master's natural son because of his name, directed the artistic activities of the workshop. Irene and Giovan Maria gave Titian a happy sense of satisfaction; he kept them close to his person and watched over their progress.

Irene had never been to Venice before, and she went around, clasping and unclasping her hands, her eyes opened wide. In the studio she worked like a demon, messing herself up with paint from head to foot, so that she had to cover herself with a wide coat which made her look like a celestial spirit. She talked about her completely modern ideals and at times expressed her sensations with the greatest ingenuousness. She was fascinated by the arguments between the cultured Verdezzotti and the Master, unpretentiously listening to their verbal acrobatics. They would glance at a passage in the 'Dialogue on Painting' and take up the theme again, as though it were a duel of wits. In the end, the Master intervened to cut short the argument, to expostulate with Irene on the proportions of a figure, or to advise his other pupil to proceed more carefully as regards composition. Nevertheless the whole atmosphere of talking and painting, eagerness to understand and to express, delighted him and kept him in touch with the new trends of taste and the ideology of the times. Irene went back to work, coughing over the sticks of charcoal that frittered away between her fingers; then she smiled, and went on smiling, though her sparkling eyes were swimming while she struggled to get back her breath.

Just because he was the greatest artist of his time, Titian felt the necessity of sheltering in the solid simplicity of the young people's company. He was so great and so old, so detached from everything, and the thought of death loomed so vastly before his inner eyes, ever increasing.

He knew that this thought was not destructive in itself, that it could even become comforting, and that it tested man as fire tests ore. But all his life the thought, tragic and of supreme importance, common to all men, had haunted him, and it was engraved for him in the beautiful features of Giorgione. Now that it presented itself to him under the guise of a pure, abstract element, though not less wounding, it made him shudder. He had learnt to disguise the hurt and to savour, by small sips, in aristocratic silence, his memories, his patient comparisons, his ideas. Death was everywhere.

They were young; he forced them to work as he had forced himself to work, as he still did today, untiringly.

He loved them for their youth. He would interrupt them and take them out with him to walk round the garden, so that they might talk to him a little and try to make him talk: he could make them understand so many things. And to understand was all that mattered.

They started out. Giovan Maria gave the Master his arm as they went down the steps, then they looked at the lagoon, at the light, the way in which everything was transformed from one moment to the next. Irene coughed a little and ran into the house to fetch a wrap. She came back; they had already begun their discussion and she looked from one to the other, her eyes shining with vivacity as she tried to seize the gist of the argument.

It might well have been an eternal argument, as enduring as the years of their youth were fragile. Titian watched them as he talked, their smooth cheek-bones, Irene's white neck. He would have liked to hold them close, like the gold of his coffers, like little Emilia, like all new and youthful things he saw palpitating near him.

In a frenzy of splendour, he overthrew death through his art, for now he was beginning to impart, as never before, light and sensuous life to the youthful figures he painted: the amazing Rape of Europa, a nude Diana surprised by Actaeon, a Venus in the act of blindfolding Cupid. And then, over and over again, he painted replicas of a Saint

Jerome who was always himself, beating his breast in terrestrial despair, while fires flared up all around, as though the mountains of the world were communing with the skies in volcanic, cosmic upheavals.

From his new power of expression emanated grandiose possibilities, a universal conception; a passage of a landscape or a sitting figure, like that of Venus blindfolding Cupid, was beginning to contain a cosmic perfection, an impregnable harmony of colour: it might be the essence of a grave gesture, the ineffable rendering of the very breath of life.

With his beard striped with ochre and his hands covered with varnish, he would move about among the canvases in the solitude of his studio. His servant Mattia came to call him, but he did not even answer. Girolamo would remind him of appointments or meetings at the works of San Marco—he sent Orazio. When he was thus immersed in his work he became intractable. People came to tell him that Michelangelo had died on the 18th February, 1564—he said he knew all about it, cutting them short. He knew all about it, he remarked, when he was informed that Salviati, Veronese and Tintoretto had competed with designs for the plan of a great picture to be executed at San Rocco, and Tintoretto had painted the entire composition in its actual measurements all in one breath. When the jurors assembled they found, instead of the plan, the complete work, which was even being offered as a gift by the too clever, the cunning *pictor celer*. He knew all about it, Titian growled. And did he also know that the Congregation of the Council, with the consent of Pope Paul IV, had ordered that all the nudities in Michelangelo's 'Last Judgement' should be covered up? The master knew all about the inevitable events, the sensational events, or the idiotic events taking place in the world. And he snorted as though to say: don't let us waste time with this idle talk, my hours are counted.

Still, he was not cynical enough to say 'I knew it' on the day when Irene had a sudden haemorrhage of the lungs, in his studio. Poor frightened child! How she had looked! How often had he told her not to consume herself in her work! Now he saw her suddenly transferred into a world of inexplicable atrocity, facing a grim future all alone. He went to her assistance, telling her that it was probably nothing serious. He had her taken home immediately; he visited her many times, accompanied by Giovan Maria. From day to day he watched her fading away—fading inexorably like all the living creatures on the earth. . . .

A short time ago his brother Francesco Vecelli had died, without ever having succeeded in becoming a good artist; now the adorable Irene was dying, without having succeeded in making herself known as an artist like Anguissola, whom she mentioned so many times. She talked and talked, deliriously, smiling, as though craving forgiveness, at her mother who was holding her close in an agony of grief. But she could not escape her destiny.

'*Si fata tulissent*' Titian wrote under the portrait which he painted of her, based on the sketches he had done in Spilimbergo. In the background he painted the symbol of the fresh, animated virginity of this young creature—a radiant, silent unicorn.

*　　*　　*

Once again, his life revolved patiently around his work and a thousand worldly preoccupations: transactions about the ownership of lands sold by the deceased Francesco at Pieve, the great picture of a Madonna flanked by St Andrew, Saint Tiziano, the Bishop of Oderzo who had founded the family, and Titian himself; accounts of expenses sustained for him by Garcia Hernandez; cases and boxes of ultramarine azure; messengers who conveyed his works to Genoa in order to send them on to Spain.

But Irene had flown away—and she had left an emptiness like all the women of whom he had been fond.

He went to spent the autumn in Pieve. Emilia embraced him reverently. She was now nearly seventeen, and she was beautiful. He took her with him to Venice on his return. But in the meantime, a cobbler, named Nicolô Rampogna, had murdered his faithful servant Mattia from Cadore, because of a private quarrel; just as forty years earlier his poor shabby Luigi had been dispatched into the other world. Death was everywhere, all the time. . . .

On the first day of the year 1566 he got up early, alive, and in good health. He went into his studio. Cornelius Cort and Nicolô Boldrini, who were always busy reproducing his paintings on copperplates, were the first to wish him a healthy and happy New Year and ever-improving work. Then came Girolamo, the good Girolamo, whose success was becoming increasingly established, followed by Jacopo, called Palma the Younger, a grand-nephew of his old friend Palma Vecchio, Marco Vecelli, and other young men. Then there came Nicolô Stoppio, the antiquary and art-dealer, who was later to take a great part in increasing the circulation of prints after Titian's paintings, as soon as the Venetian government had accorded the Master the licence to sell them. They all wished him good health and good work.

The Master smiled a little, but a deep seriousness had come upon him again; his face was grave and the piercing eyes seemed like needles that had been thrust into a mask of decrepitude. It flashed through his mind that they need not think him in his dotage, just because the year 1566 was beginning—when he was in front of his easel, he could still make short work of the lot of them! And he gave his hand to each one of them to greet them and also to convince them, by this contact, of the miracle by which God permitted him to remain so extraordinarily alive.

VI

ACCORDING to what people say he is very old,' wrote Garcia Hernandez to King Philip in 1564. 'He is supposed to be about ninety.'

They were saying he was ninety. Others thought him younger, others again maintained that he must be decrepit by now, although incredibly well preserved, owing to the chastity of his best years, when he had always led a strictly moral and temperate life.

He was in good health. Only his eyes gave him trouble, they were often watering. Emilia had sewn fine, large handkerchiefs of delicate lawn which he kept in his pocket or in the sleeve of his gown, as ladies sometimes did. And ever and again, when they were among other people and Orazio signed to him, he wiped away the tears that trickled down right into the hairs of his beard.

The company he now enjoyed most of all was that of his erudite admirer and pupil Verdezzotti, a perfect gentleman, full of tact, courtesy and delicacy. Since the death of Irene, hardly a day went by when Giovan Maria did not come to Birri Grande, either to work or to keep the Master company. Sometimes he would take him for a rare outing in a gondola. Giovan Maria was really the only person who could make him move, go out and see new faces, interrupting his absurdly tenacious industry. They would glide through the city along the fine canals. Titian half closed his eyes and indicated certain aspects of colour which could be used in painting to give entirely new effects. They passed women on the gently curving bridges—the gondola seemed to slide through under their ample skirts. Giovan Maria must not forget about love—he was already missing many fine raptures by keeping company with an old devil like himself, Titian said.

They arrived. While the gondola swayed at the foot of the steps to the Palazzo, the aged painter stepped out cautiously, supported by the servants and Giovan Maria. He wrapped his cape round himself, and the veins on his temples swelled a little. The procedure of getting into a gondola or leaving it irritated him; it was humiliating and mortifying. He pulled himself together immediately, forcing himself to step out firmly now that he entered the hall, ascended the staircase and came into the reception room.

They were expected. Some ladies dressed in the latest fashion made studied curtseys, like peacocks spreading their tails, others smiled from behind the feathers of their fans that were like many-coloured crests, and raised their faces to the light; thin curls were spread over their foreheads like crescent moons. Lovely women they were, inviting kisses, rather plump, their busts compressed in bodices of patterned damask and blossoming out above them with the lace ruffs which it was now the fashion to raise straight up—like a peacock's.

The master of the house, Domenico Venier, was a man of letters, who was having a great vogue at the time; he enjoyed inviting illustrious people, philosophers, artists, bankers, 'honoured' courtesans proficient at singing and composing verses. Verdezzotti was on the look-out to sign to the Master when some personality approached them, for Titian with his absent-minded air appeared not to see anyone, and took no notice when someone bowed to him. Actually he recognized everybody, but he liked to enjoy the luxury of not wishing to recognize them. Only when he noticed something exceptionally young and vibrant in a face, did he become fascinated. Now, for instance, a woman was moving towards him from the other end of the room, secure, erect, becoming more and more beautiful with every step that brought her nearer. It was Veronica Franco.

She made a low curtsey, paying homage to the majesty of the aged painter; as she was bending, her low-cut gown, adorned with jewelled rosettes, revealed her snowy bosom; then, as she straightened herself up again, raising her skirts a little to spread out and rearrange their folds, she revealed not only a tiny foot, but even a shapely calf clad in a silk stocking.

She begged to be accorded the high honour of visiting the studio at Birri Grande, though she was only a poor amateur artist, she said, smiling mysteriously. A wretched amateur, she called herself, but her smile conveyed that she was a woman who could make even a saint lose his head. The others immediately saw her as a forward creature, thirsting to occupy the centre of the stage—one, who like all the man-eating females of her kind, merely disguised her wantonness by boasting of four stanzas, or rhymed wails which would have been quite unbearable if Venier, the master of the house, had not corrected them. And so as to regain their authority, they drew up in battle array behind their raised fans, as if in the fort of morality, repeating the latest scandal of the Convent of the Holy Ghost, from where Sister Clemenza Foscarini had fled with Bernardo Contarini, and Sister Camilla Rota with Gerolamo Correr. It was a crying shame—the Holy Inquisition of Spain was needed there!

Veronica at barely nineteen was already beginning to use the power of her subtle fascination. Very sure of herself, amiable yet precise in the arguments of her conversation, attentive to every detail in the calculated composition of her apparel, she imparted harmony to her surroundings by the quality of her essence. 'Daughter of Pallas Athene and Cupid,' her admirers sighed. She was tall and slender, her lovely cheeks moulded expressly by the desire to smile in a regal manner; she demonstrated with great ability that she put inclination before doctrine, instead of before pleasure.

'One must have a diploma of Padua to be allowed to kiss her!' her rivals said, suggesting that no man without a university degree could win her favours. And actually more than one of the men who wooed her had been advised by her to lead a more restful life in the tranquillity of his study; nevertheless, she added, he might come again from time to time to let her see whether he had profited by it.

Now the company was sitting in a circle and talking. The bankers were anxious to explain how the end of the world, the end of Venice, would come about, foretelling that business was moving towards a crisis. Money was worth less because of the devaluation of the precious metals.

'The Americas!' they sighed. The Americas had a certain significance for the future ways of the world, but also for the small world, to them so enormous, of the commercial relations of Venice. During these years Genoa had already left Venice far behind as regards her imports.

The world was changing. Everything was changing. In the artistic world as well—had they noticed, for instance, how much attention was now being paid to the art of writing letters? For the last twenty years countless letters had been written, with an ever-increasing view to publication. Certainly there were masterpieces among them, and the epistolatory style of the late regretted Bembo was still supreme, even above the picturesque exuberance of the printed collection of Aretino's letters. But where could one now find the great poems of the Middle Ages?

'And what about Messer Ariosto?' some objected.

'And Tasso, after all!' It was known that ever since he was sixteen years old he had been composing a poem 'Del Gierusalemme' of heaven knows how many stanzas. A heated discussion ensued.

Veronica followed the argument intently, while all the men present devoured her with their eyes. All eyes were fixed on her, even those of old Sansovino, whose sparse white hairs among the red ones that were left over from his former carrotty mane gave his head the appearance of being covered with a kind of foam which was neither down nor hair.

Tasso, Palladio, Tintoretto, Veronese, the Bassanos . . . these were the new names that were now on everybody's lips. They were valid, formidable names. Titian thought of Orazio, of his defenceless talent which had been crushed by his own authority. He was now attempting to make it possible for his son to enjoy an aura of prestige after his own death; he intended to petition the Great Council to transfer the patent of the Senseria to Orazio, and to address a similar request to Philip II, concerning the Milanese pension.

All that remained for him to do was to accord the hand of Emilia to Andrea Dossena, a merchant in cereals from the Bergamo. When he had provided for this marriage by a dowry, his paternal duties would have been fulfilled. Then he intended to retire; he felt that he could not go on any longer. His eyes were troubling him, and he no longer wanted to look around and peer right and left to see how the world was made. He had lived too long, he had seen too much.

VII

TITIAN did not even go to Emilia's wedding.

With the assistance of Toma Tito, he had caused a notary to draw up a deed conferring a dowry of seven hundred and fifty ducats on the bride, and now he listened as the document was read out to him: 'Emilia, the daughter of the magnificent and most excellent painter Titian Vecelli . . .'.

She, too, was leaving him—like Lavinia, like Irene, like Cecilia. She would come back, like Lavinia, and visit him from time to time, an infant in her arms, her chin a little rounder, a new ring on her finger. And he would be bleating away at the clerk, dictating the hundredth petition asking to be paid the outstanding pension from Naples or Spain. Or maybe hearing the glass panes in the windows shaking as salutes were fired to mark the departure or the arrival of the fleet, now that Venice was once more at war with the Turks. The maid-servant had crossed herself when Orazio came home with the news that the unfortunate Admiral Bragadino, the heroic opponent of the Turks in Cyprus, had been flayed alive from head to foot—as one peels the skin off a peach.

'Oh!' the silly girl had cried, fixing her eyes on the canvas at which the Master was working; a picture of Apollo and Marsyas, Marsyas head downwards, being flayed—a perfect illustration of what Orazio was describing.

'Oh! Oh! Oh!' she continued to moan.

Father and son burst out laughing, and they laughed and laughed and could not stop. The girl, stunned and bewildered by the explosions that were shaking the windows and by the spectacle of the two gentlemen shaking with mirth, no longer knew what to think—surely the Turks would now be arriving at any moment!

No, no, they would never get to Venice, they assured her. But even more reassuring was the victory of the Venetian Republic on the 7th October, 1571, when one hundred and twenty-one battleships sailed against the infidel lunatics and won the glorious victory of Lepanto.

220

The whole of Venice went mad with joy. Christmas came, and people were singing in the streets; there were torchlight processions and countless drunken brawls. Then the preparations for the most fantastic Carnival in the entire history of the Republic were made.

All the artists of the Christian world had started painting the apotheosis of that victory—and by the time they had painted all the ships, the cannon and the banners, four years were to go by. Now through all the alleys, along the Mercerie, simulated ships with rows of cars fixed in mid-air like rakes, were dragged along, preceded by banners—and finally debouched on to the Piazza. Boys wrapped in coverlets and carpets representing Turkish warriors hopped around everywhere, and pelted each other with orange-peel.

There were regattas, buffooneries with every kind of mask, and symbolical processions. Night fell and nobody had any idea at what time they would go to bed. Finally, on the last Sunday during Carnival, there was an exceptional masquerade. Youths disguised as Turks, as negroes, as Swiss and as fishermen, defiled through the entire city with chariots representing Faith, Venice, and the known parts of the world. In the taverns there was not a single tankard with a handle left, not a goblet that was not chipped. And in the bedrooms there would not have been room for another grain of dust, so many people had come from Verona, Ferrara, Padua and from the most distant parts.

During those festive days many people begged for the honour of being allowed to visit the Master.

They arrived at Birri Grande in parties and settled down in the studio as though it had been a theatre. After a careful examination of every picture, among the most recent the 'Apollo and Marsyas', a vision as disturbing as it was profound, they were shown a painting of 'Christ crowned with Thorns', in which the Master had introduced a flaming light from the side—the power of the composition was such that the connoisseurs compared it to the classical Laocoon. They begged to be shown the celebrated 'Tarquinius and Lucrece', but that had already been sent to King Philip in Spain.

Orazio, the Boldrinis and Cort displayed folders containing the etched copies of the paintings, which were sold like hot-cross buns, even the curious caprice taken from a sketch of the Master's showing apes wreathed round with serpents in the poses of the Laocoon group. He had done this sketch to mock certain ignorant artists who refused to understand classic art.

Antonio Perez, the Secretary of State at Madrid, came to select work from his studio; Veronica Franco to look through the prints, a great number of which one of her lovers desired to buy for her. They all turned towards the Master with the pleasure and respect that his time-honoured authority commanded. They asked him to tell them about Gentile Bellini, about Giorgione, those men who already seemed personages from a book on ancient history.

Titian would put in very short appearances. He rested a great deal, to nurse his ailing eyes and to show himself fresh and energetic to his incessant visitors.

The time came when he considered it opportune to arrange for his own sepulchre. As he could not have a monument carved by Sansovino, who had died two years earlier, he decided to provide one himself, by composing a great picture which would be an exaltation of human grief round a Descent from the Cross. He talked about it to the Prior of the Frari and indicated his choice for the Chapel of the Crucifix. As a good priest, the Prior asked the artist to begin the work before stipulating the terms of the contract, saying they would discuss them later on.

Orazio studied the measurements and went over the plans with his father. Finally, among many fine new canvases, they selected the one that appeared durable enough and had the right dimensions.

VIII

WHO was to come? Who was to disembark at the landing-stage of Birri Grande? Who would still come before Death came?

He painted in the morning, as though it were the most natural thing in the world. Then, punctually, he would ask if there were visitors coming in the afternoon or tomorrow; who was coming? No one?

Giovan Maria was his most faithful visitor, and he would often bring him a little surprise—a book containing curious prints, a musician friend of his who would play on the organ. He kept the aged Master informed on the habits of this or that family, those that it was worth while talking about, of course—for only too often one would learn in what futile and provincial pursuits even the best families were wont to spend their evenings, throwing dice to discover the future, or amusing themselves with riddles, cards, or the hunting-game. For the latter, the company split into two parties: women and men were given the names of animals and fled through a hall or a garden, while the others, the hunters, followed them. It was pathetic to see fools with fat paunches tripping along behind agile young hinds or doves who flouted them, raising their many-coloured damask skirts.

A more sophisticated game was that of guessing pictures, which had been invented at the Cornaro palace. Some of those present would represent pictures by famous modern artists, and the onlookers, highly amused, had to guess which artists they were. A youth of the Contarini family, wrapped in a rose-coloured cloth and reclining on a carpet, had represented a 'Venus' by Titian. Others, sitting at a table over-laden with silver and crystal, parodied a 'Supper' by Veronese which, in imitation of Tintoretto's impetuosity, was suddenly disturbed by the irruption of young men and girls running like 'robust' angels; but their entry had been so robust that not only did the spectators immediately guess the artist's name by the typical confusion, but the table spread in Veronese's manner was accidentally overthrown, and dishes, plates and crystal goblets were smashed to smithereens.

223

Verdezzotti's constant attentions and his civil and well-informed conversation were a daily relief to the tension which came over the Master when he was not in the mood to work. When, as it occasionally happened, his young friend had to absent himself for a month from Venice in order to look after his estates in the country, the old painter kept on asking when he was due to return.

Titian had begun to paint a picture of Adam and Eve. It was more difficult for him to work at the vast canvas of the 'Pietà' for his tomb. Months went by, the seasons changed.

Emilia came to visit him with her husband and her two children, Alcide and Vecellia. While they were waiting for their grandfather to get up after his afternoon sleep, the children whispered with exaggerated importance and smoothed out their skirts. At last he appeared. The little ones fell silent, suddenly intimidated.

'So that is Cellia? Let me have a look at her!' he quavered. He had nothing with which he could amuse the little girl—nothing except the handkerchief with which he dried his tears, and he waved it in the air as though making signs from a distance. He sent Orazio to fetch some coins from his cabinet, and the two children clutched them as though they were holding the hope of a future life in their little hands.

The tenor of his days was regulated to perfection, and their contents sifted by Orazio's affectionate care. He was informed of every item of good news, but bad news was kept from him. He never learnt that the fire in the Doge's Palace in 1574 had also destroyed his great canvas representing the victory of Barbarossa at Spoleto. This battle scene had been universally known as the 'Battle of Cadore', because he had wanted to immortalize the resistance of the Venetians to Maximilian's troops during the years of his youth, in 1508, and he had faithfully reproduced the hills and valleys of his home.

However, his friends informed him joyfully of the imminent visit of Henri III, the King of France. On his return from Poland the monarch was to stay in Venice, and it was to be foreseen that he would not refuse to sit for his portrait. He was described as a most sympathetic personality. During his sojourn, Venice offered him her homage with the most exquisite distractions, as, for instance, the ball at the Palazzo Ducale, where two hundred patrician ladies appeared dressed in white and covered with jewels like statues of the Madonna. The King was heard to say that he had never seen so splendid a sight. It was not quite certain whether he was referring to the ladies, the hangings, or the paintings of the hall or to all of this together, but it soon became known that, seductive though he was, he had not entered into amorous relations with any high-born woman.

Instead, the young king had gone to see Veronica Franco. She had knelt down to receive him at the portals, pretending that she could not possibly allow him to enter so humble a dwelling. Her house boasted a legion of arrogant servants, refreshments enough to satisfy a regiment, marvellous musical instruments, parrots, flowers, all sorts of delights. In the end, the beautiful lady presented the king with a little portrait.

On the day when the royal cortège of gondolas arrived at Birri Grande, Titian wore the Imperial chain round his neck. The furniture of the house had been waxed and polished, and the selection of paintings that were to be shown was prepared.

The old artist surprised his visitors by his respectful vivacity. Sitting on a chair next to the seat occupied by the king, he caused the paintings to be displayed which he had decided to offer to his generosity. They were approved, and so was their author, the noble old man who wiped away the tears of his gratitude like an austere, rugged, senatorial tortoise.

The King roamed round the house like a genuinely friendly guest, chatting unconstrainedly about all sorts of things, even asking the name of the plant outside the window, and sniffing its small insipid flower.

Titian stood on the landing-stage together with Orazio to watch the gondolas being rowed away. Henri III turned once more to salute him, smiling at him with a gay, boyish, foreign smile, and he raised his hand and waved; he was still holding the little flower he had plucked from the vase.

Titian had the feeling that his soul was gliding away, carried off among the honours.

*   *   *

He often gazed at the lagoon from the garden, or at the sky from behind the slightly opalescent panes of the window. Like all those bowed down by the weight of their years and therefore hindered from moving around, he longed to travel, to return to Pieve and to watch once more the changing of the seasons there, also to go to the Palazzo Ducale to see the recent work that had been done there.

P

Tintoretto was doing this, Tintoretto was doing that, he was told. He was not very interested in his painting, he grumbled; he had always preferred Antonio Allegri, whom they all called 'il Corregio', a highly-gifted artist who had died too soon; though his talent was a little too feminine, he had possessed a magical touch when he painted flesh and human faces.

But all these problems had ceased to interest him.

IX

H E would have loved to return to Pieve, to look once more at every fir tree, every stone. Up there at least everybody bowed their knee when he passed by, and in church they prayed before his venerable beard, looking up at the picture he had painted of himself praying at the feet of the Madonna. Up there they did not look askance at him like those cassocked dogs of the Chiesa dei Frari with whom he had agreed on a tomb in the Chapel of the Crucifix and who were now inventing one pretext after the other . . . perhaps they would even refuse to keep their promise.

Giovan Maria slipped in a word and described the beauty of the great 'Pietà' to them, just as the Master himself had been forced to expatiate on the beauty of the 'Assumption', long ago.

Titian continued to work.

Giovan Maria drew his attention to the fact that there were still many rolls and pictures in a corner of the studio; he offered to draw up an exact list of them: already he was preparing paper and pen and tucking up his sleeves.

They must nearly all be incomplete works, ideas he had abandoned, Titian said; he could not remember. Yes, he would like to look at them. Giovan Maria brought the pictures to him, one by one; then he began to write:

'Portrait of Pomponio as a youth.'

He pulled out a damaged canvas:

'Study of Our Lady ascending into Heaven.'

'To be thrown away!' said the Master.

At last a completely finished composition came to light. It had never been exhibited among the important paintings that were placed on the easels. Perhaps the Master had kept it concealed discreetly, owing to the peculiarity of the subject. The picture represented a woman in the prime of her youth, wearing a fur cape in the Roman fashion, her head covered with the *capigliara*, one of those great turbans made of hair and silk which Isabella d'Este had brought into fashion. One recognized the self-portrait of Titian, standing before her and laying his outstretched hand on her body, which was big with child. The skull painted on one side symbolized that Death had carried off the young beauty who was to have been a mother.

Giovan Maria looked at the picture in amazement and waited, pen in hand, for directions as to what title to write on the list. But the Master had put down his palette and his brushes and was gazing at it in silence.

There is always a special expression one assumes when one is overwhelmed by a strong emotion—an expression which seeks to simulate composure. Titian's face now seemed like that of a decrepit child that finds itself disturbed and embarrassed. He signed that the picture should be brought closer, but he continued to gesticulate anxiously, waving his hand in the air. His eyes filled with tears—he might have been a man in his death agony who was seeing once again the most beautiful years of his life.

Giovan Maria, who was holding the picture up to him like a mirror, wrinkled his brow in an effort to recognize the female figure: this woman did not resemble the Madonna for whom Cecilia had always been the model, nor any of the many Venuses—the Venus who was the prototype of all the feminine beauty that Titian had glorified in every one of his pictures.

The Master's brow was mottled with red under the rim of his cap. He could not take his eyes away from the painting, and he made a slight movement, as though he were consenting to all the memories that were now crowding in on him. It seemed as though he were alone with the picture. He wiped his watering eyes and slowly scratched one of his ears, as though to conceal his embarrassment. Then he raised his hand to remove the covering from his head and said, in a thread of a voice, as though he were uttering the word for the first time in his life:

'Love.'

★　　★　　★

At the beginning of the summer, in the parish of San Marziale and in the house of a certain Vincenzo Franceschini, who had been careless enough to give hospitality to a native of Trento, the first case of plague was verified.

Precautionary measures were taken immediately. At Trento the plague had been raging for a long time. In Venice, however, notwithstanding that first 'imported' case, people were led to believe that the epidemic which was rapidly spreading was a sickness caused by the drought.

The palaces of the wealthy families, most of whom had already left for the country, were suddenly empty: everybody who could do so fled to the islands, or to stay with friends or relations in a villa as far away as possible, on the mainland.

Girolamo Mercuriale and Guglielmo Capodivacca, well-known physicians who had been urgently summoned from Padua, failed at first to realize the gravity of the situation. As a spark falling into a hay-loft during the burning summer solstice, the plague flared up, and spread through the whole of Venice, with lightning speed.

Doors were nailed up; the inhabitants escaped through the windows. Nobles and plebeians, robbers and their victims, newborn children and dying men—they were all impregnated by the same acid mire of infection. They cursed those who had succeeded in escaping, raving wildly; suffocating in the heat of August, they leaped into the filthy water of the canals and re-emerged as livid corpses, stripped of flesh.

The convents were swarming with death like gigantic ant-hills. Nuns in a frenzy of faith and fever collected in the courtyards round great fires, into which they cast baskets full of rotting corpses, and their own living bodies.

Litanies of supplication were being recited at San Marco. Cesare Vecelli fled to Pieve, and Lucrezia left with him, screaming from the gondola and calling desperately to Orazio that he must join her tomorrow—he must join her!

He hurried to the heads of the Government's medical commission to arrange for the transportation of his aged father to their home—he needed the official guarantee of the authorities, he did not mind about the expense.

They remained perplexed. 'How many people are you?' they asked him.

'The magnificent Vecellio, myself and one servant.'

It was late. They would have been willing to do something to oblige the Master, but first of all he would have to undergo a medical examination, and Orazio himself must also be examined—his eyes were staring, his face livid.

Panting, he began to run through the city. There was no one at Casa Coltrini, the Dossenas had also vanished. He felt as though he were running over burning slabs on which putrid flesh was frying, skulls splitting open, but the ground was only littered with greasy rags and fragments of broken crockery. Stumbling, he hastened on through a desert of death. The flaming heat of the dogdays was suffocating him. He stared at the motionless water of the canals.

It was late. When he arrived at Birri Grande he felt that he had reached a haven of safety. He called the man-servant—but there was no answer.

'Orsa!' he shouted, going from room to room, from the attic to the cellar. But all the rooms were empty, chests that had been forced open lay around in confusion, a coffer that had contained the silver plate had been rifled.

He found his father in the studio, slumped on a chair before the great canvas of his last, unfinished painting, in the attitude of one who slumbers.

Through the heavy air four flies were buzzing faintly; one settled on the old man's face, near the watering eye, and seemed to inject the poison of those lethal days into the orbit.

He barely roused himself and, docile as a child, allowed himself to be helped up and put to bed.

Then Orazio went round the house frantically, closing the shutters and nailing wooden crossbars across them with great nails. Every time he brought down his hammer, clenching his teeth and half closing his eyes, he saw a shower of sparks like those of his despair.

Suddenly he stopped short, sobbing, unable to go on.

X

FROM his room, the old man heard the hammering suddenly cease.

It was like the time when they had shouted under his window that poor Aretino was dead. And, just as then, the whole world seemed to be turning upside down, describing a parabola in reverse. It blotted out his memory, his sensations, his senses.

'Orazio,' he tried to call out. But he understood that death had descended on to his house. He panted, struggling for breath, attempting to hold on to life. 'Orazio. . . '. But he no longer had a voice, he could no longer see—there was nothing left.

The foul, stagnant air that contaminated everything was slowly invaded by the night.

Black lemures, wearing gloves to protect themselves from contagion, came to rob his treasures. Black, horrible lemures, dark nocturnal thieves appeared like grave-diggers around his bed, sequestering his house, inflicting the worst possible offence on him.

Perhaps he was not yet dead; perhaps, in the sultry heat and the weak light of the lantern they had set down on the threshold, he opened his eyes for a last time in his delirium. He saw forms that moved around swiftly. Seeing their shadows, he thought they were coming to help him—he could not know that Orazio was lying dead in another room, that the servant had fled and that these dark forms were those of damnable thieves who had come to rob him of the greedily amassed fruits of a lifetime.

As they manoeuvred to break open the safe, the noise penetrated his consciousness and he started. At that moment he seemed to be looking at them, and they turned round. Like certain masks that appear in the comedies of Plautus—Dossennus, Bucco, Pappus—their faces covered with black cloths, they seemed not to breathe as they moved swiftly and returned to their business with alacrity.

He raised one hand with a feeble movement. It was as though he

231

were insanely showing them the hiding-place of his riches. Encouraged in their avidity by that sign, they set about their work madly with their fingernails and their chisels.

He fell backwards and gave no further sign of life.